NIAGA
FALLS

JOEL

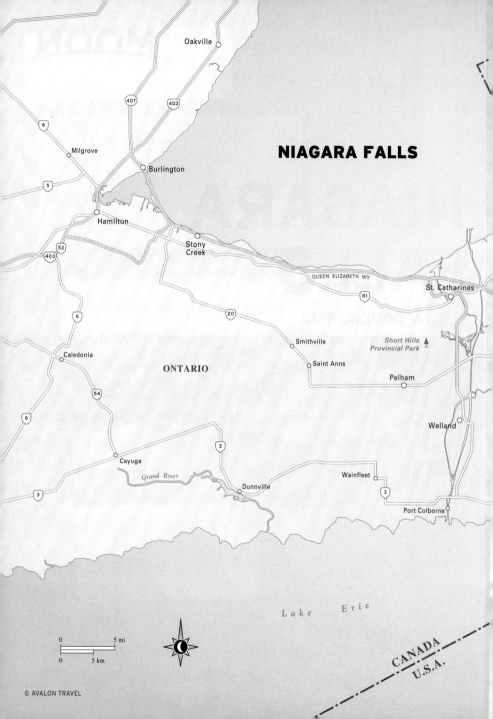

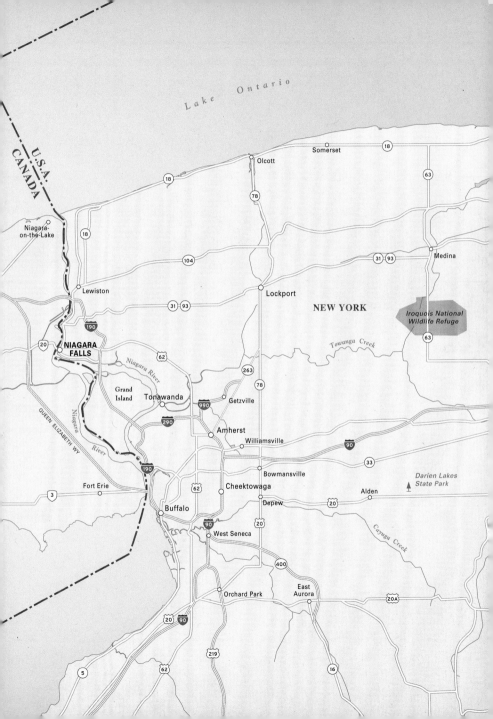

Contents

Niagara Falls

A boat draws you into the furious tumult at the base of the falls. The bright green water roils with energy, mist flying from all sides. The roar is deafening. The sun is eclipsed by plumes of mist as the boat heads closer and closer to the jaws of the torrent.

Amid the chaos, a moment of clarity emerges. This is a 17-story wall of water that has no equal in the world. This is the power of nature. This moment draws millions of people to Niagara Falls each year.

But Niagara offers more than just this moment. It's a world-class destination where you can experience nature and adventure, as well as entertainment, culture, food, and drink. Stretching across both sides of the U.S.-Canada border is a fertile wine country that produces remarkable vintages on everything from family farms to stunning modern European chalets. A 20-minute drive away is Buffalo, where a waterfront entertainment district is emerging from the ruins of the old Erie Canal. The city has embraced its blue-collar charm while preserving and redeveloping an amazing architectural legacy, which includes masterpieces by H. H. Richardson, Louis Sullivan, and Frank Lloyd Wright.

Yet it all circles back to that wall of water. You have to experience this simple but visceral power of nature for yourself.

Planning Your Trip

Where to Go

Niagara Falls, Ontario

The beauty of this area extends beyond the three waterfalls known as Niagara Falls, but the heart of the Niagara experience is at the brink of the falls. Here, you'll find the Table Rock Welcome Centre, home to several major attractions that allow you to see above, below, and behind the falls. Queen Victoria Park provides a lush open area adjacent to the falls with gardens and excellent vistas of Niagara. High-rise hotels and a glittering casino are found in Fallsview, the highly developed zone that sits atop a bluff overlooking Niagara. Downstream, the Parkway North takes you to the scenic whirlpool that reveals the power of Niagara's white water.

Niagara Falls, New York

The U.S. side of Niagara offers a different perspective on the falls. Visitors spend most of their time in Niagara Falls State Park,

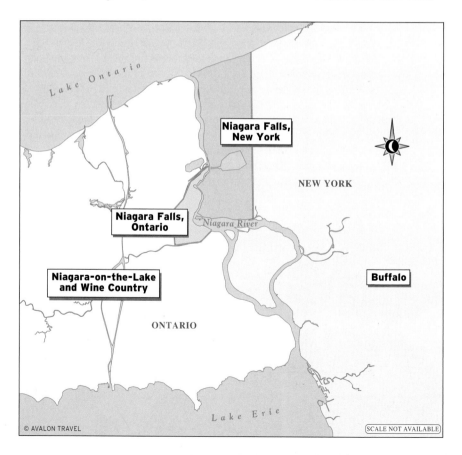

© AVALON TRAVEL — SCALE NOT AVAILABLE

which affords intimate opportunities to experience the falls. Here, you can enjoy the spectrum of Niagara's many moods, from sublime to raging. Surrounding the park is downtown Niagara Falls, with many hotels within walking distance of the falls. Little Italy offers a nostalgic and authentic taste of the city's Italian heritage. North of the Falls are hiking trails, Whirlpool State Park, and the beautiful, historic town of Lewiston. Where the river meets Lake Ontario is Youngstown, an area that has witnessed more than three centuries of conflict over the control of Niagara.

Buffalo

Buffalo is New York State's second-largest city. At Canalside, the city's waterfront district, you can kayak, sail, and fish. Downtown, buildings designed by the likes of Frank Lloyd Wright, H. H. Richardson, and Louis Sullivan are a stunning reminder of the city's affluent past, while the neighborhoods of Elmwood Village and Allentown are centers of arts and culture. To the east and northeast of the city, Lockport and Niagara County offer wine-tasting and hiking in the countryside.

Niagara-on-the-Lake and Wine Country

Niagara-on-the-Lake, perched on the southern shoreline of Lake Ontario, is a beautiful Victorian village. The area expanding outward from NOTL is a fertile crescent, home to more than 20 wineries and vineyards. To the west, the Welland Canal draws recreational boaters and ocean-going freighters alike, and is where visitors can watch massive ships traverse the canal's locks. The small towns that line the canal are charming and historic, from the garden city of St. Catharines to Fort Erie, home to the historic Old Fort Erie.

When to Go

Most people visit Niagara Falls in the 100 days of summer, mid-June through early September. The weather is pleasant, with high temperatures averaging 81°F. During this time, you may experience longer lines at attractions, especially on the Canadian side of the border and on holidays such as Memorial Day and the Fourth of July. Avoid traveling to the falls on summer holidays, due to the crowds and lengthy waits at border crossings. Hotel rates peak during summer.

Nature puts on an amazing show during autumn, September through October. This region explodes with color as leaves make their annual transformation from green to yellow, red, brown, and orange. The weather moderates, with the high temperature averaging 60°F in October. Mornings and evenings can be crisp, but the days are mostly bright and sunny. Many locals favor visiting the falls at this time, because the attractions are still open, but there is seldom a line. If you are a leaf peeper, visit this region on the Columbus Day weekend and hike to your heart's content while the fall colors

are at their peak. Wineries take on an extra-romantic ambience at this time of year.

Winter is the slowest tourism season for Niagara, and with good reason. The months of December-February are snowy, with bitter wind chills and below-freezing temperatures. Seasonal attractions are closed and the tourist areas somewhat empty. However, the freezing weather also creates an austere landscape and frozen mist from the falls envelops everything in a crystalline icy coating. The best time for a brief visit is during the Festival of Lights around the holidays in December.

In spring, March until the beginning of June, you'll find off-season rates on accommodations. As in winter, some attractions have limited hours or are not operating. The Maid of the Mist and Hornblower Niagara Cruises cannot safely ply the waters of the lower Niagara until the river is free of ice, so they don't typically start running until May. Spring arrives a little later here than in other parts of the Northeast due to ice on Lake Erie. By May the weather is more pleasant.

The Two-Day Best of Niagara Falls

For this itinerary, base yourself on the Canadian side of the border. The Fallsview Casino Resort and Marriott Niagara Falls Fallsview Hotel & Spa both offer excellent views and are close to all the major attractions.

Day 1

Purchase an Adventure Pass at the Ontario Parks Welcome Centre near the base of Clifton Hill. The clerk will ask if you'd like to reserve ticket times for Journey Behind the Falls, Niagara's Fury, and the White Water Walk. Add two hours to the current time to come up with your reservation time for Journey Behind the Falls. Reserve Niagara's Fury for one hour after that. Do not reserve a time for the White Water Walk.

Walk one block to Hornblower Niagara Cruises, and hop on a boat for an up-close (and saturated) look at the falls. Afterward, walk south along the rim of the gorge,

enjoying the excellent vista of the U.S. side of the border. In the front atrium of Table Rock Welcome Centre, you'll find the entrance for Journey Behind the Falls. Explore the falls from a tunnel dug through the gorge, emerging in time to catch Niagara's Fury, located on the second floor of the Welcome Centre.

Relax and enjoy the view from the brink of Horseshoe Falls, located at the rear of the Welcome Centre. For lunch, treat yourself to a meal at Elements on the Falls for casual fine dining with an incomparable view.

Spend a leisurely afternoon exploring Queen Victoria Park, across from the Welcome Centre. Within walking distance are the Dufferin Islands, the Floral Showhouse, and many beautiful gardens.

Hop on a green-line WEGO bus (included in the Adventure Pass) headed north along the gorge. Get off at the White Water Walk, where you can spend an hour strolling close

Take a boat trip to the base of Horseshoe Falls with the Maid of the Mist or Hornblower Niagara Cruises.

The White Water Walk gets you up close to the Niagara River's ferocious rapids.

to the river's rapids. Get on another green-line bus and head farther north, stopping at the Whirlpool Aero Car. From the viewing area, you'll have a chance to observe the dangerous and breathtaking whirlpool.

After returning to your hotel for a rest, it's time for dinner. Try the Grand Buffet at the Fallsview Casino Resort for exceptional value and a great view of the falls. After dinner, try your luck at the casino's tables, or head to Queen Victoria Park for the nightly illumination of the falls. Enjoy the beauty of the lights projected upon the falls and fireworks over the falls on Friday and Sunday evenings in the summer.

Day 2

Start early! Explore the American side of Niagara with a trip aboard the Whirlpool Jet Boats in Lewiston. Afterward, head south along the gorge and stop by the Niagara Power Vista. Take the brief drive to the bottom of the Power Vista to the fishermen's platform and see anglers catching huge trout and salmon. Next, continue south along the gorge to Whirlpool State Park, a perfect 30-minute stop for a brief walk to an excellent view of the swirling waters of the Niagara River whirlpool.

Enter Niagara Falls State Park and make for Goat Island. Here, you will find many opportunities to experience the majesty of Niagara up close. Start at the Cave of the Winds, which takes you beneath Bridal Veil Falls. Next, head to Luna Island, which will let you get as close to the brink of Niagara as possible. On the far shore of Goat Island, Terrapin Point is next. This is the best spot in the park for a view of the brink of Horseshoe Falls. Finally, walk along the south shore to Three Sisters Islands, which jut out into the upper rapids of the Niagara River.

If you're looking for a quick lunch, try the Misty Dog Grill, or if you have time, take the 10-minute drive to Little Italy and go to the Como Restaurant for an authentic Italian lunch. Return to the Canadian side via the Rainbow Bridge and rest before dinner.

Head north to St. Davids for dinner at the Ravine Winery Restaurant. After dinner, go to the Skylon Tower and watch the sunset from the observation deck, 52 stories above the falls. Take a walk down Clifton Hill for some kitschy entertainment. Take an evening ride on the Niagara SkyWheel.

Waves of Fun

The Whirlpool Jet Boats take you through the exhilarating waters of the Niagara River's rapids.

The Niagara region is a great destination for water lovers.

BOATING

- **Whirlpool Jet Boats** take you on an unforgettable ride through Class V white water in Lewiston, New York, Niagara-on-the-Lake, or near the whirlpool in Ontario.

- It's hard to think of a more relaxing way to enjoy a two-hour cruise in the Buffalo Harbor than aboard the *Spirit of Buffalo,* a 73-foot sailboat.

- Try **Grand Lady Cruises** in Buffalo for a romantic and luxurious sunset voyage along the Niagara River.

- **Lockport Locks & Erie Canal Cruises** takes you along the Erie Canal and back in time on a leisurely two-hour cruise.

- In Buffalo, the **Queen City Ferry** offers daily history tours of the Buffalo River that take you inside some of the silos that make up the "Concrete Atlantis" of Buffalo's waterfront.

- Want to be the captain of your own ship? **Buffalo Harbor Kayaks** lets you skipper your own kayak or stand-up paddleboard.

FISHING

- Some of the best freshwater fishing is in **Lake Erie, Lake Ontario,** and in the **Niagara River.** The Lower Niagara River and Lake Ontario are renowned for salmon, steelhead, and trout.

- Join a chartered boat trip with Lewiston's **Niagara River Guide Service,** during which the captain can help you land some trophy fish.

- Operating out of Buffalo, **Jim Hanley's Charter** will take you to where smallmouth bass and walleyes hide in the waters of the Upper Niagara River and Lake Erie.

SWIMMING

- The region's best beach is **Crystal Beach,** along the shore of Lake Erie. This public beach lives up to its name, with beautiful sand and warm water, thanks to Lake Erie's status as the shallowest of the Great Lakes.

- Back on the U.S. side of the border, **Beaver Island State Park** is a great place to picnic and play in the sand. The beach here is large and monitored by lifeguards.

Day Trips from the Falls

Wine Country and Niagara-on-the-Lake

There are several ways to enjoy a tour of wine country: You can drive yourself, let someone else drive for you, or take a bike tour.

Many transportation companies like Grape and Wine Tours and Grape Escape Wine Tours offer bus or van tours of wineries, which usually include visits to 3-5 wineries and a meal. Escorted bicycle tours are another popular way to tour the area. As you cycle through the countryside, visiting wineries along the way, tour guides provide narration about the region. Niagara Getaway, Grape Escape Wine Tours, and Niagara Wine Tours International provide bike tours of the winery region as well as bike rentals.

MORNING

From your hotel in Niagara Falls, make the 20-minute drive to Fort George and be transported back to the War of 1812 with costumed docents, period music, and musket demonstrations. Plan on spending 2-4 hours here. Head to Niagara-on-the-Lake for an early lunch of authentic British pub grub at the (allegedly) haunted Olde Angel Inn.

AFTERNOON

After lunch, head south out of town to Peller Estates, a stunning French château that is large, yet homey. Couches surround a fireplace, making for a cozy wine-tasting experience. Continuing south along the gorge, stop at Inniskillin Winery, which boasts some of the region's best ice wines. Return north to visit Stratus Vineyards and Jackson-Triggs Niagara Estate Winery. Each provide an excellent introduction to the diverse vintages in the Niagara region, including ice wine, chardonnay, pinot noir, riesling, and gewürztraminer.

EVENING

Make your way back to Niagara-on-the-Lake for dinner at Zees Grill. Sit out on the patio if the weather is nice. Zees' wine menu features selections from Inniskillin, Peller Estates, and Jackson-Triggs. Test out your new skills in wine pairings by choosing one of these local wines to complement your meal.

After dinner, walk along Queen Street to browse some of the shops. If you love sweets, stop at the Rocky Mountain Chocolate Factory, where chocolate lovers will be

Reenactors bring the War of 1812 to life at Fort George.

overwhelmed by the number of tempting goodies.

Buffalo: History, Heritage, and Architecture

Frederick Law Olmsted, the designer of Central Park in New York City, called Buffalo the "best-designed city in America." When touring the streets of Buffalo, it is easy to see why.

MORNING

Start your day with a tour of the Martin House Complex, designed by Frank Lloyd Wright. A brief drive gets you to the Museum District and Delaware Park, for a glimpse into Buffalo's golden era, when the Erie Canal flooded the city with prosperity. The Albright-Knox Art Gallery, The Buffalo History Museum, and the Richardson-Olmsted Complex are all within walking distance of each other and well worth a visit.

Head downtown for lunch at the Pearl Street Grill and Brewery. Consider taking the one-hour brewery tasting tour.

AFTERNOON

After lunch, walk two blocks north on Pearl Street to find Louis Sullivan's prototype skyscraper, the Guaranty Building. Directly across the street is St. Paul's Episcopal Cathedral, built by Richard Upjohn. The architect considered St. Paul's his best work.

Walk or drive to the waterfront Canalside complex. Start at the Commercial Slip, the unearthed and restored terminus of the Erie Canal. Here, you can explore the actual ruins of the canal, including the towpath and foundations of buildings that lined the waterway. Interpretive signs allow you to explore at your own pace. Hop aboard the Queen City Ferry for a historical tour of the Inner Harbor and the amazing grain elevators of Buffalo.

Head next door to the Buffalo and Erie County Navy and Military Park, which features three decommissioned naval vessels, including a WWII submarine, destroyer, and guided missile frigate. Artifacts and displays honor all branches of the military, but the real stars are the retired vets who act as docents.

EVENING

Dinner is just five minutes away at the Lafayette, a beautifully restored 1904 luxury hotel. Enjoy fine dining at Mike A's at the Lafayette, just off the main lobby. Before or after dinner, stroll through the ground floor of the hotel for a reminder of the Gilded Age in Buffalo.

Romantic Weekend Getaway

Niagara Falls calls itself the Honeymoon Capital of the World. This itinerary will help you appreciate the romantic mystique of the falls in a quick weekend getaway.

Base yourself on the Canadian side of the falls. Make reservations at the Marriott Niagara Falls Fallsview Hotel & Spa, which boasts the best spa in town. It's worth the splurge to stay in one of the hotel's two-level loft rooms, where you'll get a great view of the falls from floor-to-ceiling windows, and a fireplace and whirlpool tub in your room.

Friday

Check into your hotel, then use the afternoon to acquaint yourself with the falls area. Take a boat ride to the base of the falls with Hornblower Niagara Cruises, then go for a different perspective with Journey Behind the Falls. Head three miles downstream from the falls for a peak at the Lower Niagara's entrancing whirlpool.

Take a horse-drawn carriage ride around town as dusk approaches. You can find the carriages on Niagara Parkway, close to Murray Hill. Enjoy an intimate dinner at one of Niagara's most exclusive restaurants, AG. Be sure to order an ice wine martini as an aperitif. Make your reservation for 7:30pm to give yourself enough time to enjoy the fireworks display over the falls at 10pm.

After dinner head to the Skylon Tower. Grab a coffee or other warm beverage at the coffee shop in the base of the tower to keep you warm once you're out on the Observation Deck. This is the perfect spot to watch the fireworks display. Your perch 520 feet above the ground gives you the opportunity to look down on the pyrotechnics.

If you still have some energy left, go to Clifton Hill for a ride on the SkyWheel, some arcade games, or a kitschy trip through one of the numerous haunted houses.

Saturday

Following breakfast, head out for a tour of the wineries in wine country. The best way to relax and enjoy a tour and lunch is by bus. If you and your partner are more active types, try a bicycle tour. Great Grape Escapes offers both bus and bike tours, and will pick you up at your falls-area hotel. The bus tour covers stops at four wineries, plus a three-course meal at an excellent Niagara-on-the-Lake restaurant. The bike tour offers a picnic lunch in an orchard.

After a day of touring, it's time to relax back at the hotel. The Marriott's Serenity Spa offers couples services. Start off with the hour-long massage. Next, get a facial treatment for two, followed by 30 minutes of hydrotherapy in a shared tub.

For dinner, make your way to Elements on the Falls after the sun goes down. Here, you'll enjoy great food and an excellent view of the nightly illumination of Niagara Falls. After dinner, head over to the Fallsview Casino Resort, where you can try your luck at the tables or catch a show at the casino's Avalon Ballroom Theatre.

Sunday

If you're heading back to the States today, stop at Niagara Falls State Park after you cross the border. The park is a wonderland of natural features, and offers some different views of the falls.

Spend a few hours walking around Goat Island, being sure to check out Terrapin Point and Luna Island. From there, you can venture out onto the Three Sisters Islands, which will place you as close to the upper rapids of the Niagara River as you can safely get.

On your way out of the park, stop at the Observation Tower Platform for one last look at amazing Niagara Falls.

Journey Behind the Falls

Splurge or Save

RESTAURANTS
Splurge

- **Mike A at the Lafayette:** Buffalo's best chef offers a creative menu and unsurpassed cocktails all in a grand restored 1904 hotel.

- **Peller Estate Winery Restaurant:** Pairing locally sourced food with the proper wine is an art form here.

- **Koi Restaurant:** This first-class restaurant in the Seneca Niagara Casino serves authentic Asian dishes.

Save

- **Grand Buffet:** You can't lose at this Fallsview Casino buffet, with a world-class view and great selection of food at a reasonable price.

- **Misty Dog:** This takeout spot on the U.S. side of the falls has a large menu, including vegan and low-calorie options.

- **Pearl Street Grill and Brewery:** The food is good, the ambience and beer are great. There's no better place to be before a big event in downtown Buffalo.

HOTELS
Splurge

- **Sterling Inn and Spa:** Rekindle the romance with in-room fireplaces and a warm breakfast delivered to your bed at this inn in Niagara Falls, Ontario.

- **Giacomo:** This boutique hotel is unparalleled grandeur on the U.S. side.

- **The Mansion on Delaware:** Enjoy the services of a personal butler and relax at Buffalo's most luxurious boutique hotel.

Save

- **Rex Motel:** If your favorite aunt ran an inexpensive hotel in Niagara Falls, Ontario, this would be it.

- **Red Lounge Hostel:** This large, bright, and airy property has an international ambience and is just a short walk to the falls.

- **The Falls Motel:** On the New York side, this motel is clean, inexpensive, and family-operated.

ACTIVITIES
Splurge

- **Whirlpool Jet Boats:** An unforgettable and wild ride over class V white water.

- **Niagara Pedi-Cab Tours:** Take a romantic bicycle-powered rickshaw driven by the most knowledgeable guides in Niagara Falls, New York.

- **Grape Escape Wine Tours:** The most relaxing way to enjoy the Canadian wine country is aboard a bus with a knowledgeable guide.

Save

- **Table Rock Welcome Centre:** One of the best views of the falls is free. Find it behind the Table Rock Welcome Centre, at the brink of falls.

- **Niagara Falls State Park:** The best natural experience of the falls is here, and it's free.

SHOPS
Splurge

- **Irish Design:** Find tweed and wool clothes fit for royalty on Niagara-on-the-Lake's Queen Street.

- **Fashion Outlets of Niagara Mall:** Coach, Hugo Boss, and Ralph Lauren are just a few of the high-end stores found in this sprawling Niagara Falls, New York, outlet mall.

Save

- **Buffalo Niagara Shop:** High quality authentic souvenirs are reasonably priced here, plus staff members offer the best advice on current attractions and festivals.

NIAGARA FALLS, ONTARIO

In the shifting fortunes of the Niagara region, Niagara Falls, Ontario, is on the upswing as the preferred destination for tourists. Visitors are drawn to the Canadian side for the best view of the three waterfalls, Horseshoe, Bridal Veil, and American Falls, collectively known as Niagara Falls. From this side of the U.S.-Canadian border, millions of tourists are inspired by the complete panorama in all its glory.

Family-friendly attractions, golf courses, and accommodations offer all the amenities of a world-class destination. Though some visitors feel that the glitz and glass of the high-rise hotels obscure the natural beauty of the falls, most still favor the Canadian side over its American cousin across the river.

More than 16,000 hotel rooms are available, giving the city the second-largest visitor capacity in all of Canada. The Fallsview Casino Resort attracts 20,000 visitors each day and is the largest gaming venue in the country.

The star of the show, though, is Niagara, the raw and refreshing apex of nature's power.

HISTORY

The early history of this region is as turbulent as the mighty Niagara River. For hundreds of years, a tribe of Indians known as the Neutrals hunted and farmed this area on both sides of the river. In an effort to increase their share of the beaver pelt trade, members of the Iroquois Confederacy overpowered the Neutrals and took control of the region in the 1650s.

Europeans explored the area beginning in the 1600s. The first written description of Niagara Falls was by a Jesuit priest, Father

HIGHLIGHTS

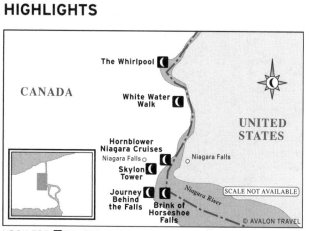

The Whirlpool

CANADA

White Water Walk

UNITED STATES

Hornblower Niagara Cruises

Niagara Falls

Niagara Falls

Skylon Tower

Journey Behind the Falls

Brink of Horseshoe Falls

Niagara River

SCALE NOT AVAILABLE

© AVALON TRAVEL

LOOK FOR ⚫ TO FIND RECOMMENDED SIGHTS, ACTIVITIES, DINING, AND LODGING.

⚫ **Brink of Horseshoe Falls:** This is where nature's power and beauty combine to become Niagara Falls. It's an experience like nothing else on the planet (page 23).

⚫ **Journey Behind the Falls:** Check out the world's most famous wall of water from tunnels dug behind Horseshoe Falls (page 24).

⚫ **Hornblower Niagara Cruises:** This cruise takes you into the fury beneath Niagara Falls. To get any closer, you'd need to be in a barrel (page 25).

⚫ **Skylon Tower:** Day or night, some of the best views of the falls are from the tower's observation deck, perched more than 500 feet above the falls (page 27).

⚫ **White Water Walk:** This boardwalk allows you to safely come face-to-face with the mighty Niagara River as it surges through the gorge, creating 15-foot-tall waves (page 29).

⚫ **The Whirlpool:** This curious bend in the Lower Niagara River is deceptively beautiful, but its swirling vortex is deadly (page 30).

Louis Hennepin, in December 1678. By the 1700s, France and England were fighting for control of the region. English forces prevailed and, in 1759, the French military finally departed.

As the American Revolution heated up, colonists loyal to England moved to Canada. Many settled in the area that is now southern Ontario on land given to them by the British Crown. Settlers cleared the land for farming, finding the soil perfect for growing fruits and vegetables. The War of 1812 brought death and destruction to the Niagara frontier, with many of the bloodiest engagements occurring along the Niagara River.

By 1881, the Town of Niagara Falls, Ontario, was established. The Canadian side of the falls was already a popular spot for visitors, but was also known as a tourist trap, where competing attractions used aggressive promotional techniques to secure customers. The Canadian government bought the land surrounding Horseshoe Falls, removed private hotels and attractions, and created Queen Victoria Park in 1885. With a goal of conservation and wise growth, the Niagara Parks Commission governs the development of the region. The Commission's partnership with various government agencies and private interest groups

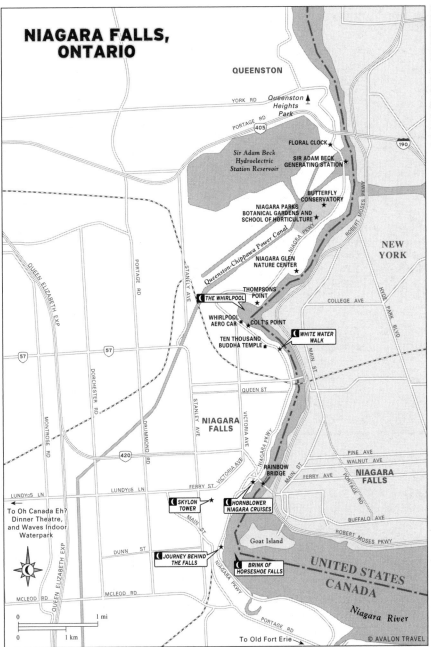

NIAGARA FALLS, ONTARIO

QUEENSTON

YORK RD
Queenston Heights Park

PORTAGE RD
405

FLORAL CLOCK ★

Sir Adam Beck Hydroelectric Station Reservoir

SIR ADAM BECK GENERATING STATION ★

BUTTERFLY CONSERVATORY ★

NIAGARA PARKS BOTANICAL GARDENS AND SCHOOL OF HORTICULTURE ★

190

ROBERT MOSES PKWY

Queenston-Chippawa Power Canal

NIAGARA PKWY

NIAGARA GLEN NATURE CENTER ★

NEW YORK

PORTAGE RD

STANLEY AVE

QUEEN RD

QUEEN ELIZABETH EXP

THE WHIRLPOOL

THOMPSONS POINT ★

WHIRLPOOL AERO CAR ★ ★ COLT'S POINT

COLLEGE AVE

HYDE PARK BLVD

WHITE WATER WALK

TEN THOUSAND BUDDHA TEMPLE ■

57   57

DORCHESTER RD

MONTROSE RD

DRUMMOND RD

STANLEY AVE

QUEEN ST

NIAGARA FALLS

VICTORIA AVE

NIAGARA PKWY

MAIN ST

420

PINE AVE
WALNUT AVE

RAINBOW BRIDGE

NIAGARA FALLS

PORTAGE RD

FERRY AVE

LUNDY'S LN

LUNDY'S LN

FERRY ST   VICTORIA AVE

To Oh Canada Eh? Dinner Theatre, and Waves Indoor Waterpark ←

SKYLON TOWER

HORNBLOWER NIAGARA CRUISES

MAIN ST

BUFFALO AVE

ROBERT MOSES PKWY

DUNN ST

Goat Island

JOURNEY BEHIND THE FALLS ★

BRINK OF HORSESHOE FALLS ★

UNITED STATES
CANADA

MCLEOD RD

MCLEOD RD

NIAGARA PKWY

PORTAGE RD

Niagara River

0   1 mi
0   1 km

To Old Fort Erie →

© AVALON TRAVEL

has yielded a destination that welcomes more than 12 million tourists each year.

PLANNING YOUR TIME

Niagara Falls, Ontario, is rich in natural and developed attractions. A three-day, two-night stay allows enough time to fully appreciate all this destination has to offer.

Plan on making both daytime and nighttime visits to the pedestrian path along the gorge that connects the brink of the falls with the Hornblower Niagara Cruises complex. This 0.75-mile path offers the best views of all three waterfalls that comprise Niagara. Viewing the falls at various times during your visit will reveal different aspects of this natural wonder.

Fewer tourists visit on weekdays than on weekends and holidays, when the area swells with visitors. The best strategy for avoiding long lines at the Hornblower Niagara Cruises complex is to arrive early in the morning, just after 10am. The **Niagara Falls Adventure Pass** (www.niagaraparks.com, $50 adults, $37 children 6-12) reserves timed tickets for Journey Behind the Falls, Niagara's Fury, and the White Water Walk.

Some attractions, including the Hornblower Niagara Cruises, Journey Behind the Falls, and the White Water Walk, are seasonal and are either closed or have restricted hours November-April. The Niagara Parks website (www.niagaraparks.com) is the best resource for information on seasonal schedules.

This area is car-friendly, but the tourist transit system (WEGO) provides excellent, inexpensive transportation with stops at all the major hotels and attractions. If your hotel is not on the WEGO route, you can park for free at the Whirlpool Aero Car lot (3850 Niagara River Pkwy.) and pick up the bus there.

ORIENTATION

Attractions generally are clustered in three zones:

Brink of the Falls: The area from Chippawa in the south to the Rainbow Bridge, which includes Queen Victoria Park, Table Rock Welcome Centre, Hornblower Niagara Cruises, and the Dufferin Islands.

Fallsview: The developed area parallel to Victoria Park, including Clifton Hill and Lundy's Lane.

Parkway North: The area from the Rainbow Bridge north toward Queenston, which includes the whirlpool, White Water Walk, and the Butterfly Conservatory.

Sights

Unless noted otherwise, the sights listed here journey south to north.

CHIPPAWA

Located just two miles from the brink of Niagara, the quiet community of Chippawa is frequently overlooked by tourists and is known as the childhood home of film director James Cameron.

Chippawa is bisected by the Welland River, which makes for numerous beautiful waterfront views. Some of the best are from **Kingsbridge Park** (7870 Niagara Pkwy., 877/642-7275, www.niagaraparksnature.com, dawn-dusk daily), which has picnic facilities, a playground, and a wading pool. Another nearby park, the **Chippawa Battlefield Site** (Niagara Pkwy. near Ussher's Creek, www.niagaraparksheritage.com, dawn-dusk daily) memorializes the Battle of Chippawa, where more than 200 Indian, Canadian, and American soldiers died fighting during the War of 1812. The park's main feature is a cairn with plaques describing the battle and the men who lost their lives and are buried here. Each year on July 5, the anniversary of the conflict, a solemn ceremony commemorates the battle and the 200 years of peace that followed.

BRINK OF THE FALLS

Marineland

Located just five minutes from the falls is **Marineland** (7657 Portage Rd., 905/356-9565, www.marineland.ca, Sat.-Sun. mid-May-June, daily July-mid-Oct., $43 adults, $36 children 5-9), a sprawling theme park with thrill rides, animal shows, and a petting zoo. Visitors of all ages will enjoy the shows in the park's main pool, where beluga whales, dolphins, walruses, and sea lions perform four times daily. You can feed and pet the beluga whales for an additional charge ($8). The aquatic performances are the main attractions here, so plan to attend a show first. The arena, King Waldorf's Stadium, is close to the entry gates; shows start every two hours.

Young children will delight in the petting and feeding pens for land animals, where they can feed deer and view other animals, including elk and bison. The park also features more than a dozen amusement park-style rides for all ages, including Dragon Mountain, the world's largest steel roller coaster.

Families with small children will want to spend a half-day at Marineland. Be prepared to walk. The various attractions are spread out on a campus that is nearly two square miles, with no trolley or bus transportation system. The park is in need of cosmetic updates.

The hours of operation vary throughout the year, with the park opening at either 9:30am or 10am. Closing hours fluctuate as well, with admission booths closing at 5pm or 6pm. The park attractions remain open until dusk.

International Control Dam Overlook

The **International Control Dam Overlook** (Niagara Pkwy., 1.5 miles south of Niagara Falls) is an important vista for understanding the natural and developed forces at work in Niagara. The control dam is a concrete structure extending 1,500 feet into the Niagara River, upstream of the falls. The dam uses a series of gates that raise and lower to control the flow and dispersion of the water over the falls.

At all times, 50 percent of the water heading down the Niagara River is diverted for hydroelectric power generation before reaching the falls. This dam helps regulate that diversion, but it also serves another important purpose: It spreads the water in an even pattern over the brink of Horseshoe Falls.

As you stand on the grassy area between the river and the parkway, note the gates in the dam—some will be up, others will be down. Look for the semisubmerged concrete weirs running parallel to the shore. The gates and weirs work in concert so that Horseshoe Falls appears to have a uniform wall of water crashing over its brink. Facing south (upstream), you'll see two tall, narrow buildings. These house the gates that also assist in regulating water diverted from the river. Those gates are built over the intake tunnels that feed the Sir Adam Beck Generating Station downstream.

Driving north from Chippawa, you'll see a service road opposite the entrance to the Rapidsview parking complex (7369 Niagara Pkwy.). Park in the Rapidsview complex and walk a few hundred yards to the service road for the best view of the dam. If you park directly at the curb of the service road, the Parks police may ask you to move, as there is no parking allowed in this area.

Dufferin Islands

The **Dufferin Islands** (Niagara Pkwy., one mile south of the falls, 877/642-7275, www.niagaraparksnature.com, 24 hours daily, free) are a wonderful area, perfect for a picnic or walk. This quiet oasis was built in response to concerns that the area surrounding the falls had lost some of its natural appeal. The park is not on the radar of most tourists, so it offers an eco-enclave for people to relax and commune with nature.

This 10-acre park features 10 small islands joined by a network of footbridges and trails. The mixture of lightly wooded areas, small green spaces, shallow streams, and trails allow refuge from the crowds and bustle of the nearby tourist areas. While the park is best appreciated on foot, you may also enjoy a slow drive along paved roads. When driving, look out for

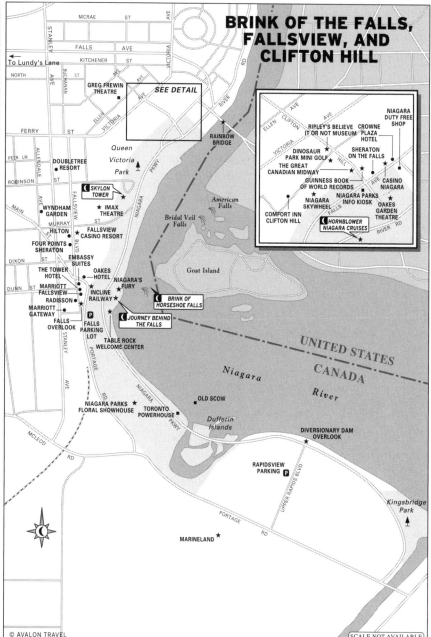

BRINK OF THE FALLS, FALLSVIEW, AND CLIFTON HILL

SEE DETAIL

← To Lundy's Lane

SCALE NOT AVAILABLE

© AVALON TRAVEL

geese and ducks using the roads to cross from pond to pond.

During most of the year, the Dufferin Islands are free of crowds. Summer weekends are the most popular times for visitors and locals who use the park for dog walks and picnic lunches. Catch-and-release fishing and birdwatching are popular activities in the summer. In the winter, animated-light displays for the Festival of Lights are erected in the park. Motorists can drive through the park and make a small donation that benefits the festival organization.

Toronto Power Generating Station and the Old Scow

The **Toronto Power Generating Station** (Niagara Pkwy.) is an abandoned power plant that generated electricity 1906-1974. Looking at the beautiful limestone structure, it's hard to believe it was a power station. When commissioned as a hydroelectric plant, it was an engineering marvel. The plant's owners wanted the exterior to match the importance of the interior, so an Italian Renaissance design was chosen—the first time beaux arts had been used for an industrial structure. Imposing ionic colonnades flank the stately main portion of the building. It stands along the shore of the river, an elegant reminder of the electric power revolution that was born at Niagara. The interior of the building is closed to the public.

Niagara Parks now owns the station and is weighing how best to repurpose the building. Locals speculate the grand structure will someday house an interpretive museum.

The grounds immediately adjacent to the station afford the best perspective of the **old scow.** A scow is a type of large boat that has a flat bottom and squared-off ends, used primarily for transporting materials like ore or sand in bulk. The old scow was carrying a load of rock when it broke loose, rapidly floated downstream, and became lodged above Horseshoe Falls in 1918. Two men aboard were rescued by the heroics of famed river man Red Hill, Sr. The scow remains lodged where it became marooned nearly 100 years ago, providing a

resting spot for gulls and other birds. You can spot the scow from the parkway while driving, but it's worth a closer examination on foot. The best vantage point is the northern end of the Toronto Power Generating Station.

Floral Showhouse

A few hundred yards from the brink of Horseshoe Falls, the **Floral Showhouse** (7145 Niagara Pkwy., 905/371-0254, www.niagaraparks.com, 9:30am-5pm daily, $5 adults, $3.75 children 6-12) is a tropical oasis filled with lush foliage and songbirds. The showhouse is an enclosed greenhouse with thousands of flowers and plants chosen for their beauty and fragrance. The main showhouse is a large, airy, indoor space featuring a waterfall and trapezoid-shaped glass roof. This spacious area has the atmosphere and intrigue of a tropical forest. Several smaller, rectangular greenhouses are attached to the showhouse, each filled with tropical plants, statuary, and trees.

Of particular interest is the *titan arum,* the world's largest lily, which grows to 10 feet. The plants on display are changed eight times a year, so there's always something different to enjoy. (Easter and Christmas displays are the seasonal highlights.) All plants are identified by signs indicating the species name. Although plants are not for sale, you'll find unique gardening-related treasures in the gift shop.

The outdoor gardens surrounding the showhouse consist of a large rose garden and reflective ponds, ideal for taking a relaxing afternoon stroll. About 30 minutes is ample time to enjoy this attraction, but flower enthusiasts could easily spend more than an hour.

◖ Brink of Horseshoe Falls

Arguably one of the most photographed sites in the world, the **brink of Horseshoe Falls** (6650 Niagara Pkwy., 24 hours daily, free) has a view like no other. The brink is a public plaza area behind Table Rock Welcome Centre, which allows you to stand at the crest of Horseshoe Falls. The space is always open to visitors and is integrated into the paved pedestrian pathway that runs all the way to Niagara-on-the-Lake from Fort Erie. Green space, trees, and benches adjacent to the plaza provide convenient places to relax and appreciate the landscape.

It is difficult to fathom how much water spills over the falls. Every second, 680,000 gallons of water pour over the brink, enough to fill the entire Empire State Building in six minutes! The crest line of Horseshoe Falls is 2,200 feet wide, joining this spot with Terrapin Point on the U.S. side. On sunny days, the vibrant green water is hypnotic and soothing, until the water slams into the lower river with 2,500 tons of force.

Mist produced by the thundering waterfall can climb 200 feet or more in the air. The wind determines where the mist will fall and there's always a possibility that standing here, you'll feel some fine precipitation. It's a good idea to carry an umbrella when visiting the brink, as well as a cloth for drying your camera lens.

This area is stunning year-round. During winter, the mist collects on every surface and freezes, creating a crystalline skin on tree branches, guide rails, and light posts, which is as beautiful as it is fragile. In autumn, the blazing reds and yellows of the changing leaves bring vibrancy to the grey of the gorge.

The pedestrian area along the brink is always open to visitors, even when the indoor areas of the Table Rock Welcome Centre are closed. Use common sense when taking pictures at the brink and do not climb on top of guardrails or support pillars. Many, many people are vying for a spot along the brink, so take photos, appreciate the vista, then let another visitor move into your spot.

Table Rock Welcome Centre

The **Table Rock Welcome Centre** (6650 Niagara Pkwy., 877/642-7275, www.niagaraparks.com, 24 hours daily, free) is the large bronze and brown structure at the brink of the falls, which houses restaurants, shops, attractions, a first aid station, and public washrooms. The bathrooms are always open, but hours of operation vary for the attractions, restaurants, and gift shops. Restaurants include takeout options as well as a coffee shop.

Paid parking ($10-20) is available across the street from the center, accessible via the crosswalk or pedestrian bridge. The complex is a major hub for the WEGO transportation service. Many visitors park across from the center and then use WEGO buses for their exploration of Niagara.

◖ JOURNEY BEHIND THE FALLS

Journey Behind the Falls (Table Rock Welcome Centre, 6650 Niagara Pkwy., 877/642-7275, www.niagaraparks.com, 9am-5pm Mon.-Fri., extended hours Sat.-Sun. Sept.-May and daily June-Aug., $16 adults, $11 children 6-12, free for children 5 and under) is, as its name implies, a chance to view Niagara Falls from inside the gorge wall, via a tunnel dug parallel to the face of the falls. The tunnels connect with two portals that allow you to look at the raging sheet of water from behind. The tunnels also lead to an outdoor observation platform at the base of Horseshoe Falls. Included in the cost of admission is a yellow plastic rain poncho. Keep it—it will come in handy later!

The journey starts with an elevator ride 15 stories underground. Upon exiting the elevator, you are immersed in a cool, dim, and dank series of tunnels, with the hum of the falls audible in the distance. The main tunnel slopes slightly downhill, leading to another tunnel on the right. This tunnel is parallel to the face of the falls. Within a few hundred yards, you'll find two portals—windows for viewing the falls from behind.

The portals have no protective glass, just a modest fence separating you from the torrent. The visual aspect of the portals (seeing falling water) is secondary to the *feeling* you experience. The roaring force of the falling water creates a subtle tremor that intensifies as you approach the safety fence. Sheets of water slash at the opening in the rock face, causing dislodged rocks to gather on the floor of the portal. Both portals are identical, so find the one with a shorter line. This portion of your journey should take about 5-10 minutes.

On your way back to the main tunnel, turn right and continue to the observation platform. The platform's upper level is enclosed and offers a protected vantage point of this amazing area at the base of the falls. Away from the some-times-drenching mist, it provides safe photo opportunities. The open viewing ports give unobstructed views of the falling torrent of Horseshoe Falls.

The lower level of the platform is for the hardy explorer looking for the full monsoon-like experience of Niagara. The difference between the upper and lower levels is like the difference between riding in a regular car ver-sus a convertible with the top down. *What* you see is the same, but *how* you see it is very different.

At the bottom of the stairway is the lower platform, a large patio area. Make certain to wear the rain poncho, because you'll likely get soaked. You're now very close to where a 17-story-tall wall of water slams into the river below. The force of this collision generates mist that seems to attack from all sides.

Those looking to minimize their exposure to the wind and mist can seek refuge on the far side of the patio area, where those elements are much lighter. If you're looking for the full expe-rience, though, face the falls and head directly to the safety rail closest to the falls. Depending on weather conditions, the experience can be refreshing or chilling, but it is always satisfying. Before you go out to the lower platform, stow all electronics underneath your poncho, ideally in a protective bag.

The last leg of your journey is the elevator ride back to the top. The line to board the el-evators usually requires a 5- to 10-minute wait. Most travelers will spend 60-90 minutes at this attraction. When taking photos in the portals, be sure your camera's flash is activated, as the light coming through the portals provides back lighting.

Portions of this attraction are limited in the winter months. From mid-December through mid-April, the lower observation deck closes for the season, and sometimes the portals are ob-scured by thick ice. Admission rates are reduced during this part of the season ($11.25 adults, $7 children 6-12).

NIAGARA'S FURY

Billed as a 4-D experience, **Niagara's Fury** (Table Rock Welcome Centre, 6650 Niagara Pkwy., 905/358-3268, www.niagarasfury.com, 9am-5pm daily, $13.50 adults, $9 children 6-12, free for children 5 and under) is a hit with children, but a bit underwhelming for adults. The attraction begins with an eight-minute ani-mation describing the birth of the falls, told through the eyes of woodland creatures. As the cartoon ends, doors open to a 360-degree the-ater space where a six-minute 4-D movie plays. During the movie, the theater's temperature fluctuates to correspond with the narrative. Water pours down the walls, the floor shakes, raindrops fall from the ceiling, and a simulated snow squall greets you. The choreographed spe-cial effects simulate the cataclysmic forces that shaped the geology of this region.

The entire experience is well under 30 min-utes. If you'd prefer to stay dry during the 4-D rainfall simulation, stand close to the exits of the theater.

⬛ Hornblower Niagara Cruises

Niagara's newest attraction is also its most am-bitious. **Hornblower Niagara Cruises** (5920 Niagara Pkwy., 905/642-4272, www.niagara-cruises.com) provides boat tours to the base of Horseshoe Falls from the Canadian side of the river. Hornblower will use new 700-passenger catamaran ships to ferry passengers to the base of Horseshoe Falls.

The ride to and from Horseshoe Falls is pleasant, providing a view of American and Bridal Veil Falls as the boat passes about 500 yards from the U.S. shoreline. The calm por-tion of the ride ends as the boat enters the choppy, roiling waters beneath Horseshoe Falls. Water assaults you from all sides, as wind-whipped mist soaks everything in its path. The ferocious torrent causes the water in the Lower Niagara River to resemble a boiling cauldron with numerous white caps and eddies surging.

Those on the top deck of the boat receive

Get close to the falls with Hornblower Niagara Cruises.

the most amount of mist. People on the lower deck receive some shelter from the wind-driven water, but everyone should plan on getting wet. If you have a waterproof camera, you'll be able to capture images throughout the journey. Others should stow their camera when the boat is directly under Horseshoe Falls (tucking the camera under your poncho is usually sufficient protection).

Hornblower is looking to top the Maid of the Mist tour, offered on the U.S. side, by offering extra services. In addition to the traditional daily 20-minute tours to the base of Horseshoe Falls, Hornblower is providing 30-minute enhanced cruises during the nightly illumination and the summer fireworks shows. Hornblower's catamarans offer amenities including washrooms, snack concessions, a deck area protected by retractable glass windows, and a bar.

Outdoor Gardens
As you walk north from the brink of the falls, you can see across the gorge to Niagara Falls.

From there, turn 180 degrees and look across the Niagara Parkway, where you'll find the outdoor gardens of **Queen Victoria Park** (Niagara Pkwy. from Table Rock to Clifton Hill, www. niagaraparks.com, 24 hours daily, free). Queen Victoria Park is a meticulously groomed landscape with lush green lawns, rock gardens, fountains, and trees. Plants have been chosen so that something is always blooming in the spring, summer, and autumn. Park benches and verdant grassy areas are perfect for a rest, with their panorama of the gorge and falls.

The **Oakes Garden Theatre** (Niagara Pkwy., www.niagaraparks.com, 24 hours daily, free) is immediately across Clifton Hill from Queen Victoria Park, a hidden gem that is easily overlooked because it appears to be part of a private attraction or hotel. It was once the site of the grand and historic Clifton Hotel, the meeting place for both Union and Confederate representatives discussing diplomatic matters during the American Civil War. Today, the Oakes Garden is the setting for many special events, including live music and festivals. The gardens feature a beautiful curved walkway adorned with pillars and latticework built into small hills that overlook a raised stage area. The falls supply a beautiful backdrop to the fan-shaped stage. The Oakes is one of the best spots to view the fireworks display over the falls at 10pm on Fridays and Sundays in summer.

FALLSVIEW
Overlook
One of the best views of the falls is from an overlook not marked on any maps and without a name. It's near the intersection of Livingstone Street and Fallsview Boulevard, just in front of the Marriott Gateway Hotel. From this humble perch, you can see Table Rock Welcome Centre, Horseshoe Falls, and the upper rapids of the Niagara River. You can also get a good sense of the distance between the Diversionary Dam, Toronto Power Generating Station, and brink of the falls.

Very few people know about this overlook, so it isn't crowded. It is a short walk from all the major high-rise hotels and the casino. Walk south on Fallsview Boulevard until you reach the end of the road. If you're driving, park along the curb on Fallsview Boulevard. Look for the WEGO bus shelter across from the taxi stand and you'll be at the right spot.

◖ Skylon Tower

The most iconic man-made landmark in Niagara Falls is the **Skylon Tower** (5200 Robinson St., 905/356-2651, www.skylon.com, 8am-midnight daily May-mid-Oct., 11am-9pm mid-Oct.-Apr., main level free). Since 1965, the concrete structure has towered 52 stories above the city, allowing for a 360-degree view of the region. On clear days, the skylines of Toronto and Buffalo are visible beyond the falls.

The main level of Skylon Tower features several gift shops, a Starbucks, and a ticket counter. The top of the tower provides fine dining in the Revolving Dining Room as well as family-style fare at the Summit Style Buffet. Above it all is the observation deck, where you'll experience some of the best panoramas of Niagara.

The elevator ride ($14 adults, $8 children 2-12, free with purchase of meal at upper restaurants) to the top of the tower is a breathtaking 52-second trip in a glass-enclosed capsule. The brief trip is a prelude to the panorama that greets you on the observation deck. The indoor observation area is enclosed in glass and climate-controlled. Decals on the windows identify points of interest that appear in the distance.

In the outdoor observation area, a wire enclosure keeps you safe, while allowing enough space for your camera lens to poke through and capture unobstructed images of the landscape.

Depending on weather conditions, plan on spending 20-30 minutes on the outdoor observation platform. Most people will spend a majority of their time looking east at the falls, and the Lower Niagara River 775 feet below. Looking north, you may be able to glimpse Toronto (40 miles away) and its CN tower, which is roughly twice as tall as the Skylon Tower.

Looking for a unique camera shot? Face the windows of the enclosed observation area with your back to the landscape. Use the camera to capture your reflection in the windows with the beautiful panorama in the background.

The observation deck is a great place to experience the nighttime beauty of the falls. The view of the nightly illumination from this perch is without parallel. During summer's twice-weekly fireworks shows, viewers in the tower watch the display from above as the fireworks explode beneath the level of the observation deck. You'll need to arrive by 9:30pm and stake out a place along the eastern edge of the platform for the best view of the fireworks.

Kids are drawn to the Family Fun Centre, an arcade located in the lower concourse level of the tower. Here you'll find dozens of interactive amusements and small coin-operated rides. Several fast-food restaurants (Pizza Pizza, Mr. Sub, and Dairy Queen) and bathrooms are also on this level. Upon exiting the building from the concourse level, you'll find the entrance for the 3-D/4-D movie theater that is part of the Skylon complex. The movie, theater, and 4-D effects are somewhat dated, so spend your limited touring time elsewhere.

Clifton Hill

Historically, Niagara Falls has always had circus-like attractions for tourists. Years ago, private museums intrigued visitors with Egyptian mummies, two-headed calves (still on display at Ripley's Believe It or Not!), reconstructed skeletons of large animals, and oddities like Sitting Bull's moccasins. Today, that spirit of carnival and weirdness is found along the street known as Clifton Hill. Clifton Hill is home to numerous arcades, creepy fun houses, mini-golf courses, and wax museums. For those traveling with children, Clifton Hill is a good place to spend an afternoon.

The **Great Canadian Midway** (4950 Clifton Hill, 905/358-3676, www.cliftonhill.com, 9am-2am daily, free admission, game prices vary) is a spacious, loud, energetic arcade with more than 300 of the latest interactive games, as well as some old-school amusements like Skee-Ball. Games operate on tokens purchased at the front desk or automated exchange kiosks.

Advertising flyers with discount coupons for tokens are on racks located on the walkway into the midway complex.

Take a relaxing ride and enjoy a spectacular view on the **Niagara SkyWheel** (4950 Clifton Hill, 905/358-4793, www.cliftonhill.com, 9am-2am daily, $11 adults, $7 children 12 and under). This gentle giant of a Ferris wheel is as tall as Niagara Falls—about 175 feet. Rides in the fully enclosed climate-controlled gondolas last about 12 minutes. The safety and comfort of the gondolas ensure a good ride for the entire family, including those uncomfortable with heights. Take your camera along, as this is one of the best perches to snap images of the falls. Each gondola carries up to six people and provides an excellent 360-degree view of the falls, Clifton Hill, and beyond. The best time to enjoy this attraction is during the day or during the twice-weekly summer fireworks display.

Tee off at **Dinosaur Adventure Golf** (4960 Clifton Hill, 905/358-3676, www.cliftonhill.com, 10am-midnight daily, $10 adults, $7 children 12 and under). Navigate two 18-hole courses with a prehistoric theme. Many of the 50 dinosaur statues will growl at you along the course. Try to keep your concentration as a 50-foot-high volcano erupts periodically, sending smoke and flames into the air.

Oddities abound in **Ripley's Believe It or Not!** (4960 Clifton Hill, 905/356-2238, www.ripleysniagara.com, 10am-10pm daily, $14 adults, $8 children 6-12). You can easily spend 90 minutes or more in this museum. There are more than 800 items on display, including shrunken heads, weird animals, and bizarre artifacts. This attraction is best for children who can read or have someone read to them.

Lundy's Lane

Lundy's Lane is a major corridor that leads to the Fallsview area and is known for its numerous hotels, restaurants, and shops. Once the site of the bloodiest battle in Canada's history, it now has a wonderful heritage museum.

The **Niagara Falls History Museum** (5810 Ferry St., 905/358-5082, www.niagarafalls-museums.ca,10am-9pm Thurs., 10am-5pm Fri.-Wed., $5 adults, $3 children 6-18) is small, but packed with interesting displays telling the story of the falls. Kids can try on military uniforms, shoulder replica muskets, and lift cannon balls from the War of 1812 era. There's also a "feet on" interactive exhibit that allows you to attempt to walk a simulated high wire. The museum was renovated in 2012, just in time for the 200th anniversary of the war. Take 60-90 minutes to appreciate this wonderfully interactive history museum.

Before you leave the museum, grab a free walking map of Drummond Hill Cemetery and walk two blocks west to experience **Lundy's Lane Battlefield** (6110 Lundy's Lane, 905/358-5082, www.visit1812.com, dawn-dusk daily, free). On this spot during the War of 1812, 6,000 British and American soldiers clashed in fighting that lasted five hours. Casualties were high, with each side recording about 800 dead, injured, or missing. The Battle of Lundy's Lane is regarded as the bloodiest day of battle in that war, yet when the smoke cleared, neither side could claim victory.

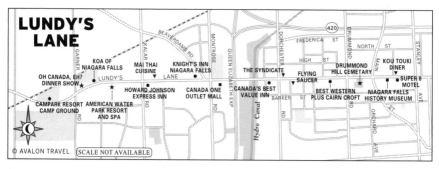

Feel the power of the river's rapids on the White Water Walk.

Following the War of 1812, visitors arrived to commemorate the battle, with soldiers from the war acting as guides. Observation towers, formal monuments, and grave markers were dedicated. As time passed, the battlefield transitioned to a cemetery.

Today the cemetery and battlefield are peaceful reminders of the sacrifices of that battle. Using the walking map, you can find many interesting places, including the area where a funeral pyre was hastily constructed to incinerate the dead. The grave of Canadian heroine Laura Secord is here as well. Secord survived a 20-mile walk through enemy territory during the war to alert the British of an impending American attack. The round-trip walk from the museum and the tour of the battlefield takes 60-90 minutes.

PARKWAY NORTH

When Winston Churchill visited Canada, he called the stretch of the Niagara Parkway heading north from Niagara Falls "the prettiest

Sunday afternoon drive i
mile portion joining th
Clock runs along the edge
veals many natural wonder
Niagara-on-the-Lake.

◖ White Water Walk

Following the Niagara Parkway north, you'll find the **White Water Walk** (4330 Niagara Pkwy., 877/642-7275, www.niagaraparks.com, 10am-4:30pm daily Apr.-mid-June and Sept.-mid-Oct., 9am-7:30pm mid-June-Aug., $11 adults, $7 children 6-12) about 1.5 miles past the Rainbow Bridge. The White Water Walk gives you the opportunity to safely stroll alongside the turbulent waters of the lower rapids without getting wet.

After descending more than 200 feet in an elevator, you'll walk along a quarter-mile stretch of the Niagara River's edge, with some of the most awe-inspiring portions of the lower rapids. In this narrow part of the gorge, water surges at 30 miles per hour, slamming against giant rocks along the riverbed, creating constant waves ranging 9-15 feet high. This raging white water is the backdrop for a scene in the film *Superman II,* in which Lois Lane is saved by quick-thinking Clark Kent.

Stroll at your own pace on the White Water Walk, pausing to read the informative signs. The walkway is raised, providing a safe, child-friendly, and dry way to see the rapids. The boardwalk is wheelchair-accessible; however, two attached viewing platforms require the use of stairs. Most visitors complete the walk in 30 minutes, but photographers and others fascinated by the roar of white water could easily spend an hour here. This attraction is a WEGO stop (green line, White Water), but also allows free curbside parking along Niagara Parkway.

Ten Thousand Buddha Temple

Directly across from the White Water Walk is the **Ten Thousand Buddha Temple** (4303 River Rd., 905/371-2678, www.chamshantemple.org, 9am-5pm daily, free), also known as the **Cham San Monastery.** This stunning pagoda and serene three-acre campus are home to a group of monks dedicated to spreading peace ...e understanding of dharma philosophy. ...e focal point inside the seven-level pagoda is ...a magnificent 40-foot Buddha statue. The public area of the temple is open daily; free tours of the entire shrine (including the main pagoda) are offered on weekends June through October.

Park in the free lots surrounding the campus. Visitors are asked to remove their shoes to view some indoor areas of the temple; ask permission before taking photographs.

◖ The Whirlpool

Three miles downstream from the falls, the Niagara River takes an abrupt right-hand turn. This area of the river forms a **whirlpool** that is violent and magnificent to behold. The whirlpool is a remnant of an ancient waterfall basin filled with loose rocks. As the Niagara River receded over the past 12,000 years, it intersected this bowl of loose rock and the course of the river changed.

Looking down at the river, note how the water enters the whirlpool and slams into the far gorge wall, turning counterclockwise. The water is forced to cross under the main flow and bubbles up on the other side. It is this force that creates the ever-churning vortex known as the whirlpool. Over the years, this has proven to be the most dangerous stretch of the Niagara, where everything caught in the river collects before heading downstream or disappearing forever.

The river is generally about 30- to 40-feet deep. The whirlpool's depth is more than 100 feet. It has swallowed objects that are never seen again. Even the powerful jet boats that blast along the surface of the river will not cross the white water of the whirlpool. The swirling eye of the whirlpool is always-moving, dangerous, and should be avoided. Prior to the jet boats, an attraction using Zodiac vessels plied the whirlpool, ending with tragic results within its first season of operation.

There are two main ways to safely view the whirlpool on the Canadian side of the gorge. The **Whirlpool Aero Car** (3850 Niagara Pkwy., 877/642-7275, www.niagaraparks.

com, 10am-5pm daily mid-Mar.-June and Sept.-Oct., 9am-8pm daily July-Aug., $13.50 adults, $8.50 children 6-12) allows passengers to glide over the whirlpool aboard an aerial tram. The aero car departs from Colt's Point on its slow journey to Thompson's Point, on the far side of the whirlpool. The 10-minute ride transports passengers 210 feet above the whirlpool, affording excellent views of the gorge and surging water below. The aero car's capacity is 40 people (standing room only); it is not wheelchair-accessible.

Ticket sales end 30 minutes before closing time. Sometimes service may be interrupted due to high winds, so call ahead if you are visiting during bad weather. The staff member traveling on-board can take a group photo with your camera, if requested. A café and public restrooms are available at the gift shop. Parking is free.

The second way to see the whirlpool is at **Thompson's Point** (Niagara Pkwy., dawn-dusk daily, free), a spot unknown to many tourists. Thompson's Point affords a great view of the Niagara River as it drops 50 feet in elevation, creating awe-inspiring rapids. It is the perfect perch to see the counterclockwise flow of the water as the river enters the whirlpool, crosses underneath itself, and then completes its trip to Lake Ontario.

Thompson's Point has many of the same views as Colt's Point (where the aero car departs from), but is less crowded and more panoramic. Thompson's Point is positioned so that you can better observe the river as it enters and exits the whirlpool. From here, you have a better sense of the entire natural system that creates the counterclockwise vortex. If the aero car is operating, stand on the left side of the platform to feel the vibration of the cable car's mechanism beneath your feet. The aero car pauses for a moment at Thompson's Point before returning to Colt's Point.

Thompson's Point is easy to miss. Driving north on the Niagara Parkway, slow down as you near the entrance for the Whirlpool Golf Course and Restaurant. Look for a small sign for Thompson's Point just before a service road

© THE NIAGARA PARKS COMMISSION

Glide 200 feet above the raging river aboard the Whirlpool Aero Car.

on your right, which leads to free parking. Take a short walk to the observation area.

Niagara Parks Botanical Gardens and School of Horticulture

No matter what season you visit the **Niagara Parks Botanical Gardens and School of Horticulture** (2565 Niagara Pkwy., 905/356-8554, www.niagaraparks.com, dawn-dusk daily, free), you'll find something in bloom. This 100-acre campus is home to Canada's only residential horticultural school.

A creative and artistic perennial garden with seasonal plants in hanging baskets greets you at the campus entrance. There are more than 3,000 species of flowers and plants, including a Victorian rose garden with more than 2,400 rose plants. Horticulture enthusiasts could easily spend an entire afternoon wandering the grounds, exploring the herb, rock, shrub, lily, and vegetable gardens. Tree species include crab apples, conifers, spruce, dogwood, and Japanese maples.

A limited number of students are admitted to this prestigious college, and their hard work and passion are evident in the lush and beautiful landscapes throughout the campus. Roaming the grounds is free; parking for the gardens is $5.

Butterfly Conservatory

Relax and watch the butterflies flutter by at the **Butterfly Conservatory** (2565 Niagara Pkwy., 905/358-0025, www.niagaraparks.com, 10am-7pm daily July-Aug., 10am-5pm daily Sept.-June, $13.50 adults, $8.50 children 6-12). Take a break from the roaring power of the falls by enjoying the delicate beauty of more than 2,000 butterflies housed in the conservatory.

Start by viewing a brief informative video on the lives of these colorful creatures. Stroll indoors at your own pace, stopping to observe the butterflies in this lush tropical environment. Sometimes the butterflies will investigate you, landing on your arms, shoulders, and head. Bring your camera and remember to dress appropriately, as the conservatory is kept warm and humid year-round.

The conservatory experience should take about one hour to complete. There's a gift shop and café. The WEGO bus stops here; parking is $5.

Sir Adam Beck Generating Station

The story of turning Niagara's raw energy into clean, inexpensive electric power is told at the **Sir Adam Beck Generating Station** (14000 Niagara Pkwy., 905/357-2379, www.niagaraparks.com, 10am-5pm daily late May-Aug., 10am-4pm daily Sept., 11am-4pm daily Oct., $10 adults, $6.50 children 6-12). The only way to experience this attraction is on a fully guided, 45-minute tour that includes a 10-minute video, interactive displays, and a look at the generator gallery.

This tour is heavy on information, but a bit light on visuals. Security precautions limit visitor access, so tours tell rather than show the story of power generation. Still, for people interested in science and engineering, this is an hour well spent. Visitors must leave bags and backpacks in storage lockers (free) at the tour's start.

Limited parking is available at the plant. Overflow parking is at the Floral Clock, just down the parkway. If you are traveling to the Beck Generating Station, take advantage of the scenic viewing area on the parkway across from the station, with views of the Robert Moses Power Project on the U.S. side of the river.

Floral Clock

Flower fans should find time to stop at the **Floral Clock** (14004 Niagara Pkwy., www.niagaraparks.com, dawn-dusk daily, free), a 40-foot-wide outdoor clock with a face made of thousands of plants organized in a beautiful design. The design is changed twice a year and typically uses more than 15,000 bedding plants. During daylight hours, you can stroll behind the clock, where you'll find a door leading to a small room with images of all the designs over the years. Those with green thumbs will want to take photos and explore a bit more than most visitors, who will be satisfied with a five-minute stop here.

Entertainment and Events

NIGHTLIFE

Clifton Hill is very lively after the sun sets. It erupts with noises and flashing lights, calling people to its arcades, restaurants, bars, museums, and attractions. Much of the area is geared to families with kids. Clifton Hill is a spectacle in stark contrast to the natural beauty of the falls, but there is some charm in the kitsch, the wax museums, haunted houses, funky bowling alley, and food stands, all of which create an artificial glow, like a small slice of Las Vegas.

Clubs

At the crest of Clifton Hill, **Rumours Night Club** (4960 Clifton Hill, 905/358-6152, www.rumoursnightclub.com, 8pm-2:30am Fri.-Sat., 19 years and over) caters to the well-dressed under-30 crowd. This dance club requires a $10 cover charge for the gents on Fridays; on Saturdays, everybody pays $10.

For a good laugh, try **Yuk-Yuks Comedy Club** (5705 Falls Ave., 905/262-5233, www.yukyuks.com, Thurs.-Sat., $11-$16) inside Casino Niagara, adjacent to Clifton Hill. The headliner talent here is top-notch and ticket prices are very reasonable. Shows are at 9pm Thursday and Friday; Saturday 8pm and 10:30pm. You must be 19 or over to attend.

Casinos

When **Casino Niagara** (5705 Falls Ave., 905/374-3598, www.casinoniagara.com, 24 hours daily) first opened in 1996, it was meant as a temporary location while a larger, permanent casino was being built. Once the permanent casino, Fallsview Casino Resort, was complete and operating, the Ontario government decided to keep Casino Niagara open. Casino Niagara is much smaller than Fallsview, but still has a lot for gamers, including 2,700 slot machines, 40 tables for gaming, and poker rooms. There are four restaurants and free live music 9pm-1:30am on weekends on the main gaming floor.

The **Fallsview Casino Resort** (6380 Fallsview Blvd., 888/325-5788, www.fallsviewcasinoresort.com, 24 hours daily) is Canada's largest gaming facility. This casino primarily attracts Toronto residents, and draws a sizable crowd no matter the time of day. This world-class casino has 3,000 slot machines and more than 100 gaming tables. From penny slots to high-limit VIP rooms, it's a safe bet that you'll find something to wager on.

The 1,500-seat Avalon Ballroom Theatre at the Fallsview is designed for intimate performances—all seats are within 100 feet of the stage. The venue routinely attracts performers such as Bill Cosby, Jay Leno, Keith Urban, Diana Krall, and musical revue acts. Live music from regional bands is played on weekends at Club 365, a lounge bar on the main gaming floor. Gamers and those attending performances at Ontario casinos must be at least 19 years old.

Performances

Another Las Vegas-style nightlife attraction is found at the **Greg Frewin Theatre** (5781 Ellen Ave., 905/356-0777, www.gregfrewintheatre.com, shows Fri.-Sat. 7:30pm, seasonal weekday shows, tickets $25-60). Highly accomplished, world-renowned illusionist Greg Frewin will astound you with his magic show featuring music, dancers, and tigers. The entertainment is perfect for families, couples, and groups, and it will leave you marveling at Frewin's magical acts. Sometimes the theater hosts tribute bands on weekdays. Ellen Avenue runs parallel to Victoria Avenue and is joined by Clifton Hill. Parking is free.

If you have an appetite for dinner theater, consider the **Oh Canada, Eh? Dinner Show**

(8585 Lundy's Lane, 800/467-2071, www.ohcanadaeh.com, 6:15pm Mon.-Sat. mid-Apr.-mid-Oct., $40-70). Set in a rustic log cabin, the show features your servers as its stars. More of a musical than a comedy, its songs celebrate and satirize Canadian culture. Tickets include a family-style dinner, which allows second helpings. The show is appropriate for all ages and accessible for everybody, not just those from the Great White North. Gratuities are not included in the ticket cost.

THE ARTS

The **Mount Carmel Chateau Park Art Centre** (7021 Stanley Ave., 905/371-3922, http://chateaupark.ca, 9am-4pm daily, tours $5-13, reservations required) is an oasis of tranquility and reflection, immediately adjacent to the buzz of Fallsview. The art center is part of a larger retreat campus and monastery operated by the Carmelite Friars of the Mount Carmel Monastery. The monastery is a work of art, built in 1894 and surrounded by 12 acres of gardens, lawns, and statues. The gallery offers an impressive number of paintings, sculpture, and pottery by contemporary Canadian artists. If you take the self-guided tour ($5), allot one hour to view the art gallery and another hour to appreciate the building and grounds. The chapel's stained-glass windows are truly magnificent.

Another gallery emphasizing the works of Canadian artists is the **Niagara Falls Art Gallery** (8058 Oakwood Dr., 905/356-1514, www.niagarafallsartgallery.ca, 1pm-4pm Mon.-Fri. July-Aug., noon-4pm Sat. Sept.-June, $5). The permanent collection features many paintings by William Kurelek, who captured the lives of Canadians in the 20th century on the country's great prairies. The John Burniak collection of falls-related art is a must-see: It tells the stories of Niagara through the eyes of artists from the 1700s through the present day. Take the McLeod Road exit (#27) off the QEW (Queen Elizabeth Way) heading east. Oakwood Drive is the first right turn after the exit. The gallery is about seven minutes from the Fallsview area.

FESTIVALS AND EVENTS

The most popular nighttime activity in Niagara is watching the **illumination of the falls.** Every night, 21 powerful lights illuminate all three of Niagara's waterfalls, starting just after dusk. From January through April, the illumination ends at 10pm; during the rest of the year, the lights stay on until midnight.

The lights project soft colors onto the falls, creating an amazing, surreal effect. The best place to appreciate the illumination is along the gorge rim, from the brink of the falls to the Rainbow Bridge. The slowly changing colors are visible from different vantage points, as well as from the Skylon Tower and Niagara SkyWheel.

Another nighttime tradition is the **fireworks display** over the falls, visible at 10pm on Friday and Sunday evenings from late May through September 1. You can watch the pyrotechnics from the same places as the illumination. Particularly good vantage points are the Skylon Tower, the lawn near the Parks Police Headquarters, and the Rainbow Bridge. The fireworks last 10 minutes and also occur on holidays such as Canada Day and the Fourth of July.

Each year, the biggest festival in Niagara Falls is the **Festival of Lights** (citywide, www.wfol.com, mid-Nov.-Jan.). More than one million tourists visit the falls during the festival to view 120 animated light displays at the Dufferin Islands. There are religious and cultural displays, as well as those with seasonal scenes and Disney characters. The festival is best explored on foot or by car. The park is transformed into a winter wonderland of lights as you slowly drive on the main road. At the park exits, volunteers collect donations—typically people give $5-10 per car—which help fund the festival.

When winter is over, it's time for **Springilicious** (Queen St., 905/356-5444, www.sprigilicious.ca, 1st weekend of June, free). This grassroots festival, occurring over the first weekend of June, celebrates the best of Niagara Falls in food, music, and drink. There's a carnival and rides for the kids, a local

Every night, 21 high-powered lights illuminate the falls.

© THE NIAGARA PARKS COMMISSION

talent contest, and free music performances each evening on the main stage. Running concurrently with Springilicious is the **Niagara Falls Beer Festival** (www.springlicious.ca), set along Queen Street and showcasing innovative beers from local microbreweries.

Also celebrated on Queen Street is **Canada Day** (Queen St., 905/356-7521, www.niagarafalls.ca, July 1, free). This patriotic holiday, celebrated on July 1, commemorates the unification of the Canadian Provinces, which eventually led to their sovereignty. The festivities include a parade along Queen Street, entertainment on the main stage at City Hall, food vendors, and a car show. The evening culminates in a fireworks display over the falls at 10pm. Traffic can be heavy with tourists and locals enjoying the fireworks.

Shopping

NIAGARA FALLS FARMERS MARKET

For more than 50 years, some of the freshest food in Niagara Falls has been found year-round at the **Niagara Falls Farmers Market** (5943 Sylvia Pl., www.niagarafalls.ca, 6am-noon Sat.). A modest indoor area hosts a handful of sellers while more than a dozen vendors set up shop in the adjoining lot. You'll find whatever is in season at the market, including tomatoes, corn, beans, mushrooms, strawberries, apples, and peaches. Some vendors sell baked goods and homemade canned goods. To locate the farmers market, find the Niagara Falls History Museum on the corner of Ferry Street and Sylvia Place; the market is behind the museum in the public parking lot on Sylvia Place.

MALLS

In general, retail prices for clothing and other goods tend to be higher than those in the United States. Residents of Southern Ontario often travel across the border to purchase clothing, shoes, and accessories. However, there are name-brand stores and bargains to be found at the **Canada One Outlet** (7500 Lundy's Lane, 905/356-8989, www.canadaoneoutlets.com, 10am-9pm Mon.-Sat., 10am-6pm Sun.). Among the 40 stores are Roots, Coach, Tommy Hilfiger, Guess, Nike, and Levi's. The mall is conveniently located on Lundy's Lane near the QEW overpass.

Some big box retailers are close to the falls. **Canadian Tire** (6840 McLeod Rd., 905/358-0161, www.canadiantire.ca, 8am-9pm Mon.-Fri., 8am-6pm Sat., 8am-5pm Sun.) is a discount retailer with an automotive shop, handy in the event of car trouble. Less than a half-mile west on McLeod Road is **Walmart** (7481 Oakwood Dr., 905/371-3999, www.walmart.ca, 7am-11pm daily), with groceries, clothing, and a pharmacy.

More than a dozen convenience stores and pharmacies are in Niagara Falls, many of them clustered along the Lundy's Lane corridor. **Nicholbys** (5613 Victoria Ave., 905/356-6103, www.nicholbys.com, 24 hours daily) is a clean, reasonably priced convenience store in the heart of the Fallsview area.

Sports and Recreation

PARKS

There is no shortage of green spaces in Niagara Falls. The city maintains 96 parks, many of which are community parks with baseball diamonds, soccer fields, a shelter, benches, and playgrounds.

There are two large parks not operated by the city. Niagara Parks Commission is responsible for **Queen Victoria Park,** the green space immediately along the rim of the gorge from the brink of the falls to Clifton Hill, and **Niagara Glen Park** (3050 Niagara Pkwy., www.niagaraparks.com, dawn-dusk daily, free). Niagara Glen has ample free parking, dozens of picnic tables and grills, as well as a large pavilion with additional tables. This park is also home to the trailhead for the Niagara Glen hiking trails. At Glen Park, check out the **Niagara Glen Nature Centre** (905/354-6678, www.niagaraparks.com, 10am-5pm daily June-Aug., 10am-5pm Sat. Sept.-Oct., free), a treasure trove of information on the parks system, hiking trails, animals, and plants found in the Glen. Park naturalists can guide you to the best hiking trails in the Glen based upon your skills and experience.

HIKING

The city has 20 walking/hiking trails (www.niagarafalls.ca) within its limits, most of which are well under two miles and generally flat.

The best hiking in this region is in two areas along the gorge, the Whirlpool Trail and the Niagara Glen Paths, which are also quite dangerous for inexperienced hikers. Trails here lead to stretches of the Niagara River including the whirlpool and lower rapids. Trying to wade or swim in these stretches can lead to injury or death.

All Niagara Parks trails are open year-round, but they are not maintained in winter. It is up to the individual hiker to determine if snowfall affects the trails to the degree that they are not passable.

The best source of information on local hiking trails is the **Niagara Glen Nature Centre** (3050 Niagara Pkwy., 905/354-6678, www.niagaraparks.com, 10am-5pm daily June-Aug., 10am-5pm Sat. Sept.-Oct.). Staff at the center can answer questions about trail locations and conditions, as well as the level of difficulty.

Whirlpool Trail

The **Whirlpool Trail** (off Niagara Pkwy., just north of the Whirlpool Aero Car, 905/354-6678, www.niagaraparksnature.com, dawn-dusk daily), is a challenging hike. It starts with more than 300 wooden stairs down the slope of the whirlpool wall. From the stairs, it's about one mile to the water's edge. You'll encounter steep drops as you walk through a mature ravine forest.

At the bottom of the trail, the massive swirling whirlpool unfolds before your eyes. As you look up, you may see the aero car quietly hovering over the water. Occasionally the din of the water's movement is interrupted by a jet boat filled with soaked passengers. Walking

HIKING IN NIAGARA

Here are some of the guidelines issued by Niagara Parks for hikers:

- Pack out trash.

- Stay on the marked trail.

- No fires are permitted.

- Respect wildlife; appreciate animals from afar. Do not approach animals.

- Use common sense—trails are not maintained during winter months and present extra hazards.

Niagara Parks hiking guidelines are in compliance with Leave No Trace (www.leavenotrace.ca). Check the website for information on ethical hiking.

clockwise along the shore (downstream), you'll eventually meet up with the River Path, which connects to the Niagara Glen Paths. This point is 1.5 miles from the trailhead. At this point, many hikers choose to return to the beginning of the Whirlpool Trail. Those who want to keep exploring the Niagara Glen Paths may want to start at the trailhead of the Niagara Glen system, rather than from the Whirlpool Trail.

To find the Whirlpool trailhead, proceed north along Niagara Parkway, passing the aero car attraction. After the next intersection at Whirlpool Road, look for a small parking lot on the right side of the road. Park and look for the stairwell.

Niagara Glen Paths

Within Niagara Glen Park lies the trailhead for the **Niagara Glen Paths** (3050 Niagara Pkwy., 905/354-6678, dawn-dusk daily). The paths consist of seven trails that add up to a robust five miles. Individual paths are named and blazed with the following color codes: Terrace Path (red), Cliffside Path (white), Trillium Path (light blue), Cobblestone Path (purple), Woodland Path (yellow), Eddy Path (green), River Path (blue).

Starting from the 55-foot-tall steel staircase, take the trail north to the Cliffside Path. Following this path, you'll intersect with the Terrace Path. Head down (turn left), and you'll encounter stone stairs and amazing boulders. The Terrace Path ends when you reach the River Path that runs along the river's edge. This portion of the Glen Paths reveals the splendid Carolinian Forest with its beech and tulip trees.

As you head upstream along the River Path, you'll see the green water and the steep wall of the gorge on the U.S. side of the river. This relatively flat terrain contains sumac, sassafras, and cedar trees. Eventually you will reach the Eddy Path that reconnects you to the Cliffside Path. End the hike by returning to the steel staircase and trailhead. In Niagara Glen Park, head down the grassy hill toward the large pavilion. Continue to the rim of the gorge and you'll find the stairs.

BIKING

Biking is quickly gaining in popularity in the Niagara region. The **Niagara Recreational Trail** (www.niagaraparksnature.com) provides a safe, paved 35-mile path along the Niagara River from Lake Erie to Lake Ontario.

In the Niagara Falls area, two shops offer bike rentals. **Mac's Bike Rentals** (5956 Clark Ave., 289/969-6227, www.macsbikesniagara.com, 9am-6pm May-Oct., $30 full-day rental) has many styles of bikes. Each rental includes a helmet, lock, and self-guided tour map. Park your car at the rental shop for free, or they'll deliver and pick up the bike for you (also for free).

Zoom Leisure (6289 Fallsview Blvd., 866/811-6993, www.zoomleisure.com, 9am-5pm daily June-Aug., reservations required Sept.-May, $30 full-day rental) has several locations along the Niagara Recreational Trail. Helmets, locks, and maps are included in rentals. Drop-off and pick-up service is available, and is free if you're located within five miles of one of their shops. In addition to bike rentals, Zoom also offers bike tours of various destinations guided by a staff member. Guided tour packages ($69-119) include meals, wine sampling, and more.

ICE SKATING

Skating and ice hockey are popular year-round in Niagara Falls. There are two city ice arenas: the **Gale Center** (4171 4th Ave., 905/356-7521) and the **Willoughby Memorial Arena** (9000 Sodom Rd., 905/295-6554). Both have public skating times and equipment rentals. Information on ice time availability for both arenas changes frequently, so call ahead or check online (www.niagarafalls.ca).

During winter's Festival of Lights, a temporary skating rink is constructed across from the Table Rock complex. Known as the **TD Rink at the Brink** (6650 Niagara Pkwy., 905/374-1616, www.wfol.com, 4pm-9pm Mon.-Thurs., noon-10pm Fri.-Sat., noon-9pm Sun. Dec.-Feb., $8 all-day pass), it offers something no other ice rink does: a live view of Horseshoe Falls. Skate rental is $6.

© THE NIAGARA PARKS COMMISSION

skaters enjoying TD Rink at the Brink

Accommodations

FALLSVIEW AREA

The **Wyndham Garden Niagara Falls** (6170 Stanley Ave., 800/207-4421, www.wyndham.com, $160) is a property offering good value to guests. There's a heated indoor pool, a good-sized fitness center, and free high-speed Internet. The WEGO bus stops just outside the hotel.

Floor-to-ceiling windows with unobstructed views of the falls are a draw at **The Tower Hotel** (6732 Fallsview Blvd., 866/325-5784, www.niagaratower.com, $250). This boutique hotel is designed for romantics and has an in-house wedding chapel. This 42-room boutique hotel is renowned for its unobstructed views of the falls. The hotel is atop a tower located close to the casino and the incline railway. The circular shape of the tower forced designers to create oddly shaped rooms that trend small (refrigerators and microwaves are in the closet).

The Fallsview rooms have the best view, but are smaller than the Cityview rooms. During summer, it's worth splurging for the Fallsview room. In the off-season, reserve a Cityview room and ask for an upgrade at check-in. The staff is very friendly. There's no self-parking, but the valet service ($20/day) allows unlimited in-and-out access at no extra charge.

Stay in the middle of the action at the **◖ Fallsview Casino Resort** (6380 Fallsview Blvd., 888/325-5788, www.fallsviewcasinoresort.com, $249). If you like the convenience of being close to gaming and world-class entertainment while still being close to the falls, this is your hotel. All 374 rooms in this hotel are large in comparison to other properties in the area. Suites feature large whirlpool tubs and extra space for relaxation. Ask for a room with a view of the falls, preferably on the 12th floor or higher. Corner suites offer the best opportunity to see American and Horseshoe Falls from your room. If you bring a car, signing up for the casino's perks card can earn you reduced-cost or free parking. If a show at the casino is sold out, check the box office at noon; some unclaimed comp tickets may still be available.

The fireplaces in the rooms of the **❰ Sterling Inn and Spa** (5195 Magdalen St., 289/292-0000, www.sterlingniagara.com, $185) may put a spark in your romantic getaway at the falls. This boutique hotel provides couples with a special experience. Rooms are spacious, and most are equipped with whirlpool tubs. Have a warm breakfast delivered to your room for a special treat.

If you're keen on staying in a room with a beautiful view of the falls, you'll have to choose a chain hotel. Choose the **❰ Marriott Niagara Falls Fallsview Hotel & Spa** (6740 Fallsview Blvd., 866/576-5456, www.marriott.com, $220), because it's in the heart of everything, just a few blocks from the casino, and very close to the incline railway that takes you down to Table Rock. Make sure to reserve a room facing the falls (the higher the floor, the better). There are two Marriott hotels on Fallsview Boulevard—check your hotel's address so you don't register at the wrong property.

Clean, cheap, and close: That's the best way to describe the **Rex Motel** (6247 McLeod Rd., 905/354-4223, www.rexmotel.com, $70). This no-frills, family-owned gem is five minutes away from the glitz of Fallsview. The owners greet all guests and provide suggestions for area attractions. The rooms include fresh towels folded into swan shapes, along with free Wi-Fi.

LUNDY'S LANE

Lundy's Lane hotels are farther away from the falls, but generally have lower prices. The **Best Western Cairn Croft Hotel** (6400 Lundy's Lane, 800/568-8520, www.bestwestern.com, $175) is a solid value with 165 rooms and a beautiful indoor courtyard area and pool. Parking is free and the hotel is a stop on the WEGO route.

The **Super 8 Niagara Falls** (5706 Ferry St., 800/536-1211, www.super8.com, $110) is neat and clean. Prices for this 190-room hotel are a good value, especially since it has an indoor pool and free parking. The only drawback is that motor coach groups use the hotel, so there can be congestion at checkout times and at breakfast in the restaurant.

Canada's Best Value Inn (7034 Lundy's Lane, 888/315-2378, www.canadasbestvalue-inn.com, $70) lives up to its name by providing decent accommodations at a reasonable price. This 45-room, two-story motel has an outdoor pool. Free wireless Internet and breakfast are included. As a bonus, it's just a block away from several restaurants, including the world-famous Flying Saucer Drive-In.

If you're camping, the **Campark Resort** (9387 Lundy's Lane, 877/226-7275, www.campark.com, $45 campsite, $67 cabin) is a good option. It has 400 campsites, including traditional sites for tents and large RV sites with water, power, and cable TV connections. Modern cabins with beds, kitchenettes, and other amenities can be rented year-round. A large outdoor pool, hot tub, splash pad, and playground offer a welcome respite after a long day of touring. Don't want to drive your RV into town? Daily shuttle-bus service is provided.

PARKWAY NORTH

Driving north from the falls, there is a cluster of family-operated bed-and-breakfasts. Among the best is the **Redwood** (5227 River Rd., 905/358-1990, www.redwoodbb.ca, $145). Overlooking the gorge, Redwood has three luxurious rooms, each with an en-suite bathroom and television; two of the rooms have fireplaces. The proprietors are a mother-and-daughter team who express their Italian heritage in the provided breakfast.

The **Greystone Manor Bed & Breakfast** (4939 River Rd., 905/357-7373, www.greystone-manor.ca, $125) sets the standard for service in this region. It features four rooms, each with a private bath. If you desire even more privacy, reserve the Topaz Room, a renovated carriage house with its own private entrance and balcony. The gracious host, Rob, offers outstanding customer service and attention to detail, whether you require a late check-in after being delayed at the border or if you have dietary restrictions. With lower room prices than most hotels, the Greystone is highly recommended.

The amenities at **Accommodations Niagara Bed and Breakfast** (5069 River Rd., 866/346-7727, www.accommodationsniagara.com, $130) make it a comfortable place to stay. Each of the four rooms has a fireplace, whirlpool tub, coffee maker, microwave, TV, and an air-conditioner. Guests will feel at home here.

Children will absolutely love their stay at the 🄲 **Great Wolf Lodge** (3950 Victoria Ave., 888/878-1818, www.greatwolf.com, $330). The prices are not cheap, but they include admission to the world-class, indoor water park (available to guests only). The park features numerous water slides (one goes uphill), a wave pool, a splash area for the little ones, and a whirlpool hot spa for adults only. The hotel provides a nightly story hour that gives parents time to relax. The facility is safe, clean, and a joy for kids year-round.

Food

DINERS AND BUFFETS

Breakfast for under $2 and authentic alien decor? Look no farther than the **Flying Saucer Drive-In** (6768 Lundy's Lane, 905/356-4553, www.flyingsaucerrestaurant.com, 6am-3am Mon.-Fri., 6am-4am Sat.-Sun., $12). The Saucer sports a distinctive, 1950s spaceship motif served tongue-in-cheek with a little kitsch on the side. This local diner legend is known for its ambience, portion sizes, and late-night hours. The Canadian Burger three-quarter pounds of beef, jack cheese, and back bacon, is out of this world.

For good value and an even better view, head to the 🄲 **Grand Buffet** (Fallsview Casino Resort, 6380 Fallsview Blvd., 888/325-5788, www.fallsviewcasinoresort.com, 8am-11pm daily, $22) located inside the Fallsview Casino Resort. It has everything you'd expect at a casino buffet—a wide variety of main dishes and over-the-top desserts—and a great view of the falls. There's a discount of $2 if you sign up for a player's card. You cannot enter the restaurant unless you are 19 or over, per casino regulations.

GASTROPUBS

The Syndicate (6863 Lundy's Lane, 289/477-1022, www.syndicatebrewery.ca, 11:30am-11pm daily, $22) locally sources its ingredients, including meat, so the menu changes based on

their availability. The meal price includes a soup or salad, an entrée, and dessert, an exceptional value. Pair your meal with wine or one of the craft beers available on tap. This eatery affords a real break from the chain restaurants; reservations are strongly recommended.

FINE DINING

Regarded by many as Niagara's top fine-dining establishment, 🄲 **AG** (5195 Magdalen Ave., 289/292-0005, www.agcuisine.com, 5:30pm-9:30pm Tues.-Sun., $41) earns its reputation by using locally sourced, seasonal ingredients. The restaurant adds a touch of class to a town with many chain restaurants catering to price-conscious tourists. Consider ordering an ice wine martini to complete your meal.

At 🄲 **Elements on the Falls** (6650 Niagara Pkwy., 905/354-3631, www.niagaraparks.com, 11:30am-9:30pm daily, $21), the food is as good as the view. Conveniently located in the Table Rock Welcome Centre, Elements provides casual fine dining. Because of its location, this restaurant is an excellent romantic spot for viewing the fireworks over the falls or the nightly illumination. The menu is eclectic, featuring gourmet burgers as well as Cajun calamari. Of particular note is the Stevensville pork loin, served with double-smoked bacon and maple jus. For dessert, the apple barge is a wonderful phyllo pastry bowl filled with apples, raisins, and ice cream. Choose any of the local ice wines served here to pair with this warm apple dessert.

ITALIAN

Niagara Falls is blessed with several good Italian restaurants, and **Casa Mia Ristorante** (3518 Portage Rd., 905/356-5410, www.casamiaristorante.com, 11:30am-2:30pm and 5pm-10pm Mon.-Fri., 5pm-10pm Sat.-Sun., $35) may be the best. Casa Mia is a good value, and serves authentic Italian meals prepared by the same family that started the business in 1988. If you appreciate homemade sauces and pasta, you'll happily dine here. The restaurant is about a 10-minute drive from downtown, but well worth the trip.

JAPANESE

Don't let the drab exterior fool you: **Taki Restaurant** (5500 Victoria Ave., 905/357-7274, www.niagaratakirestaurant.com, 11:30am-9:30pm daily, $23) is an authentic Japanese treat inside. The fish is fresh, the menu comprehensive, and there's even a kid's platter. Save room for the black sesame ice cream.

GREEK

In a world full of Greek diners, the **KouTouki** (5745 Ferry St., 905/354-6776, www.koutoukiniagara.com, 11:30am-11pm daily, $21) is a genuine Greek restaurant. The difference here is the focus on authentic Mediterranean food and wine. Located at the start of the Lundy's Lane strip, this local gem is a nice break from the touristy chain restaurants. Lunch is quick, tasty, and averages about $9.

MEXICAN

You'll find excellent "Fresh-Mex" at **Frijoles** (3465 Portage Rd., 289/296-3999, www.frijolesfreshmex.com, 11am-8pm Mon.-Wed. and Sat., 11am-9pm Thurs.-Fri., $8). "Fresh-Mex" is Mexican-inspired food with a touch of Southern California. Burritos and tacos are made to order with your choice of beef, pork, chicken, fish, vegetables, beans, or everything mixed together. The food here is healthy, but you can cheat a bit by trying one of the Dorito Taco Bags. Also recommended are any of the eight homemade salsas and sauces.

STEAK HOUSES

If you're looking for a great steak dinner, take a chance on **Lucky's Steakhouse** (5705 Falls Ave., 905/374-3598, www.casinoniagara.com, 5pm-10pm Wed.-Sun., $35). Steaks, chops, and prime ribs are the stars here, although seafood, chicken, and pasta are available. Consider the 34-ounce porterhouse steak for two ($68) or the 16-ounce prime rib for $35. You will not leave hungry. Lucky's is on the second floor of the Casino Niagara complex on Falls Avenue.

Information and Services

Niagara Falls, Ontario, is a mid-size city of 82,000 residents. Although many government signs and notices are bilingual (English and French), English is the official language of Ontario.

The U.S. and Canadian dollars fluctuate in relative value. Sometimes the currencies are at par, while at other times, there is a significant difference. To obtain the best rate for your dollars, exchange them at a bank before your trip. Better yet, use a credit card that does not charge fees for processing purchases made in Canada.

Crime is low in Canada, especially in the tourist areas of Niagara Falls. Niagara Parks has its own police department. Many of its officers use bikes to monitor traffic and keep rubbernecking tourists moving along the parkway. The City of Niagara Falls and the Province of Ontario have their own police forces as well. For an emergency, dial 911, just as in the United States.

Getting There and Around

BY AIR

There is no airport in Niagara Falls, although smaller regional airfields are nearby. Most visitors to the falls are day-trippers from New York City who land at the **Buffalo Niagara International Airport** (BUF, 4200 Genesee St., Cheektowaga, 716/630-6000, www.buffaloairport.com), rent a car there, and then drive 20 miles to Niagara Falls and cross the border. Taxis are plentiful at the Buffalo airport, 24 hours a day. A taxi ride to the falls costs $85.

BY CAR

The usual mode of transport for visitors to Niagara Falls is by automobile. One international bridge joins Niagara Falls, Ontario, with Niagara Falls, New York—the Rainbow Bridge. Border inspection wait times at the bridge are difficult to predict, but updates are available via the Niagara Bridge Commission website (www.niagarafallsbridges.com). Hourly updates are also available by calling 800/715-6722.

Driving in Ontario is virtually the same as in the United States, except that speed limit signs use the metric system. Pedestrians always have the right of way within a designated crosswalk—motorists must stop. When driving along the very scenic Niagara Parkway, keep in mind that many drivers are visitors to the region and may be paying more attention to the scenery than to other cars or traffic lights.

The main thoroughfare in southern Ontario is known as the QEW, or Queen Elizabeth Way. The QEW joins Niagara Falls to Toronto.

A flashing green light at an intersection indicates that it is safe to make a left-hand turn (equivalent to a green arrow light).

Parking is expensive in Niagara Falls. Prime tourist lots operated by Niagara Parks charge close to $20 per day.

BY BUS

The **WEGO** (www.wegoniagarafalls.com) bus system is simple and easy to use. Passes good for 24 hours are $7 for adults and $4 for children 6-12. The system uses four color-coded routes to cover the tourist area of Niagara Falls. You must purchases a pass before boarding the bus. Passes are available at more than 30 falls-area hotels (look for the "We Sell WEGO" signs in your hotel's lobby) and at the four official welcome centers operated by Niagara Parks.

Bus schedules are available on the WEGO website, bus shelters, or at the Niagara Park's welcome centers. WEGO buses are accessible and feature a rack on the front of each bus that can accommodate two bicycles.

BY TRAIN

Traveling by rail from Toronto to the falls is easy. **VIA Rail** (www.viarail.ca) trains leave from Union Station in Toronto for the **Niagara Falls train station** (4267 Bridge St.) at least seven times daily. The one-way cost is $17. The train station at the falls is also on the WEGO purple line. **Amtrak** (www.amtrak.com) trains coming across the border from the United States, on the Maple Leaf route, stop at this station twice daily. The trip from the Buffalo station to the station in Niagara Falls, Ontario, is 90 minutes, with fares starting at $19 for a standard coach seat. As this is an international crossing, have your passport available when you obtain your ticket.

A cab ride from the train station to the Fallsview area is under three miles and costs less than $10. A taxi stand is located directly outside the train station. Cab drivers know the train schedule, so you shouldn't have a hard time finding a cab once your train arrives.

INCLINE RAILWAY

The **Falls Incline Railway** (Portage Rd. near Main St., www.niagaraparks.com, 10am-6:30pm daily with increased hours in summer, $2.50 one-way, free for children five and under) is an easy way to traverse the 100-foot-tall ridge that separates the Fallsview area of hotels from

Table Rock Welcome Centre. Each tram car holds 40 passengers and is fully enclosed for year-round comfort.

The railway is located off Portage Road, one block from Main Street. Pedestrians can use a footbridge that connects the railway with the Embassy Suites and Marriott Hotels and crosses over Portage Road. Round-trip fare is $5 and an all-day pass is $6. If you don't want to use the railway, you'll have to take Murray Hill Road to travel from Table Rock Welcome Centre to the Fallsview area.

NIAGARA FALLS, NEW YORK

Although the U.S. side of Niagara Falls is sometimes overshadowed by the glitz of the Canadian side, it still has a lot to offer visitors. The charm of the U.S. side lies in its natural splendor. It once was regarded as *the* destination for the region. Curious travelers from around the world flocked to Niagara Falls, New York, to embrace the natural beauty and power of the falls. The U.S. side provides many opportunities to see the rainbows and rushing water of the falls.

The park at Niagara Falls is the oldest state park in the country and has retained much of its natural beauty since opening in July 1885. America's preeminent landscape architect, Frederick Law Olmsted, designed the park to maximize access to all of Niagara's many moods. It is on the American side that the class

VI white water of the upper rapids will leave you in awe. Here, too, the deceptively gentle flow of the water near Luna Island draws you in for reflection. On Bath Island, you can enjoy an intimate and quiet lush green picnic spot protected from raging rapids nearby.

While the best view of Niagara Falls is from the Canadian side, the natural wonder of the falls is best experienced on the U.S. side, where you can reach out and touch Bridal Veil Falls. As the water roars over the falls at 70,000 gallons a second, it's a thrill you won't soon forget.

The treasures of the Niagara region are also found beyond the falls. North along the gorge is Lewiston, a beautiful and historic town nestled at the base of the ridge where the falls began 12,000 years ago. Lewiston is a place

© NYSDED-PHOTO BY DARREN MCGEE

HIGHLIGHTS

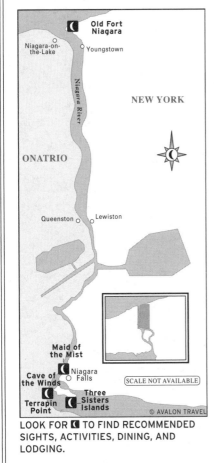

SCALE NOT AVAILABLE

Old Fort Niagara

Niagara-on-the-Lake

Youngstown

NEW YORK

ONATRIO

Niagara River

Queenston

Lewiston

Maid of the Mist

Cave of the Winds

Niagara Falls

Terrapin Point

Three Sisters Islands

© AVALON TRAVEL

◖ Maid of the Mist: Any trip to the falls must include this boat tour into the heart of Niagara's awe-inspiring power (page 48).

◖ Cave of the Winds: Walk beneath one of Niagara's mighty cascades (page 54).

◖ Terrapin Point: This is the best land-based observation area (page 55).

◖ Three Sisters Islands: Get up close to the raging upper rapids of the Niagara River on three beautiful islands (page 55).

◖ Old Fort Niagara: Over 300 years old, this fort once protected the gateway to the New World (page 68).

LOOK FOR ◖ TO FIND RECOMMENDED SIGHTS, ACTIVITIES, DINING, AND LODGING.

NIAGARA FALLS, NEW YORK

where the arts and culture flourish, with a Norman Rockwellian main street that leads to the river and spectacular sunsets. Farther north, Fort Niagara, the longest continually occupied military structure in North America, stands sentinel as it has for nearly 300 years, guarding the confluence of the Niagara River and Lake Ontario. Here, reenactors bring to life the history of the gateway to the New World, the scene of bloodshed among Native American, French, and British combatants.

HISTORY

To the native peoples who lived here, Niagara Falls was a mystical place. Although none of the inhabiting tribes left written records, their oral traditions tell of gods who lived behind the mighty waterfall. By the time the British

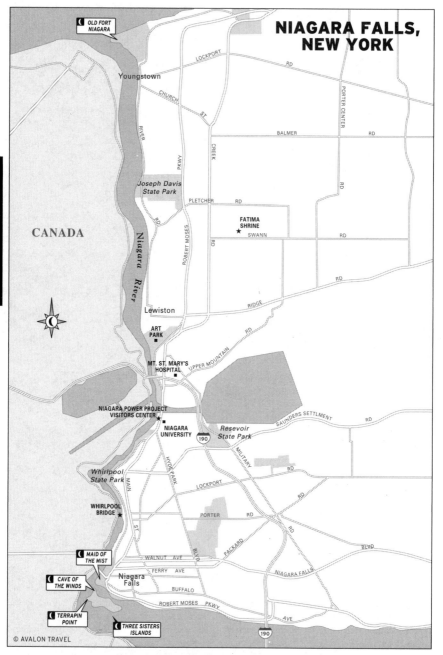

NIAGARA FALLS, NEW YORK

OLD FORT NIAGARA

Youngstown

CANADA

LOCKPORT RD

CHURCH ST

CREEK

PORTER CENTER

BALMER RD

RD

Joseph Davis State Park

PLETCHER RD

FATIMA SHRINE

SWANN RD

ROBERT MOSES PKWY

RD

Niagara River

Lewiston

RIDGE RD

ART PARK

MT. ST. MARY'S HOSPITAL

UPPER MOUNTAIN

NIAGARA POWER PROJECT VISITORS CENTER

NIAGARA UNIVERSITY

190

SAUNDERS SETTLMENT RD

Resevoir State Park

Whirlpool State Park

MAIN ST

HYDE PARK

MILITARY RD

LOCKPORT

WHIRLPOOL BRIDGE

PORTER RD

MAID OF THE MIST

CAVE OF THE WINDS

TERRAPIN POINT

THREE SISTERS ISLANDS

Niagara Falls

WALNUT AVE

FERRY AVE

BUFFALO

ROBERT MOSES PKWY

BLVD

PACKARD

BLVD

NIAGARA FALLS

AVE

190

© AVALON TRAVEL

had expelled the French from this region in 1759, the Iroquois Indians were trading, working with, and fighting for (and against) the European settlers. Until the American Revolution, the Iroquois kept most white settlers out of the area; however, the Iroquois sided with the British during the conflict and were eventually forced from their lands for their opposition to the American cause.

The Europeans who settled here were awed by Niagara's beauty, but also saw the raging Niagara River as a source of power. Prior to being named Niagara Falls, New York, this settlement was known as Manchester. Local folk imagined the economy paralleling that of Manchester, England, a prosperous mill and manufacturing town. As a result, industrial mills marred Niagara's shoreline for many years as manufacturing and tourism competed against each other. Tourism prevailed after New York State purchased the land surrounding the falls from private owners, finally creating the park that exists today. More than 150 buildings, including factories, hotels, and mills, were removed to return Niagara to a more natural state. World-renowned landscape architect Frederick Law Olmsted designed the park and set guidelines that direct the stewardship of the park to the present day.

In July 1885, the Niagara Reservation Park opened, making it the oldest state park in the United States. The history of the city of Niagara Falls is as turbulent as the water coursing through the upper rapids. The lure of cheap and plentiful electric power brought many industries to the area, and the city's population grew to 102,000 by 1960. At present, the city has fewer than 50,000 inhabitants; its decline mirrors that of other northeastern U.S. cities that experienced a loss of manufacturing and jobs during the 1970s. Today, the city is depressed, having lost more than half of its population since 1960. The average household income here is just $18,000 a year.

The area immediately surrounding the state park is clean, safe, and experiencing new development. New programs featuring live music, themed activities, and increased vendor opportunities are rejuvenating the city streets

adjacent to the park. In 2012, famed high-wire walker Nik Wallenda traversed Horseshoe Falls, a feat that focused attention on the area. In addition, New York State has finally provided funding for important enhancements to major attractions within the park.

PLANNING YOUR TIME

Niagara Falls is an ideal one-day destination and a good base for several day trips. Plan on visiting the major attractions, Maid of the Mist and Cave of the Winds, early in the day, when waiting times are short. Reserve some time in the evening to view the nightly illumination of the falls and fireworks on Friday and Sunday nights in the summer. If your travel plans require crossing the border, give yourself plenty of time. It can sometimes take more than an hour for customs and immigration inspection.

One of the most popular day trips is a visit to Lewiston and Fort Niagara. These attractions are best appreciated together because of their distance (Lewiston is about seven miles north of the falls and the fort is another six miles beyond.) Seeing both towns involves a five- to six-hour day with a blend of driving, walking, and sightseeing.

ORIENTATION

The city's **downtown** area is immediately adjacent to Niagara Falls State Park, with hotels, restaurants, and attractions all within walking distance of the park. The epicenter is Old Falls Street, which runs from the Seneca Niagara Casino to the pedestrian entrance of the park.

Little Italy is about one mile from the park, along Pine Avenue. Here you'll find small shops, authentic Italian restaurants, and a sense of what the city was like at its zenith in 1950. Pine Avenue becomes **Niagara Falls Boulevard,** and morphs from a walkable neighborhood into a four-lane thoroughfare with accommodations and retail stores. The boulevard is known for its value-priced hotels and family-operated motels, and it provides access to I-190.

Traveling on I-190 north from the city leads to the village of **Lewiston** and **Fort Niagara.** These two destinations are more pastoral and historic than urban Niagara Falls.

Sights

NIAGARA FALLS STATE PARK

Each year, more than eight million people journey to **Niagara Falls State Park** (Prospect St., 716/278-1796, www.niagarafallsstatepark.com, 24 hours daily, parking $10), drawn by its 400 acres of unparalleled beauty and splendor. Although many waterfalls are taller than Niagara, none are more prodigious. Visitors come here to feel the power of nature and experience a boat ride on the chaotic, roiling waters beneath the world's most famous waterfall. There are manmade diversions here, but make no mistake, the main attraction is the 750,000 gallons per second of water hurtling over American Falls, delivering 2,700 tons of force into the water below. Within the boundaries of the park, you'll find the famed Maid of the Mist boat tour, the Cave of the Winds, Terrapin Point, and Three Sisters Islands.

At the entrance to the park, walkways, hedges, and signs will direct you toward the visitors center, which houses an information desk with maps and brochures, as well as clean bathrooms. The lower level of the visitors center has a gift shop, restaurant, interpretive historical displays, and the Adventure Theater.

The Adventure Theater shows a 40-minute film with highlights of Niagara's history as well as stunning helicopter shots of the gorge and falls. It depicts the mythical "Maid of the Mist," a Native American woman who threw herself over the falls (supposedly to either save her tribe or to avoid a forced marriage), along with early European explorers and daredevils who challenged Niagara. The 275-seat theater is comfortably air-conditioned. The main entrance for the park is found along Prospect Street, across from the Hard Rock Café near the bus drop-off loop.

◖ Maid of the Mist

There are few experiences like the **Maid of the Mist** (Niagara Falls State Park, 716/284-8897, www.maidofthemist.com, 10am-5pm Mon.-Fri., 10am-6pm Sat.-Sun. Apr.-mid-May and Sept.-early Oct., 10am-6pm daily late May-late June, 9am-8pm daily late June-early Aug., 9am-7:30pm daily early Aug.-late Aug., 10am-5pm daily early Oct.-late Oct., $17 adults, $10 children 6-12). What begins as a gentle, 20-minute boat ride suddenly transforms into a journey into the heart of the falls. From the safety of the vessel, you are buffeted by heavy mist. It's awe-inspiring to see the 17-story-high thundering wall of water that slams into the Lower Niagara River. For more than 150 years, this ride has thrilled millions of tourists and is the top attraction in Niagara.

Once you're aboard the boat, relax and enjoy the view. After the boat pulls away from the dock, it passes American Falls. Notice the stairs along the left (north) side of the falls. This is part of the Crow's Nest, and can be accessed after the boat ride.

As the boat moves onward, you'll approach Bridal Veil Falls, flowing between Luna Island and Goat Island. You'll see brave folks underneath this waterfall, experiencing the Cave of the Winds. There's a deceptively calm stretch of water, the quiet before the storm. Thousands of waterfowl can be seen resting or building nests in the rocky ledges of the gorge.

The chatter of the birds gives way to the ominous din of Horseshoe Falls. As the boat enters the basin beneath the falls, water thunders down from a precipice 17 stories above. Wind whips mist from all sides as the boat bobs upon a boiling cauldron of water. For five intense minutes, the boat fights the surging waters and the unpredictable wind dictates visibility.

Riders on the upper deck or in the lower bow area receive the brunt of the mist. People looking to avoid getting soaked can find limited shelter on the lower deck in the middle of the boat. How wet you get depends mostly on the wind's velocity and direction, so there's no guarantee that you'll stay dry. The poncho

DISCOVERY PASS

One of the first considerations you'll face when touring Niagara Falls State Park is the decision to purchase the Discovery Pass, which allows you to visit five major attractions with one voucher. Purchasing the pass will save you more than 30 percent compared to purchasing each attraction separately.

INCLUDED IN THE DISCOVERY PASS

Attraction	Adult	Child 6-12	Child 5 and under
Maid of the Mist	$15.50	$9.00	Free
Cave of the Winds	$11.00	$6.00	Free
Niagara Adventure Theater	$11.00	$7.50	Free
Niagara Gorge Discovery Center	$3.00	$2.00	Free
Trolley (day pass)	$2.00	$1.00	Free
Aquarium of Niagara	$10.00	$6.00 (ages 3-12)	Free (2 and under)

If you intend on spending an entire day in the park, the pass is the way to go. However, if you are planning to spend a few hours at the park and just want the highlights, then try going à la carte. In either event, the trolley is an inexpensive way to make your way through the park.

NIAGARA FALLS, NEW YORK

provides sufficient protection for your camera and phone during the heaviest periods of misting.

As the boat travels back to the dock, consider heading to the rear of the lower deck. The boat's stern provides an excellent vantage point for capturing the panorama of the gorge. The Maid of the Mist boat ride affords a rare opportunity to photograph the falls and gorge from water level in the Lower Niagara River.

The ticket booths are near Prospect Point, about 500 yards from the visitors center. Board the boat via the elevators at the base of the Observation Tower. Avoid a long line for the Maid of the Mist tour by arriving before 11am, though you won't usually wait longer than 20 minutes (except on U.S. holidays like Independence Day and Labor Day). If you plan to visit both sides of the border, there are advantages to taking the tour on the U.S. side. It is less expensive and there are usually shorter lines. There's also an added attraction, included in the price of the boat ride, called the Crow's

Nest, which leads you up a set of stairs along American Falls.

After exiting the boat, continue past the elevators and you'll see the **Crow's Nest.** The Crow's Nest is an excellent natural observation deck at the base of American Falls, set atop giant boulders that are the remnants of a massive rockslide. The stairs that lead to the Crow's Nest are somewhat steep, but safe, and they permit an up-close view of American Falls. Keep your rain poncho from the Maid of the Mist if you plan to visit the Crow's Nest. At the entrance to the Crow's Nest are park benches (a great place to catch your breath) and bathrooms. Buying a ticket for the Observation Tower ($1) will also gain you access to the Crow's Nest, if you aren't riding on the Maid of the Mist.

OBSERVATION TOWER

The **Observation Tower** (9am-10:30pm daily Apr.-late Oct., 10am-4:30pm daily late Oct.-Mar., included in Maid of the Mist ticket, à

MAID OF THE MIST TIPS

© NIAGARA TOURISM AND CONVENTION CORPORATION

The Maid of the Mist takes you to the base of Horseshoe Falls.

- You are issued a flimsy rain poncho before you board the boat. When wearing the poncho, your neckline, shins, and feet are exposed. Wear sandals, shorts or capris, and V-neck tops to avoid getting exposed clothing and shoes soaked.

- After receiving your poncho, resist the urge to put it on immediately. Stopping to figure out how to wear the poncho causes a chain reaction pile-up behind you. You don't need the poncho until well after the boat leaves the dock. Wait until you board the boat to don your raincoat, especially on hot days.

- The boat does not have seats, so all passengers stand throughout the journey. No matter where you stand, you are going to get wet. If you want the full experience, stand in the front of the boat or on the top level. If you want to stay drier, choose a spot on the lower deck in the middle of the boat.

- After exiting the boat, you are greeted by large blue plastic bins in which you may place your poncho for recycling. Keep your poncho if you are going to climb the stairs along American Falls before heading back up the elevators to the observation deck.

- The majority of the journey is dry. You'll have plenty of warning to put cameras, phones, and tablets under your poncho as you approach the falls. Use common sense and your electronics will survive the voyage.

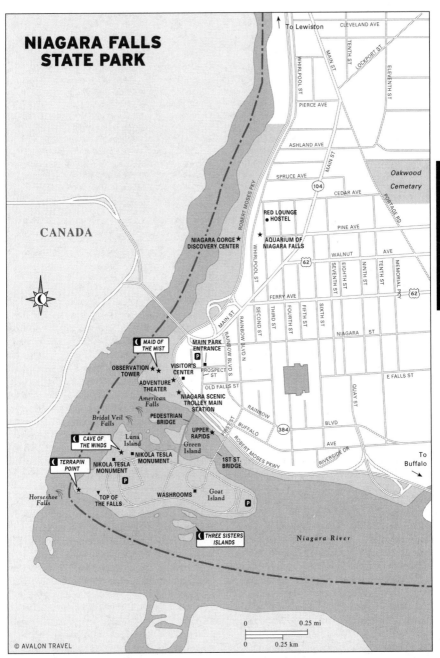

NIAGARA FALLS, NEW YORK

NIAGARA FALLS
STATE PARK

CANADA

To Lewiston
CLEVELAND AVE
TENTH ST
LOCKPORT ST
ELEVENTH ST
MAIN ST
WHIRLPOOL ST
PIERCE AVE
ASHLAND AVE
MAIN ST
PORTAGE RD
SPRUCE AVE
Oakwood
Cemetery
(104)
CEDAR AVE
ROBERT MOSES PKY
RED LOUNGE
HOSTEL
PINE AVE
NIAGARA GORGE ★
DISCOVERY CENTER
AQUARIUM OF
NIAGARA FALLS
WHIRLPOOL ST
(62)
WALNUT
AVE
SEVENTH ST
EIGHTH ST
NINTH ST
TENTH ST
MEMORIAL PKY
FERRY AVE
(62)
SECOND ST
THIRD ST
FOURTH ST
FIFTH ST
SIXTH ST
NIAGARA ST
MAIN ST
RAINBOW BLVD N
MAID OF
THE MIST
MAIN PARK
ENTRANCE
P
OBSERVATION ★ ★
TOWER
VISITOR'S
CENTER
PROSPECT
ST
RAINBOW BLVD S
E FALLS ST
ADVENTURE ★
THEATER
OLD FALLS ST
QUAY ST
American
Falls
NIAGARA SCENIC
TROLLEY MAIN
STATION
Bridal Veil
Falls
PEDESTRIAN
BRIDGE
RAINBOW
FIRST ST
BUFFALO
BLVD
CAVE OF
THE WINDS
Luna
Island
UPPER ★
RAPIDS
(384)
TERRAPIN
POINT
NIKOLA TESLA
MONUMENT
Green
Island
NIKOLA TESLA
MONUMENT
1ST ST.
BRIDGE
ROBERT MOSES PKWY
To
Buffalo
P
RIVERSIDE DR
Horseshoe
Falls
★
TOP OF
THE FALLS
WASHROOMS
Goat
Island
P
THREE SISTERS
ISLANDS
Niagara River

0   0.25 mi
0   0.25 km

© AVALON TRAVEL

TURNING OFF THE FALLS

If you stood at Prospect Point in August 1969, you could not have appreciated the raging beauty of the Niagara River as it plummeted over the brink of the falls. That's because the U.S. Army Corps of Engineers had de-watered American Falls earlier that summer. A temporary earthen dam was built across the river that feeds American and Bridal Veil Falls so that scientists could study the bedrock and assess whether it needed to be shored up. Engineers checked out the rocks gathered beneath the falls with an eye on removing them for aesthetic purposes.

While the technicians drilled and measured the rocks, a temporary walkway was constructed so tourists could walk on the dry riverbed just a few yards away from the rocky brink. Record numbers of tourists came to see the oddity throughout the summer and fall. In November, the earthen dam was removed and water once again flowed over the falls. In the end, the Army Corps of Engineers recommended that only a few minor changes should be made to the falls and the rocks at the bottom of American Falls should remain.

la carte $1) serves two primary functions: to provide a panoramic view of the three waterfalls that comprise Niagara, and to house the elevators that lead to the docks of the Maid of the Mist. From afar, the tower resembles an incomplete bridge; its platform extends more than 200 feet from the gorge wall. The views here are among the best on this side of the border. If you stand atop the metal benches on the platform, you can get a great photo of your loved ones as they stand along the guardrail, with the falls in the background.

The Observation Tower is among the best bargains in all of Niagara. Admission is included in the cost of the Maid of the Mist ticket, or can be purchased à la carte ($1). The tower is closed during foul weather or high winds.

Prospect Point

Prospect Point is located at the brink of American Falls, near the Observation Tower Platform. It affords an excellent view of the entire American Falls crest line and the upper rapids of the Niagara River. The upper rapids form as the riverbed drops more than 55 feet in elevation while the river runs east around Goat Island. A pedestrian bridge 300 yards upstream from Prospect Point has the best view of the churning, frothy white water of the upper rapids. At night, lights along the shoreline

illuminate the upper rapids, a surreal spectacle to behold.

Goat Island

Goat Island sits between Horseshoe Falls and Bridal Veil Falls, affording perhaps the most visceral on-land experience of Niagara on the U.S. side of the border. The island parts the river in two, creating different areas for the water to channel its moods. The island is home to the best sightseeing in the park, as well as walking paths, woods, picnic areas, concessions, and the park police. Visitors often spend most of their time in the park on Goat Island. The major attractions here are Terrapin Point, the Cave of the Winds, and the Tesla Statue. Goat Island is also the gateway to Luna Island and the Three Sisters Islands.

The island is named for the goats kept on the island by a British settler in the late 1700s. Subsequent attempts to name it Iris Island (after the goddess of rainbows) failed, and the name Goat Island has stubbornly stuck.

To drive onto Goat Island, use the bridge at the foot of First Street. On the island, there are two parking lots ($10) for vehicles (including campers). On foot, Goat Island is accessed via the pedestrian bridge that joins the mainland portion of the park, Bath Island, and Goat Island.

© NIAGARA TOURISM AND CONVENTION CORPORATION

NIAGARA FALLS, NEW YORK

Goat Island, seen here between Horseshoe and American Falls, provides many of the best views and experiences in Niagara Falls State Park.

POWER ARCH

In 1896, the world's first commercial hydro-electric power plant, Adams Power Plant, sent electricity from Niagara Falls to Buffalo, signaling a new age in long-distance power transmission via Nikola Tesla's alternating current design. Though the plant was eventually demolished, the **Power Arch** was left intact. This three-story-tall stone arch served as the facade of the plant's main building. It was moved to Goat Island from the southern part of the city in 1967 to serve as a memorial to Niagara's important industrial heritage. It's located about 200 yards away from the Cave of the Winds ticket office.

TESLA STATUE

Although his engineering and discoveries impact our lives to this day, many people look quizzically at the **statue of Nikola Tesla** on Goat Island. Tesla was a genius, with more than 300 patents to his name, responsible for inventing alternating current, fluorescent lighting, wireless communication, and remote control devices. The bronze statue, by sculptor Frano Kršinić, was dedicated in 1976, a gift to the park from the Yugoslavian government. The statue depicts a contemplative Tesla looking down at notes in his lap. Like Tesla, the statue is larger than life—about 10 feet tall. Feel free to scale the statue and sit in the lap of the man who is said to have invented the 20th century.

LUNA ISLAND

Luna Island is a small scrap of land that separates American and Bridal Veil Falls. It offers spectacular views of both falls and the gorge, and several spots allow close access to the beautiful and menacing brink of Niagara.

Take a moment to stand in the south corner of Luna Island, immediately next to the brink of Bridal Veil Falls. The green water flows rhythmically, providing a sense of peace.

© NYSDED-PHOTO BY DARREN MCGEE

At Cave of the Winds, walk under the torrent of Bridal Veil Falls.

But a peek over the brink exposes the thundering, falling water, which reveals the duality of Niagara, where beauty and force contrast sharply. You'll experience this most intensely on the U.S. side, where you can get close to the water and don't have to fight the crowds on the Canadian side.

To reach Luna Island, walk down the flight of steps at the northernmost tip of Goat Island, then cross the small bridge.

◖ CAVE OF THE WINDS

The **Cave of the Winds** (Niagara Falls State Park, 716/278-1730, www.niagarafallsstate-park.com, 9am-9pm Sun.-Thurs., 9am-10pm Fri.-Sat. mid-May-early Sept., 9am-7pm Sun.-Thurs., 9am-9pm Fri.-Sat. early Sept.-mid-Oct., 9am-5pm daily mid-Oct.-late Oct., $11 adults, $8 children 6-12) is a self-guided tour along a series of decks leading to the foot of Bridal Veil Falls. The Hurricane Deck is the last of these, located directly under Bridal Veil.

Standing on the Hurricane Deck takes courage and stamina, since you're saturated by cascading water; the souvenir rain poncho provides little protection. Children often find this attraction equal to, if not better than, the Maid of the Mist. On a hot summer day, this torrent of water can be rejuvenating.

If you have a camera or cell phone, place them in the plastic bag provided and let someone hold it while you stand out on the deck. Visitors who want to stay dry on the tour can stay on the upper decks and simply enjoy the dramatic view of the falls from there.

There are rarely long ticket lines, but they're shorter earlier in the day. You may enjoy this self-guided tour at your own pace; most visitors spend about an hour here.

Purchase tickets on Goat Island at the main concessions area (near the Tesla statue). You'll be given a plastic bag, rain poncho, and sandals that are required for safety reasons. Place your street shoes in the plastic bag, then proceed from the concessions area to the large stone building that houses the elevators going down to the attraction. Recycling bins are

OVER THE FALLS WITHOUT A BARREL

Four people have survived a plunge over Horseshoe Falls, including a seven-year-old boy. All survived the 17-story plunge without the aid of a barrel or other protective device.

It is mind-boggling to consider how such a miracle could transpire. The most popular explanation postulates that the falls act like a giant bubbler. If you've ever seen high divers perform, you may have seen a bubbler at work—compressed air is introduced into the water at the point where a diver will land. The bubbler reduces surface tension and the bubbles act as small air-filled pillows that lessen the impact on the diver. It's possible that large pockets of ever-shifting air bubbles are constantly being generated at the base of the falls, providing sweet spots where landing is less damaging to a human body.

Testing the theory is not only foolhardy, but illegal. People attempting to go over Horseshoe Falls face a fine of nearly $10,000.

available for your rain poncho and sandals following the tour.

◖ TERRAPIN POINT

Terrapin Point is the westernmost point of Goat Island, and forms the brink of Horseshoe Falls. It provides the most dramatic views of the falls from the U.S. side. Terrapin Point is downhill from the main body of Goat Island. You'll enjoy sweeping views of the upper rapids of the Niagara River, the brink of Horseshoe Falls, and the tumult of the Lower Niagara River at the base of the giant waterfall.

Terrapin Point is a beautiful area with a microclimate that changes with the wind. One moment, it's sunny and clear, with a double rainbow over the gorge. The next minute, a cooling blanket of ultrafine mist blows in, generated by the force of the water hurtling over the 175-foot precipice. The thickness and height of the mist plume are a function of the temperature difference between the water and the air. The greater the difference, the larger the mist plume. The vagaries of the wind determine where the mist falls. Bring your camera and an umbrella.

The point is accessed via stairs and a paved path, about 300 yards away from the Top of the Falls restaurant. For safety reasons, Terrapin Point is closed to visitors during the winter season, usually starting in December, due to hazardous accumulations of snow and ice. Its re-opening date is determined by the spring thaw.

◖ Three Sisters Islands

Many tourists overlook **Three Sisters Islands,** which jut out from the southern side of Goat Island into the upper rapids of the Niagara River. The islands—Celinda, Angelina, and Asenath—are named after the children of Parkhurst Whitney, a distinguished officer in the War of 1812 and a local hotelier. These small, lightly wooded, and enchanting islands are about a half-mile upstream from Terrapin Point. Paved pathways with guardrails give visitors a chance to get close to the raging upper rapids of the river. Signs warn against leaving the designated paths, but some curious visitors explore the water's edge on the island farthest out into the rapids.

Niagara Gorge Discovery Center

The **Niagara Gorge Discovery Center** (701 Whirlpool St., 716/278-1796, www.niagarafallsstatepark.com, 9am-5pm Sat.-Sun. late Apr.-late June and early Sept.-late Oct., 9am-5pm Sun.-Thurs., 9am-7pm Fri.-Sat. late June-early Sept., $3) is a rock-solid attraction for visitors interested in the geology that shaped the gorge. Opened in 1971, the facility is circular and designed to resemble a hydroelectric water turbine. Rock hounds and geology geeks could easily spend 45 minutes here enjoying the interactive exhibits, movies, and the virtual elevator ride, all of which illuminate the ancient forces of nature that shaped the Niagara Gorge. The rock-climbing wall and the video detailing the collapse of the Schoellkopf Power Plant are some of the most popular exhibits. Even visitors with only a passing interest in geology will find these exhibits engaging, educational, and accessible.

The Gorge Discovery Center is part of Niagara Falls State Park. Park for free at the lot on Whirlpool Street, then use the pedestrian bridge to safely cross over Robert Moses Parkway. Pedestrians can walk to the center by using the paved path along the rim of the gorge. From Prospect Point, continue north, then pass under the Rainbow Bridge.

Niagara Scenic Trolley

The **Niagara Scenic Trolley** (716/278-1730, www.niagarafallsstatepark.com, 9am-10pm Sun.-Thurs., 9am-11pm Fri.-Sat. mid-June-early Sept., 9am-8pm Sun.-Thurs., 9am-10pm Fri.-Sat. early Sept.-mid-Oct., 9am-6pm daily mid-Oct.-early Jan., $2/day) transports visitors to the state park's attractions, with hop-on/hop-off service. It navigates a three-mile course around the park, stopping at key points including the visitors center, Niagara Gorge Discovery Center, Goat Island, and all parking lots. The trolley is an attraction in itself, with live narration provided by knowledgeable park employees.

AQUARIUM OF NIAGARA

The **Aquarium of Niagara** (701 Whirlpool St., 716/285-3575, www.aquariumofniagara.org, 9am-6pm daily, $10 adults, $6.50 children 3-12) is small, but makes the most of its size. Most of the activity is inside the aquarium and centers on the large main tank where harbor seals and sea lions perform. There is an outdoor pool for interactive feeding of the sea lions ($5). The penguin display features adorable Peruvian penguins (feedings at 10am and 3pm daily). Numerous smaller tanks contain saltwater and freshwater fish, including sea horses, electric eels, and sturgeons.

Though the facility seems dated, the

Learn about the region's geology at the Niagara Gorge Discovery Center.

exhibits and animals are well kept by the caring, cheerful staff. Check the schedule for hourly demonstrations with penguins, harbor seals, and sea lions. The aquarium is good for families with small children, who can expect to spend about 90 minutes here. It's near the Niagara Gorge Discovery Center and accessed via a short walk over the pedestrian bridge that crosses the Robert Moses Parkway.

DOWNTOWN NIAGARA FALLS

Downtown Niagara Falls is bordered by Niagara Falls State Park to the south and west, Niagara Street to the north, and 4th Street (and the casino) to the east. This tourist area is safe, clean, and lively—especially during summer. Visitors can get regional information and advice at the **Niagara USA Official Visitor Center** (10 Rainbow Blvd., 716/282-8992, www.niagara-usa.com, 9am-7pm daily June 1-Sept. 15, 9am-5pm daily Sept. 16-May 31). For the most official, up-to-date information on events and new attractions, the visitor center should be your first stop.

Seneca Niagara Casino & Hotel

At 26 stories high, the glistening **Seneca Niagara Casino & Hotel** (310 4th St., 716/299-1100, www.senecaniagaracasino.com, 24 hours daily) towers over the downtown area. This full-service casino welcomes gamers, with more than 4,000 slot machines and 100 gaming tables, and both smoking and nonsmoking areas. The casino's decor combines Native American art and mythology with contemporary design. Ongoing updates and renovations keep the gaming areas and hotel rooms looking fresh.

Nationally acclaimed entertainers perform at

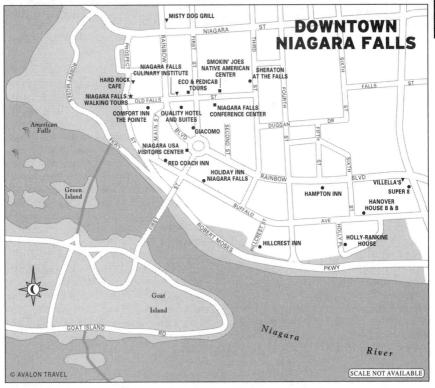

NIAGARA FALLS, NEW YORK

© JOEL A. DOMBROWSKI NIAGARA FALLS WALKING TOURS

Walking tours are a good way to experience the natural beauty of Niagara Falls State Park.

the 2,400-seat Event Center and the 440-seat Bear's Den. In winter, when many downtown restaurants are closed or have restricted hours, the casino's nine restaurants are open, some 24 hours daily.

The casino is nearly impossible to miss from any vantage point in downtown. Look for the tall metallic-blue building. You must be 21 to play the slot machines or enter the gaming floor of the casino. The casino lobby and restaurants are open to patrons of all ages.

SIGHTSEEING TOURS

Tours of Niagara Falls can add a great deal of enjoyment to your visit. However, most of the major attractions are clustered, reducing the need for transportation. Most private tour operators include only two paid attractions (Maid of the Mist and Cave of the Winds), which account for less than half of a tour's typical $80-90 price tag.

The price may be worth it, though, because these tours are guided and provide transportation, with most operators offering hotel and campground pickups that save you parking fees. Before purchasing a tour, inquire whether all guides are properly licensed and if they escort guests throughout the tour or simply drop them off at attractions with return pickup times. **Bedore Tours** (800/538-8433, www.bedoretours. com) provides pickups at all hotels, motels, and campgrounds in the area. **Over the Falls Tours** (716/283-8900, www.overthefallstoursniagara. com) offers tours on both sides of the border.

Niagara Falls Walking Tours (716/222-2432, www.niagarawalkingtours.com, $15) gives scheduled and private walking tours of the park with an emphasis on history and humor. **Niagara Pedicab** (716/345-5446, www.niagarapedicab.com, $30 and up) is an ecofriendly way to view the park scenery from your personal rickshaw pedaled by a guide.

Entertainment and Events

NIGHTLIFE

After a long day of communing with rocks and water, you might be ready for some rock and roll at the **Hard Rock Cafe** (333 Prospect St., 716/282-0007, www.hardrock.com 11am-11pm Sun.-Thurs., 11am-midnight Fri.-Sat.) The Hard Rock has continuous music videos, a reasonable selection of beers, and a ton of cool rock'n'roll memorabilia affixed to the walls. Look for the sketch by Jim Morrison, Jimi Hendrix's guitar, and the pair of Bono's signature sunglasses. The Hard Rock hosts live music with no cover charge every Friday evening.

You'll find entertainment daily at the **Seneca Niagara Casino** (310 4th St., 716/299-1100, www.senecaniagaracasino.com, 24 hours daily). Waitstaff will serve drinks while you're gaming, or you can sit at the bar in **Club Stir** and enjoy free live music 5pm-1:30am Friday-Sunday.

Within stumbling distance of downtown is the **Third Street Tap Room** (439 3rd St., 716/282-8277, 7pm-2am Tues.-Thurs., 6pm-3am Fri.-Sat.). A casual atmosphere with local clientele and reasonable drink prices makes this a good place to unwind. Creative drink specials include s'mores-flavored martinis.

THE ARTS

There is something for everyone at the **Niagara Arts and Cultural Center** (NACC, 1201 Pine Ave., 716/282-7530, www.thenacc.org, 9am-5pm Mon.-Fri. noon-4pm Sat.-Sun., free). NACC features works from more than 70 local artists, including paintings, sculpture, and crafts, and displays change frequently. NACC is a converted high school building with 60 artist studios, two theaters, two galleries, and a TV production soundstage. Check the NACC's online events calendar for the most up-to-date information on the gallery exhibits.

Native American folklore and art come to life in at **Smokin Joes Native Center** (333 1st St., 716/831-2585, www.sjnativecenter. com, 9am-9:30pm daily, free). The main draw is a 40-minute live performance of Native American dance and song that describes a spirit's journey from ancient to contemporary times, called "A Native Journey into the Spirit of the Mist" (7:15pm and 8:30pm Mon.-Sat., 8pm Sun., $20 adults, $13 children 6-12). The authentic music, dancing, singing, and traditional clothing vividly bring the tale to life. Audience members can stay after the show to meet the performers, who will also pose for photographs. The Native Center also has a boutique that sells souvenirs and authentic Native American goods.

FESTIVALS AND EVENTS

Daily entertainment is a regular occurrence downtown, specifically along the Old Falls Street cobblestone corridor. This three-block area runs from the Seneca Niagara Casino to the pedestrian entrance of the state park. During the summer, daily events include exercise classes, movie screenings, music concerts, lectures, and family activities. A current schedule is online (www.fallsstreet.com).

The top nighttime activity in Niagara Falls is the **illumination of the falls** (dusk-10pm daily Jan.-Apr., dusk-midnight daily May-Dec.). The falls are bathed in softly colored light by 21 xenon gas-powered lights stationed on the Canadian side each evening. Though the illumination is difficult to see from the U.S. side, there are a few places with a good view. Terrapin Point (Apr.-Nov.) is the best spot during summer and fall. During winter, the best vantage point is also in Niagara Falls State Park, at Stedman's Bluff, the point on Goat Island that overlooks Luna Island. The **illumination of the upper rapids** (dusk-10pm daily Jan.-Apr., dusk-midnight daily May-Dec.) is also visible each night along the Niagara River from the First Street Bridge to Prospect Point. The

NIAGARA FALLS, NEW YORK

pedestrian bridge located midway is a great spot for taking photos.

During the high season (late May-Sept. 1), **fireworks** light up the skies over Niagara Falls on Friday and Sunday at 10pm. The 10-minute displays are a wonderful climax to a day of sightseeing. They can be seen almost anywhere along the rim of the gorge in the park. The top two vantage points are Luna Island and the Observation Deck, with the Rainbow Bridge pedestrian walkway as a good alternative.

The **Niagara Falls Blues Festival** (www. niagarafallsbluesfest.org, free) focuses on the "Three Bs"—blues, barbecue and beer. Thousands of people gather at Old Falls Street in September for three days of blues music performed by nationally acclaimed artists. Dozens of food vendors sell tasty barbecue delights. Typically, the entertainment begins at 4pm Friday and noon Saturday and Sunday. Bands play until 11pm nightly. The festival is usually held the second weekend in September, but that can vary by year, so check the website.

Old Falls Street rocks throughout summer during the **Hard Rock Cafe Concert Series** (www.hardrock.com, 6pm-10pm Sat. July-Aug., free). On Saturdays in July and August, Old Falls Street is transformed into an outdoor theater for music acts from the 1970s, 1980s, and 1990s. Performances are free; check the Hard Rock website for a list of artists playing each Saturday.

Shopping

The area immediately surrounding the park has many nearly identical souvenir shops. A refreshing alternative is **Made in America** (1 Niagara Center, 2nd floor, 716/304-3622, www.madeinamericastore.com, 9am-5pm daily Apr.-Oct.). Set in the tall blue-glass building adjacent to the main entrance of the state park, the store sells souvenirs with an authentic American flavor, along with clothing.

For non-touristy shopping, you'll need to travel outside of the downtown area. A little more than five miles from downtown, you'll find the **Fashion Outlets of Niagara Mall** (1900 Military Rd., 716/297-2022, www.fashionoutletsniagara.com, 10am-9pm, Mon.-Sat., 11am-6pm Sun.). There are more than 150 retail stores, such as Coach, Ralph Lauren, Hugo Boss, and Eddie Bauer. Many Canadian shoppers cross the border to find a better selection, lower prices, and lower taxes on clothing and electronics. This complex is adjacent to a **Wal-Mart** (1549 Military Rd., 716/298-4484, www. walmart.com), which, in turn, leads to Niagara Falls Boulevard and another corridor of retail big-box stores.

Recreation

HIKING AND BIKING

Niagara Falls has several biking and hiking paths. The entire state park is designed to promote access by foot and bike. The portion of the Robert Moses Parkway running from the Niagara Gorge Discovery Center to Devil's Hole Park is dedicated to bikers and hikers, as well as those simply out for a stroll.

Gorge Rim Trail

Just outside the Niagara Gorge Discovery Center is the **Gorge Rim Trail** (716/278-0820, www.niagarafallsstatepark.com, dawn-dusk daily, free) trailhead. The Gorge Rim Trail is an easy hike that stretches from the state park to the Robert Moses Power Plant, a one-way distance of 6.2 miles. This multipurpose trail goes along the top of the gorge and is mostly paved. As you proceed north, there are excellent views of Canada, the rapids, and the whirlpool. Rest stops have interpretive signs describing the industrial heritage of the area. This trail feeds into others that descend into the gorge for views of the rapids and whirlpool. A kiosk at the trailhead has good informational posters and brochures about the entire 15 miles of trails that travel from the falls north toward Lake Ontario.

Bike Rental

Bike rental shops in the Niagara Falls region cater to locals and visitors pursuing the pleasures and health benefits of cycling. There are two excellent options in Niagara Falls, although both rent bikes June-September only. **The Red Lounge Hostel** (723 3rd St., 716/286-0707, www.redloungeniagara.com, 7am-7pm daily June-Sept.) rents bikes for $10 an hour and offers a unique, bicyclist-only guided tour ($15).

Ride Niagara Bicycle Rentals (Old Falls St. and Rainbow Blvd., 716/278-2121, www.fallsstreet.com, 10am-6pm Tues.-Sat., noon-5pm Sun. June-Sept.) equips you with everything needed for a two-wheel adventure, including helmets and bike locks. Also included are maps with bicycle-friendly routes to explore. Rentals start at $15 for a half-day.

Accommodations

Niagara Falls hotels are found in two geographic regions—downtown and Niagara Falls Boulevard. Downtown properties are typically more expensive, as they are within walking distance of the state park. Niagara Falls Boulevard hotels are less expensive, but they are older and require a five-mile drive to the falls. Hotels earn most of their revenue during summer, so don't expect any bargains then. In winter and early spring, some hotels are willing to negotiate rates. Rates listed here reflect high season costs.

DOWNTOWN

As tall as Niagara Falls, ⬛ **The Giacomo** (222 1st St., 716/299-0200, www.thegiacomo.com, $300) towers over the other lodgings in the falls region. This boutique hotel is a restored art deco building just two blocks from the state park. It sets the standard for service in the area. In addition to large, comfortable rooms, the complimentary breakfast is excellent. Visit the lounge on the top floor for its view of American Falls and the rapids.

The **Seneca Niagara Casino Hotel** (310 4th St., 716/299-1100, www.senecaniagaracasino.com, $200) is the largest hotel in the state outside New York City. It has more than 600 rooms and suites, many updated in 2013. There's a large indoor pool and spa, and nine restaurants on-site. The hotel is just three blocks from the state park.

The **Hillcrest Inn** (1 Hillcrest St., 716/278-9676, www.hillcrestniagara.com, $140) is a bed-and-breakfast close to the state park. With comfortable rooms and a warm, welcoming ambience, it's like your home away from home.

The **Red Lounge Hostel** (723 3rd St., 716/286-0707, www.redloungeniagara.com, $28 dorm) is everything you want in a hostel—clean, close, and inexpensive. The owners formerly managed an international five-star hotel. The large, airy, coed dormitory-style rooms have free Wi-Fi. Plenty of information is available here on how to enjoy Niagara on a student budget.

NIAGARA FALLS BOULEVARD
Many motels in Niagara Falls harken back to the 1950s, when thousands of families and honeymooners drove to the falls from throughout the northeast United States. The **Falls Motel** (5820 Buffalo Ave., 716/283-3239, www.fallsmotel.com, $120) is among a handful worth staying at. Rooms are small, well kept, and clean. The family owners take pride in making sure that your stay is comfortable and rewarding. The front desk can provide up-to-date information on seasonal attractions, weather, and transportation.

The **Best Western Summit Inn** (9500 Niagara Falls Blvd., 716/297-5050, www.

The Seneca Niagara Casino has more than 600 rooms and 24-hour gaming.

bestwesternnewyork.com, $110) has clean rooms and free Internet access. It's close to the Fashion Outlets of Niagara Mall, and provides a complimentary continental breakfast that's actually worth waking up for.

Food

DOWNTOWN
For a great meal and a ton of ambience, dine at the **◖ Red Coach Inn** (2 Buffalo Ave., 716/282-1459, www.redcoach.com, 7:30am-9:30pm Sun.-Thurs., 7:30am-10:30pm Fri.-Sat., $25). The cuisine is American, while the decor is reminiscent of an English Tudor manor. Entrees are satisfying and desserts are decadent, with one serving usually perfect for two adults. In winter, call ahead and ask for a table near the large open-hearth fireplace. In warmer months, dine on the open patio overlooking the upper rapids of the Niagara River.

Don't judge **Villella's Ristorante** (795 Rainbow Blvd., 716/284-9778, 11am-9:30pm daily, $15) by its exterior. The eatery is attached to a Super 8 motel on a busy street corner at the edge of downtown. The dining area is nothing special, but the traditional Sicilian food is extraordinary. Start with the fresh bread and homemade dipping oil, then relish a uniquely Sicilian appetizer, the *arancini* (fried rice balls). Of the large-portioned and fresh entrées, the veal parmigiana is a local favorite. This small restaurant is often full, so reservations are a good idea.

AN OFFER YOU CAN'T REFUSE

For many years, the American Mafia controlled the city of Niagara Falls. Running the organization was Stefano Magaddino, an old- school Sicilian mafioso known for his brutality and cunning. As prohibition enforcement forced legitimate distillers and distributors to stop alcohol production, Magaddino filled the void. Moving from Buffalo to Niagara Falls, he profited from bootlegging owing to the proximity of Canada to his turf.

Magaddino earned the name "The Undertaker," as he operated a chain of funeral homes in the area. Smuggling operations expanded into labor union racketeering, extortion, gambling, loan sharking, and narcotics. Magaddino was influential on the national stage as well, where he became a member of the mob's "commission" of top dons. The Undertaker eschewed the limelight, choosing to run his Niagara Falls operation from the shadows. He survived at least two assassination attempts and died of natural causes in 1974. Interfamily rivalry went on to rip the local mob apart, reducing its influence in the area.

Wine on Third (501 3rd St., 716/285-9463, www.wineonthird.com, 4pm-midnight Mon.-Wed., 4pm-1am Thurs., 4pm-2am Fri.-Sat., noon-10pm Sun., $25) is an upscale café, perfect for a romantic dinner with wine. The cuisine is contemporary American, and the wine list is good. When the weather permits, eat outside along 3rd Street and people-watch.

For good food fast, the ◖ **Misty Dog Grill** (431 Main St., 716/285-0702, 11am-10pm daily Apr.-Oct., $6) can't be beat. Located in the heart of downtown (look for the giant ice-cream cone on Main Street near Niagara Street), this take-out stand has a surprisingly large menu, great for families on a budget. They have kid-friendly food such as hot dogs, burgers, and fries, plus plenty of other choices, including wraps, sandwiches, and salads. If you want to try authentic chicken wings and cannot travel to Buffalo, try them here.

The odds are good that you'll find something for every appetite at the **Seneca Niagara Casino** (310 4th St., 716/299-1100, www.senecaniagaracasino.com). The best steak in town is at **The Western Door** (877/873-6322, www.senecaniagaracasino.com, 5pm-9:30pm Sun.-Thurs., 5pm-10pm Fri.-Sat., $45). Reservations are recommended. The **Koi**

Restaurant (877/873-6322, www.senecaniagaracasino.com, 5pm-9:30pm Sun.-Thurs., 5pm-midnight Fri.-Sat., $30) serves traditional and contemporary Asian dishes. At the **Blues Burger Bar** (877/873-6322, www.senecaniagaracasino.com, 11am-11pm daily, $10), you enjoy a satisfying burger along with a side dish and drink at the restaurant, or order your meal for takeout.

LITTLE ITALY

The venerable ◖ **Como Restaurant** (2220 Pine Ave., 716/285-9341, www.comorestaurant.com, 11:30am-9pm daily, $18) allows you to dine where the mob did. If you like homestyle Italian food, with huge portions served in an old-school restaurant atmosphere, then the Como is for you. This restaurant may not knock your socks off, but it will give you an authentic glimpse into the world of Niagara Falls in the 1960s, when mafia don Stefano Magaddino frequently ate at the Como.

Get hot, fresh, and cheap Mexican food at **Colosso Taco** (2440 Pine Ave., 716/284-1498, 11am-1am Mon.-Tues., 11am-3:30am Wed.-Thurs., 11am-4am Fri.-Sat., 11am-4pm Sun., $4). The tacos are satisfactory, the roll-ups outstanding!

Information and Services

The downtown area has a handful of souvenir shops and hotel gift shops that sell basic items like toothpaste and aspirin. Expect high prices, a limited selection, and limited store hours. The closest 24-hour convenience store is **7-Eleven** (402 Niagara St., 716/285-4497, 24 hours daily), across from the casino. The closest urban supermarket is **Save-A-Lot** (1740 Pine Ave., 716/285-6820, www.save-a-lot.com, 9am-8pm daily).

The best place for information on Niagara Falls is the **Niagara USA Official Visitor Center** (10 Rainbow Blvd., 716/282-8992, www.niagara-usa.com, 9am-7pm June 1-Sept. 15, 9am-5pm Sept. 16-May 31). Many for-profit souvenir shops display the internationally known blue sign with a question mark, purporting to be a tourist information center. Niagara USA provides unbiased information about the falls and the outlying areas.

Getting There and Around

BY AIR

The **Buffalo Niagara International Airport** (BUF, 4200 Genesee St., Cheektowaga, 716/630-6000, www.buffaloairport.com) is a 25-minute drive from Niagara Falls. Expect to pay $60 for a cab ride from the airport to downtown Niagara Falls. Taxi service providers at the airport are generally reliable and safe, with no advanced reservations required.

BY CAR

If your hotel is in the downtown area, you don't need a car to visit Niagara Falls State Park. Downtown hotels are within walking distance, and the park is best explored on foot or via the hop-on, hop-off **Niagara Scenic Trolley** (716/278-1730, www.niagarafallsstatepark.com, 9am-10pm Sun.-Thurs., 9am-11pm Fri.-Sat. mid-June-early Sept., 9am-8pm Sun.-Thurs., 9am-10pm Fri.-Sat. early Sept.-mid-Oct., 9am-6pm daily mid-Oct.-early Jan., $2/day). If your hotel is outside the downtown area, drive to the park. Parking is plentiful at numerous private lots ($5) or within the state park ($10), including the main lot and the lots on Goat Island. You can pay and park at the main lot, then move your car to the Goat Island lot for no additional charge, as long as you show your receipt at the parking attendant booth. During winter, when there are few tourists, parking at the state park is sometimes free, especially on Goat Island.

The downtown area has free on-street parking. Signs along the curb designate where free two-hour parking is permitted. Streets close to Niagara Falls State Park with two-hour parking spots include: Old Falls Street, Rainbow Boulevard (near the Turtle Building), Main Street, 1st Street, and 3rd Street.

Municipal parking lots are plentiful and reasonably priced. Car park ramps are located at 219 Niagara Street and 360 Rainbow Boulevard. Parking costs $1 an hour with a maximum charge of $12. A surface lot popular with RV owners is at 238 3rd Street (cars $5/day, RVs $11/day).

Private parking lots are convenient but have their downsides. Private lot attendants sometimes wear clothing similar to Parks Department uniforms and use orange flags to draw tourists into their parking lots, then lure them into adjacent souvenir stores with the promise of a free prize, map, or information, followed by a sales pitch for tours. These lots are close to the park, however, and can save you a few bucks.

BY BUS

Trailways (www.trailwaysny.com) and **Greyhound** (www.greyhound.com) bus lines pick up and drop off passengers daily at the **Quality Hotel & Suites** (240 1st St., 716/282-1212, www.qualityniagarafalls.com).

Niagara Frontier Transit Authority (716/855-7211, www.metro.nfta.com) provides local bus service. Routes 55 and 55T pick up passengers in the downtown area and serve key areas of the city, such as the Pine Street business district. Fares are $2 each way for both routes; the Trolley Route (55T) is free for guests staying at participating hotels (ask at your hotel's front desk for a trolley pass).

BY TRAIN

Amtrak (www.amtrak.com) stops at the **Niagara Falls train station** (2701 Willard Ave.) twice daily via the Empire route, and once daily via the Maple Leaf route. From Buffalo, the train ride takes about an hour (on either route). Fares start at $13 each way. The Empire route terminates at Niagara Falls, New York, while the Maple Leaf continues across the border and stops at Niagara Falls, Ontario. You can take the train from the Canadian side to visit Niagara Falls State Park, but be prepared to use a taxi to get from the train station to the park, and vice versa.

From the train station, you'll need to take a taxi 2.5 miles ($8-10) to reach the park and downtown area. Taxis wait at the train station during scheduled stop times, so you shouldn't have trouble getting a cab once you arrive.

North of the Falls

The Niagara region's beauty does not end at Niagara Falls, and neither should your travels. Following the river north, you'll find outstanding hiking, history, and attractions. Along the 15 miles of the Lower Niagara River, you'll see a deadly whirlpool, an imposing power plant, an outdoor arts campus, and a 300-year-old military fort.

Lewiston is a historic village with gorgeous hills, fertile plains, and a beautiful waterfront. In December 1813, the town was raided and destroyed by British soldiers and Native American warriors bent on revenge for American atrocities committed during the War of 1812. The picturesque village is now a tourist destination in summer and fall, thanks to its quiet beauty and the quaint shops that line Center Street.

At the place where the river ends and Lake Ontario begins, stands Old Fort Niagara, the longest continually occupied military structure in North America. Surrounding the fort is the village of **Youngstown,** a launching point for excellent boating and fishing, and site of beautiful sunsets.

SIGHTS
Whirlpool State Park

Less than three miles north of the falls is one of the most amazing natural features of the entire region: the whirlpool. A great way to appreciate it is from **Whirlpool State Park** (off Robert Moses Pkwy., 716/284-4691, www. nysparks.com, dawn-dusk daily, free). The views of the raging river below are beautiful and breathtaking.

When you arrive at the park, pass through the stone shelter and take the paved path to the left, which will lead you to the rim of the gorge. Once there, you'll grip the guardrail as you glimpse the rapids at the bottom of a sheer 200-foot-drop. The class VI white water churns menacingly down the narrow river, surging headlong into the massive whirlpool. The whirlpool basin is a relic from a waterfall that existed long before the last ice age. The Niagara River tears through this basin and makes a sharp right-hand turn as it heads downstream toward Lake Ontario.

When the river water level is high, the water

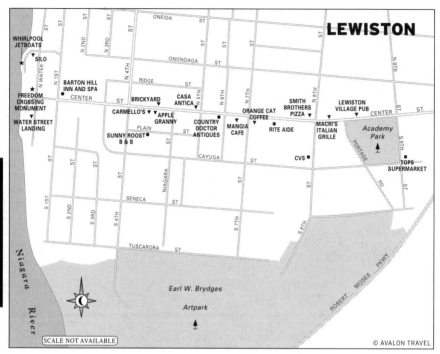

slams into the far wall of the gorge and circles counterclockwise, passing on its journey to Lake Ontario. This phenomenon forms a whirlpool, which is perhaps the most dangerous stretch of the river. The ever-moving vortex is more than 200 feet deep and tosses floating objects such as tree trunks like matchsticks. Even the modern, super-powerful jet boats do not cross this section of the river, but instead turn to avoid the capricious power of the whirlpool.

As you travel along the rim of the gorge, be aware of your footing. Some spots have washed out and present a hazard. Keep children close by, as the gorge is steep and unforgiving. At the path's end, you have a view of the more serene part of the river as it flows north toward the power plants and eventually Lake Ontario.

The path completes a circuit (0.3 mile), leading you back to the shelter where you started. There are many picnic tables and grills here, along with interpretive materials, signs,

restrooms, and a water fountain. You'll find Whirlpool State Park an ideal place to picnic and enjoy a wonder of nature.

Devil's Hole State Park

The ominously named **Devil's Hole State Park** (Robert Moses Pkwy. and Rte. 104, 716/284-5778, www.nysparks.com, dawn-dusk daily mid-May-Nov., free) is a partly wooded, 42-acre park. It sits upon the remnants of an ancient stream that poured over the wall of the gorge, creating a small waterfall. The stream is now a mere seasonal trickle down the gorge wall. It was here in September 1763 that more than 100 British soldiers and civilians were killed during a Native American ambush meant to sever the settlers' portage route around the falls.

The park is primarily a starting point for hikers and others who descend the 400 stairs down the gorge to enjoy the view of the rapids

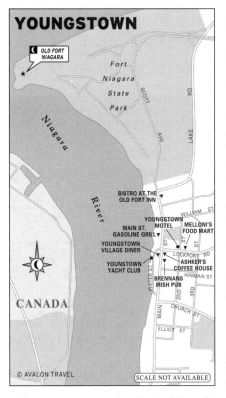

YOUNGSTOWN

OLD FORT NIAGARA

Fort Niagara State Park

Niagara River

BISTRO AT THE OLD FORT INN

YOUNGSTOWN MOTEL
MAIN ST. GASOLINE GRILL
MELLONI'S FOOD MART
YOUNGSTOWN VILLAGE DINER
YOUNSTOWN YACHT CLUB
ASHKER'S COFFEE HOUSE
BRENNANS IRISH PUB

CANADA

WILLIAM ST
LOCKPORT RD
HINMAN ST
CHURCH ST
ELLIOT ST

© AVALON TRAVEL   SCALE NOT AVAILABLE

and power plant, or try their luck at fishing for trout and salmon. There is ample parking and several tables with grills for picnicking.

Niagara Power Vista

Adjacent to Devil's Hole State Park is the **Niagara Power Vista** (5777 Lewiston Rd., Lewiston, 716/286-6661, www.nypa.gov, 9am-5pm daily, free), the visitors center of the Niagara Hydroelectric Power Plant. It is difficult to fully grasp the size of this massive facility until you enter. Built into the side of the Niagara Gorge, this plant produces clean, inexpensive energy transmitted throughout New York State. The portion of the plant open to visitors has displays and interactive, kid-friendly exhibits that explain how the Niagara River is harnessed to generate electricity.

While there, be sure to visit the fishermen's

platform at the base of the power plant. Access the platform from Hyde Park Road, turning right onto Power Authority Service Road, and parking at the bottom. The anglers will be glad to show the impressive trout and steelheads on their stringers.

Artpark

The most popular attraction in Lewiston is **Earl W. Brydges Artpark** (450 S. 4th St., 716/754-4375, www.artpark.net, dawn-dusk daily, free), a sprawling, 150-acre complex dedicated to the enjoyment of all art forms. It features two large performance venues: an indoor stage with seating for 2,400 and an outdoor amphitheater for 10,000 people. The amphitheater is an amazing space for a concert because the stage backdrop is the Niagara River Gorge. Check out the Tuesday in the Park summer concert series where you can see major acts like Chicago, the Doobie Brothers, and Lynyrd Skynyrd for just $10.

In addition to musicals and dramatic performances, Artpark provides week-long classes (known as "camps") for young people to explore drama, music, and graphic arts. Nature's artistry is on stage here as well. Artpark has picnic shelters and hiking trails, with excellent shoreline fishing in the Lower Niagara River.

Whirlpool Jet Boats

The **Whirlpool Jet Boats** (115 S. Water St., Lewiston, 888/438-4444, www.whirlpooljet.com, $61) provide an adventuresome, 45-minute ride through the lower rapids of the Niagara River. Prepare to get wet! This attraction promises thrills and delivers as boats slash through the rapids during its nine-mile round-trip. Bring extra clothes and a towel, and consider wearing a bathing suit during the ride. The ride is available in two options: wet or dry. For the "wet jet" ride, sit in the front row. The dry ride (in a glass-enclosed boat known as the Jet Dome) is wonderful, but not as thrilling.

This attraction can also be accessed from two locations on the Canadian side of the border. The Niagara-on-the-Lake site is farther downstream, so requires an extra 15 minutes

INDUSTRY ALONG THE NIAGARA RIVER

As you approach Niagara Falls from the south, along the Robert Moses Parkway, you'll notice the juxtaposition of the beautiful Niagara River on your left and rusted factory infrastructure on your right. The city has always tried to balance the seemingly conflicting goals of natural preservation with promoting heavy industry.

For many years, big names in manufacturing had a presence at the falls, lured by the cheap electric power, a willing labor force, and the availability of local land and waterways for pollution disposal. Companies such as Alcoa, Union Carbide, Hooker Chemical, DuPont, Carborundum, and Occidental have since left or significantly scaled back production.

The area along the parkway was an important incubator for new technology. The secret Manhattan Project turned to the electrochemical industries of Niagara Falls to produce the world's first atomic weapon during World War II. What remains is a hulking infrastructure of aging chemical plants functioning at partial capacity and a lot of brown field cleanup.

in the jet boat. However, the exciting, adventure-filled portions of the attraction are identical from all locations.

Freedom Crossing Monument
Lewiston's **Freedom Crossing Monument** is a dramatic yet uplifting monument that pays tribute to the brave people of Lewiston who helped transport fugitive slaves to Canada via the Underground Railroad. The bronze statue portrays a family of escaped slaves as they board a rowboat for the journey across the Niagara River to freedom. Also depicted in the monument is Josiah Tryon, the Lewiston man who risked his own freedom by assisting the fugitive slaves along the Underground Railroad. The monument is located between Center Street and the banks of the Niagara River, near the Silo restaurant.

Fatima Shrine
The inspiring **Fatima Shrine** (1023 Swann Rd., Lewiston, 716/754-7489, www.fatimashrine.com, 9am-5pm daily Jan.-mid-Nov., 9am-9pm mid-Nov.-Dec., free) is formally known as the **National Shrine Basilica of Our Lady of Fatima.** Thousands of Roman Catholics make a pilgrimage to this site each year to see the glass-domed basilica, Avenue of the Saints, and the bell tower. This 16-acre site is for prayer and contemplation, but secular

people also appreciate the beauty of religious art and statuary. Also on the shrine's campus is the Pilgrim Center, which has a gift shop and cafeteria.

◖ Old Fort Niagara
Well worth the 25-minute drive north from Niagara Falls is **Old Fort Niagara** (Fort Niagara State Park, Youngstown, 716/745-7611, www.oldfortniagara.org, 9am-7pm daily July-Aug., 9am-5pm daily Sept.-June, $12 adults, $8 children 6-12). The fort dates back to 1679 when the French constructed an outpost that became Fort Niagara. During the French and Indian War, France and Britain grappled for control of North America. After the British won, they occupied the fort until 1796, several years after the United States had won the Revolutionary War.

During the War of 1812, British troops again took control of the fort, finally leaving in 1815. The United States has since maintained control of Fort Niagara, which eventually served as a camp for German prisoners during World War II. Fort Niagara has the distinction of being the longest continually occupied military base in the United States.

Plan on spending at least two hours wandering the expansive grounds of the fort. A well-produced video at the visitors center is definitely worth viewing, as it gives context to the

© NYSDED-PHOTO BY DARREN MCGEE

Relive more than 300 years of history at Old Fort Niagara in Youngstown.

fort's long history. Costumed reenactors demonstrate how soldiers and civilians lived and died in the 1700-1800s. There are live musket- and canon-firing demonstrations, blacksmithing, and food preparation.

The most impressive building within the fort is the French Castle. The French built this two-story structure in 1726, cleverly disguising a functional garrison as a trading post. The castle housed officers' quarters, soldiers' barracks, a chapel, and jail cells. Next to the French Castle is the Bake House, which is essentially two giant stone ovens and dates back to 1756. The cooks would build a fire inside the oven, then let it burn until a few embers remained. Then they swept the embers from the oven and placed bread inside to be cooked by the stored heat.

Make a stop at the Powder Magazine to see where the fort's ammunition was stored. Built in 1757, this thick masonry building was designed to withstand hits from cannon fire without exploding. Today it has been restored so visitors can appreciate the lengths to which

armies went to their powder safe and dry. As you walk the perimeter of the fort, imagine the strategic importance of this facility, guarding the mouth of the Niagara River and gateway to the New World. The view of Lake Ontario is stunning—on clear days, you can see Toronto on the northern shore.

The fort is no longer a functioning military base, although the Coast Guard operates out of the dock on its grounds. The legions of reenactors seen here throughout the year—French, British, American, and Native American—are all volunteers. The largest annual event here is the commemoration of the 1759 siege of the fort when Britain took control of it from France. Each year, during the weekend closest to July 9, more than 1,000 reenactors stage battles that recall the history-changing conflict. In addition to battle scenes, reenactors also create camps to show how people lived, ate, and amused themselves during the 1750s.

Surrounding the fort is **Fort Niagara State Park** (Rte. 18F, Youngstown, 716/745-7273, www.nysparks.com, 9am-5pm daily Sept.-June, 9am-7pm daily July-Aug., free) with picnic facilities, a swimming pool, and boat launches.

ENTERTAINMENT AND EVENTS
Nightlife
The village of Lewiston has just 2,700 people, so some of the best nightlife consists of meandering along Center Street on a quiet evening, watching the sunset from a park bench along the riverbank, or eating an ice-cream cone near the water's edge. Nightlife here typically centers on a meal, with drinks from the bar. Few establishments focus on libation and music, which is ironic since many believe that the cocktail was invented here in the 1800s.

Local historians say Catherine Hustler, proprietor of Hustler's Tavern, invented the cocktail when she used the feather of a domestic bird (a cockerel) to stir a gin-based drink in the early 1800s. Although the Hustler Tavern is no more, it was the only building left unmolested by the British when they burned the village in 1813. Legend has it that the redcoats couldn't bear to raze the tavern they had enjoyed so often before the war. Mrs. Hustler and her husband were quite the hosts. After they entertained author James Fenimore Cooper, he included them as fictional characters in one of his books.

More traditional nightlife activities are enjoyed at the **Lewiston Village Pub** (840 Center St., Lewiston, 716/405-7017, www.lewistonvillagepub.com, 3pm-2am Mon.-Thurs., 11am-3am Fri., noon-3am Sat., noon-2am Sun.). With more than 40 beers on tap, it has a casual atmosphere that makes you feel right at home. The knowledgeable barkeeps allow you to sample beers before settling on the perfect pint.

The Arts
The **Castellani Art Museum** (Niagara University, Lewiston, 716/286-8200, www.castellaniartmuseum.org, 11am-5pm Tues.-Sat., 1pm-5pm Sun., free) is located on the Niagara University campus in Lewiston. It has more than 5,700 works of modern art by artists such as Picasso, Dali, and Warhol.

Festivals and Events
SUMMER
In summer, the **Lewiston Council on the Arts** (716/754-0166, www.artcouncil.org) sponsors free blues concerts in **Hennepin Park** at the gazebo (4th and Center Sts., Lewiston) at 7pm on Mondays. If you need to cheer up after the blues, come back on Wednesdays to hear the seven-piece Lewiston Jazz Project—also at 7pm and free.

In August, the **Lewiston Art Festival** (716/754-0166, www.artcouncil.org, free) draws more than 175 artists who display more than 20,000 pieces of art. The festival is so large that Center Street is closed to traffic from 4th to 8th Streets for the weekend. Look for a visitors booth at 5th and Center Streets for information on exhibitors.

FALL
In early September, the **Niagara County Peach Festival** (www.lewistonkiwanis.org, free) is the largest festival in the county, with amusement rides, a parade, and cooking contests. During the three-day fest, various peach confections can be purchased, a Peach Queen is crowned, and judges inspect the chins of young men to find the best peach fuzz. There is also live music and a shuttle bus service.

Lewiston's **Marble Orchard Ghost Walks** (476 Center St., www.artcouncil.org, 7pm Sat. Sept.-Oct., $15) are a real scream! Local actors present the ghoulish past of Lewiston's former residents inside the Marble Orchard. A costumed guide leads you through this family-friendly haunt recounting the burning of Lewiston, mysteries of the Underground Railroad, and other events, such as the disappearance of the man who threatened to reveal the secret rituals of the Freemasons.

RECREATION
Hiking and Biking
The **Whirlpool Rapids Trail** (Whirlpool State Park, off Robert Moses Pkwy.,

© NYSDED-PHOTO BY DARREN MCGEE

Hennepin Park is the site of free concerts.

716/284-5778, www.nysparks.com, dawn-dusk daily mid-May-Nov., free) is a difficult 1.4-mile trail with stairs, wooded paths, and some boulders to navigate. The hike is well worth the effort, as it takes you down to the water's level and up close to the class VI rapids and the whirlpool. Use caution, as the whirlpool and rapids are unforgiving to people who accidentally fall in. The trail is open to hikers 8 years and older. Alcoholic beverages, camping, and fires are prohibited. To find the trailhead, exit out the back of the stone shelter in Whirlpool State Park and follow the path to the rim of the gorge (with a beautiful view of the whirlpool). Continue in a clockwise direction on the path and in less than half a mile, you'll find stairs marking the start of the trail.

A little farther north along the gorge is the 2.5-mile **Devil's Hole Trail** (716/284-5778, www.nysparks.com, dawn-dusk daily mid-May-Nov., free). This trail is a moderate one, with approximately 300 stone stairs to climb. Upon descending them, you'll see the Devil's

Hole Cave, a natural feature shrouded in legend (and, sadly, covered in graffiti). The limestone cave is safe to enter, but watch for trash and broken bottles discarded here. Be careful: Indian legend says that any person who enters the cave is destined for tragedy! Should you survive the cave's curse, continue down the stairs to the stone picnic tables. This is a great spot for a rest or snack, but remember to pack out all your trash. The trail winds along the gorge floor and boasts excellent views of the lower rapids of the Niagara River, giant boulders, and lightly wooded areas. Heading south along the river path, you'll arrive at stairs that ascend to Whirlpool State Park. Once topside, head back (north) along the Gorge Rim Trail before arriving back at Devil's Hole Park and the end of the loop.

Parks
Joseph Davis State Park (4143 Lower River Rd., Lewiston, 716/754-4596, www.nysparks.com, dawn-dusk daily, free) has excellent large-mouth bass fishing in old quarry pits filled with

water. There are picnic facilities, a nature trail, and a 27-hole disc golf course.

Fishing and Boating

A boat launch is available at the **Village of Lewiston Marina** (145 N. 4th St., Lewiston, 716/754-8271, dawn-dusk daily, free Mon.-Wed., $14 Thurs.-Sun.), also known as the Sands Dock.

There are several areas for shore fishing, including the fishermen's platform at the base of the Niagara Power Vista, along the hiking trails in Artpark, and the waterfront at the Lewiston Marina.

Obtain a fishing license (one-day, week-long, or annual license) by phone or online (866/933-2257, www.nyfgisales.appsolgrp.com) or in person at most sporting goods stores. One-day non-resident licenses are $15. Fish are abundant in the Niagara River and anglers can expect to encounter bass, perch, pike, salmon, sunfish, and trout. A complete list of fish species, licensing requirements, and angling tips are provided at the New York State Department of Conservation website (www.dec.ny.gov).

Winter Activities

All state parks in this area, including Whirlpool, Devil's Hole, Joseph Davis, and Fort Niagara, are accessible for **cross-country skiing** and **snowshoeing.** However, there are no local outfitters that rent this type of equipment, so visitors must bring their own.

ACCOMMODATIONS
Lewiston

The **Barton Hill Hotel and Spa** (100 Center St., 716/754-9070, www.bartonhillhotel.com, $225) has an unbeatable waterfront view. Built in 2005, the hotel has the charm of a historic country inn, but the amenities of a modern luxury boutique hotel. All 78 rooms feature fireplaces, and some include whirlpool tubs and balconies that overlook the Niagara River. River view rooms cost more, but are well worth the extra expense. Request one of the corner suites on the third and fourth floors. The spa service here is exquisite. Try the Queen or King

© NIAGARA TOURISM AND CONVENTION CORPORATION

Barton Hill Hotel and Spa

for an Hour spa package, for a treat. The main drag of Lewiston is just a few minutes' walk uphill.

Sunny's Roost (421 Plain St., 716/754-116, www.sunnysroost.com, $125) has everything you could want in a B&B: four clean and comfortable rooms, friendly innkeepers, and excellent breakfasts. It's one block off Center Street, with excellent proximity to shops and restaurants. This 100-year-old home used to be a rectory for St. Peter's Roman Catholic Church.

Youngstown

Would you like a room, a cabin, or an entire cottage? You'll find all three at the **Lakeview Motel and Cottages** (2000 Lake Rd., 716/791-8668, www.lakeviewmotelandcottage.com, Mar.-Nov., $85-195). The rates are reasonable—motel room ($85), cabin ($95), cottage ($195)—and they're close to Lake Ontario.

FOOD
Lewiston

The **Silo Restaurant** (115 N. Water St.,

716/754-9680, www.lewistonsilo.com, 10am-10pm daily May-Sept., $3-12) is a local institution and a place to take the family for hot dogs, hamburgers, and a view of the Niagara River. Set in a renovated coal silo, this family restaurant is famous for the "haystack" ($12), one pound of rib-eye steak with melted mozzarella and toasted hash browns served on a large roll.

Just down the waterfront from the Silo Restaurant is **Water Street Landing** (115 S. Water St., 716/754-9200, www.waterstreetlanding.com, 11:30am-9pm Mon.-Fri., 10am-11pm Sat.-Sun., $16-40), known for its waterfront view and ambience. The dining room is quiet and a bit formal, while the patio and pub are relaxed, but busier. The food and service are generally better in the dining room. Try the crab cakes remoulade appetizer ($10) for a tasty treat.

Carmelos (425 Center St., 716/754-2311, www.carmelos-restaurant.com, 4:30pm-9pm Tues.-Thurs., 4:30pm-10pm Fri.-Sat., $14-35) is regarded as the best restaurant in the village. This intimate neighborhood eatery serves excellent Italian and modern American fare. The menu changes frequently because the chef uses locally grown, seasonal ingredients. You'll enjoy world-class food at local prices here.

Youngstown

In the shadow of Old Fort Niagara, enjoy fine dining at **Bistro at the Old Fort Inn** (110 Main St., 716/745-7141, www.bistroattheoldfortinn.com, 4pm-9pm Sun. and Tues.-Thurs., 4pm-10pm Fri.-Sat., $9-30). The restaurant's Acapulco-born and -trained chef has a menu of Latin flavors prepared with a French technique. The lobster with tequila beurre blanc combines Mexican tequila with French white butter. A baby grand piano in the dining room is a nice upscale touch. There is live music Friday-Saturday. If this restaurant had been here in 1759, the French never would have left.

INFORMATION AND SERVICES

A handy source of information for the Niagara River region is the **USA Chamber**

of Commerce (895 Center St., Lew 716/754-9500, www.niagarariverregio 8:30am-4:30pm Mon.–Fri.). The **post** (150 S. 8th St., Lewiston, 716/754-is conveniently located one block sc Center Street.

There is a **Tops supermarket** (906 St., Lewiston, 716/215-1350, www markets.com, 5am-1am daily) and **pharmacy** (795 Center St., Lewiston, 7 2370, www.cvs.com, 8am-10pm daily the main street in the village.

In Youngstown, there is a **Ri Pharmacy** (214 Lockport Rd., 716/74 and a supermarket, **Melloni's** (200 Li Rd., 716/219-4105, 7am-9pm daily) **Niagara Bank** (421 2nd St., 716/278 has a 24-hour ATM.

GETTING THERE AND AROUND
Lewiston

The municipal **bus service** (www. nfta.com) connects Lewiston to the Niagara Falls, via Route 50. The fare 50-minute ride is $2 each way. There eral bus stops along the main thorou Center Street.

Most visitors drive, accessing the vil I-190, Exit 25B. Those traveling from I Falls can take the more scenic Robert Parkway that winds along the gorge rin of about 20 minutes.

Once in Lewiston, you'll find the ma oughfare, Center Street, very walkabl most attractions along a half-mile s There is ample parking at both the e: (at the Tops supermarket) and west end Street municipal parking lot) of Center During winter (Dec.-Mar.), street p is not allowed 3am-6am to facilitate removal.

Youngstown

There are no municipal or comm buses that serve Youngstown, so mo: tors arrive in the village via car. T mile, 25-minute trip from Niagara F

BUFFALO

The second largest city in New York State, Buffalo has rebounded, transitioning from a rust belt city to a renaissance one. In 1900, there were more millionaires per capita in Buffalo than any other American city. The city now rivals Chicago as a living museum to the great American designers such as Frank Lloyd Wright, Louis Sullivan, Henry Hobson (H. H.) Richardson, and Edward Brodhead Green.

Today, the quickly developing waterfront, once a slumbering giant, is now awakening. Sailing, fishing, kayaking, and swimming are accessible and affordable. While residents embrace and endure the cold winter, they welcome the warmth of the spring, summer, and fall with festivals and events every weekend.

Residents call this area Buffalo-Niagara because Buffalo and Niagara County are perfect neighbors, offering a dual city and country experience. The fertile lands of Niagara County are ideal for growing many fruits and produce remarkable wines. The area's 20 wineries are known for the variety of their vintages, from fruit wines to an obscure favorite that tastes like a Tootsie Roll.

The glory days of the Erie Canal are still alive here, where you can voyage back in time with a canal boat ride. This area is also known for its role as the last stop on the Underground Railroad, the route for escaped slaves who found permanent freedom across the water in Canada.

HISTORY

History buffs refer to the history of this region in two distinct eras—Before Canal (BC) and

HIGHLIGHTS

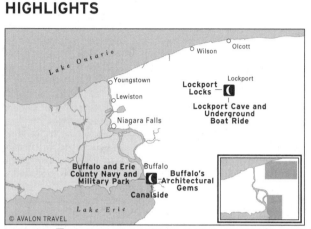

© AVALON TRAVEL

LOOK FOR ⟨ TO FIND RECOMMENDED SIGHTS, ACTIVITIES, DINING, AND LODGING.

⟨ **Buffalo's Architectural Gems:** View stunning works by many great American architects, including Louis Sullivan, Robert Upjohn, Daniel Burnham, H. H. Richardson, and Frank Lloyd Wright (page 78).

⟨ **Canalside:** This vibrant cultural space has emerged as the epicenter of Buffalo's renaissance (page 79).

⟨ **Buffalo and Erie County Navy and Military Park:** Experience the dramatic stories of war vets while touring decommissioned

Navy vessels moored in the nation's largest inland naval park (page 81).

⟨ **Lockport Locks:** These timeless gateways take you on a gentle journey back to the time when the Erie Canal was the world's first superhighway (page 95).

⟨ **Lockport Cave and Underground Boat Ride:** Explore subterranean industrial history while enjoying the longest underground boat ride in the United States (page 96).

After Digging (AD). The Erie Canal opened in 1825 and fundamentally changed every aspect of life for those living in this area.

At the start of the War of 1812, Buffalo was a village of approximately 500 people. During the war, it grew due to its proximity to Canada. The United States sent troops to the region to fight along the Niagara frontier. In December 1813, British troops and their Indian allies burned Buffalo and Niagara Falls, New York, to the ground as the violence escalated to include attacks on civilians. Following the end of hostilities in 1814, Buffalo was rebuilt and enjoyed moderate growth.

Completed in 1825, the Erie Canal was merely 40 feet wide, four feet deep, and had a speed limit of four miles per hour. This was the country's first superhighway. The terminus of this highway, Buffalo became the crossroads of the nation. Immigrants heading west and natural resources being sent east stopped in Buffalo. Some immigrants stayed, swelling the German, Irish, Polish, and Italian working-class communities that fed the city's insatiable demand for labor. Ships had to be loaded and grain mills filled. Manufacturers needed men with strong backs and even stronger constitutions to meet the requirements of a growing country.

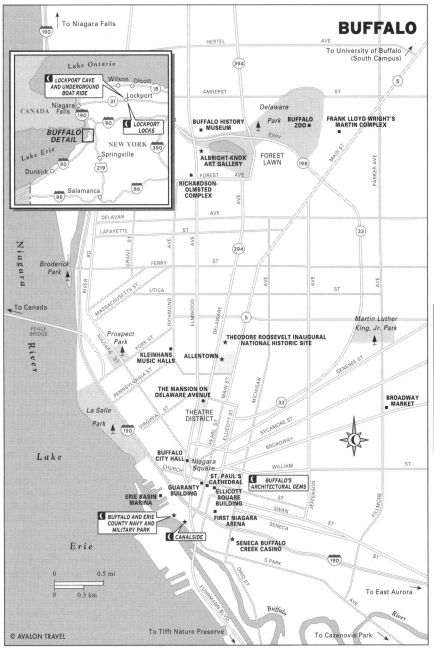

BUFFALO

To Niagara Falls

To University of Buffalo
(South Campus)

HERTEL AVE

AMHERST ST

BUFFALO HISTORY MUSEUM

Delaware Park

BUFFALO ZOO

FRANK LLOYD WRIGHT'S MARTIN COMPLEX

ALBRIGHT-KNOX ART GALLERY

FOREST LAWN

RICHARDSON-OLMSTED COMPLEX

FOREST AVE

DELAVAN AVE

LAFAYETTE AVE

FERRY ST

Broderick Park

MASSACHUSETTS ST

UTICA ST

To Canada

PEACE BRIDGE

Prospect Park

THEODORE ROOSEVELT INAUGURAL NATIONAL HISTORIC SITE

Martin Luther King, Jr. Park

Niagara River

KLEINHANS MUSIC HALLS

ALLENTOWN

THE MANSION ON DELAWARE AVENUE

BROADWAY MARKET

La Salle Park

THEATRE DISTRICT

Lake Erie

BUFFALO CITY HALL

Niagara Square

CHURCH

ST. PAUL'S CATHEDRAL

BUFFALO'S ARCHITECTURAL GEMS

SYCAMORE ST

BROADWAY

WILLIAM ST

GUARANTY BUILDING

ERIE BASIN MARINA

ELLICOTT SQUARE BUILDING

SWAN ST

SENECA ST

BUFFALO AND ERIE COUNTY NAVY AND MILITARY PARK

FIRST NIAGARA ARENA

CANALSIDE

SENECA BUFFALO CREEK CASINO

Erie

S PARK AVE

To East Aurora

0   0.5 mi

0   0.5 km

To Tifft Nature Preserve

Buffalo River

To Cazenovia Park

© AVALON TRAVEL

BUFFALO

Inset: BUFFALO DETAIL

Lake Ontario

LOCKPORT CAVE AND UNDERGROUND BOAT RIDE

Wilson   Olcott

Lockport

CANADA

Niagara Falls

LOCKPORT LOCKS

NEW YORK

Springville

Lake Erie

Dunkirk

Salamanca

Burgeoning commerce yielded wealth and influence. By the turn of the 20th century, two of Buffalo's sons, Millard Fillmore and Grover Cleveland, had occupied the White House. By the 1930s, railroads were becoming more popular, reducing the importance of the Erie Canal. But the region kept growing as manufacturers such as Ford, Chevrolet, Bethlehem Steel, Allied Chemical, Carborundum, DuPont, and Dunlop Tire expanded. However, forces outside of Buffalo's control conspired to strangle the region's manufacturing fortunes. The opening of the St. Lawrence Seaway and ever-expanding Welland Canal allowed most shipping to bypass Buffalo. Thousands of labor jobs were lost as manufacturers throughout the Northeast ceased production or moved to areas with lower taxes and less regulation.

Today, Buffalo's fortunes are beginning to reverse, as various sectors, including government, banking, and healthcare are employing Buffalo's capable and well-educated workforce. Following years of inactivity, Buffalo's waterfront, Canalside, has emerged as a new entertainment center for the region. Entrepreneurs and preservationists have joined forces to save and renovate landmarks, creating new spaces for living and entertaining. The region is capitalizing on its organic strengths—world-class architecture, a beautiful waterfront, and proximity to Canada—to reclaim its place as Queen City of the Great Lakes.

PLANNING YOUR TIME

Buffalo and its northern neighbor Niagara County can be explored in two days by focusing one day on Buffalo and another day on Niagara County's attractions. Make Buffalo your base for travel. It has the greatest concentration of lodgings in the downtown area, and many different types, from hostels to boutique hotels. There are many attractions such as the waterfront that you can easily walk to from downtown Buffalo.

From Lockport in Niagara County, you can access the winery region by going either west or east. Part of your route should include the shore of Lake Ontario, the northern edge of Niagara County.

Sights

◧ ARCHITECTURAL GEMS

Buffalo has been called a living architectural museum. The city's grand buildings represent many of the masters of American architecture, including Louis Sullivan, Frank Lloyd Wright, H. H. Richardson, and Daniel Burnham. These landmarks were built during Buffalo's meteoric rise in wealth following the completion of the Erie Canal.

Louis Sullivan's **Guaranty Building** (140 Pearl St., 716/854-0003, www.hodgsonruss.com/guarantybuilding, 8am-5pm Mon.-Fri.) may be the most prominent jewel in Buffalo's architectural crown. Completed in 1896, it was officially registered as a national landmark in 1975, and is now an office for a law firm. Sullivan is considered the "father of the skyscraper." The 13-story building was an aggressive use of technology and design for its day.

The Guaranty Building is all about verticality, featuring beautiful lines and a terracotta tile exterior. Situated on the corner of Church and Pearl Streets, the building is best appreciated from a distance before examining it up close. Prepare to stretch those neck muscles as you gaze upward to behold this monument. Notice the intricate designs covering the exterior—Sullivan fully utilized the ornamental beauty of terra-cotta to decorate the building with designs of flowers and trees. If you visit during the week, enter the atrium to see the interior at the 1st-floor reception area. The friendly guards at the reception desk are happy to answer questions about the building. Scheduled tours of the building's interior are not offered at this time.

Directly across from the Guaranty Building, **St. Paul's Episcopal Cathedral** (128 Pearl St., 716/855-0900, www.stpaulscathedral.org) occupies an unusual triangular plot of land. This Gothic Revival cathedral was consecrated in 1851. It's the work of renowned architect Richard Upjohn, considered America's foremost builder of Gothic churches. Due to its triangular lot, St. Paul's could not be built in the traditional cruciform style, in which the main aisles of the church form a cross. This magnificent church houses three pipe organs and a Tiffany stained glass window on the northeast side of the structure.

The **Martin House Complex** (125 Jewett Pkwy., 716/856-3858, www.darwinmartinhouse.org) is considered by many scholars to be Frank Lloyd Wright's best example of the Prairie House concept. The Martin House design features long horizontal exterior lines, cantilevered roofs, wide eaves, and flowing interior spaces free of walls. Wright referred to this structure as his "opus" and wrote that the Martin House was "a well-nigh perfect composition."

The estate is comprised of five interconnected structures and a visitors welcome center. In order to enter any of the houses, you must join one of the four docent-led tours (Wed. and Fri.-Mon., $15-30). Pre-purchase your tickets, as tours frequently sell out, especially in the summer months. The Martin House Complex is in a residential neighborhood and street parking is limited, so use the nearby Buffalo Zoo parking lot. Tour staff will provide you with a free token for the zoo parking lot. Photography is strictly prohibited inside complex buildings.

The **Richardson-Olmsted Complex** (400 Forest Ave., 716/849-6070, www.richardsonolmsted.com), a state asylum built in stunning Romanesque revival style, was the largest commission for H. H. Richardson. The parklike grounds and farmland surrounding the hospital were designed by Frederick Law Olmsted, who also designed Buffalo's park system and Niagara Falls State Park.

When development of the Buffalo State Asylum for the Insane began in 1870, the complex was a state-of-the-art facility that reflected a new doctrine in treating mental illness. The buildings became the embodiment of Dr. Thomas Kirkbride's therapy methods favoring a holistic approach to rehabilitation. Richardson designed a hospital that divided patients by severity of illness, while allowing them access to sunlight, ventilation, and outdoor recreation.

Over 20 years, 11 imposing buildings sprang up on the complex's 200 acres. The iconic main building features Gothic towers. Over the intervening years, the campus was divided and developed. Some buildings were knocked down, while others were abandoned.

Today, the focus is on preserving and restoring the complex. An ambitious multiyear plan will eventually transform the Richardson-Olmsted Complex into a mixed-use campus featuring a boutique hotel, conference space, and the home of Buffalo's planned Architecture Center.

The complex is only accessible to visitors via guided tours ($10 and up). Tour schedules change as more of the structure is refurbished, so visit the website for specific tours times. Twilight tours accentuate the Gothic ambience of the complex. Indoor photography is not allowed. Enter the complex at the gate at the intersection of Richmond and Forest Avenues.

◖ CANALSIDE

After languishing for many years, Buffalo's waterfront is now the epicenter of activity, specifically the public space known as **Canalside** (716/574-1537, www.canalsidebuffalo.com, 24 hours daily, free). This includes the Central Wharf and the unearthed and restored **Commercial Slip,** the original terminus of the Erie Canal. Throughout the area's 21 waterfront acres, interpretive signs explain the history of the area, shedding light on the canal's role in commerce, technology, labor, and the Underground Railroad. Open year-round, Canalside is most active June-August, when there are daily entertainment events, most of

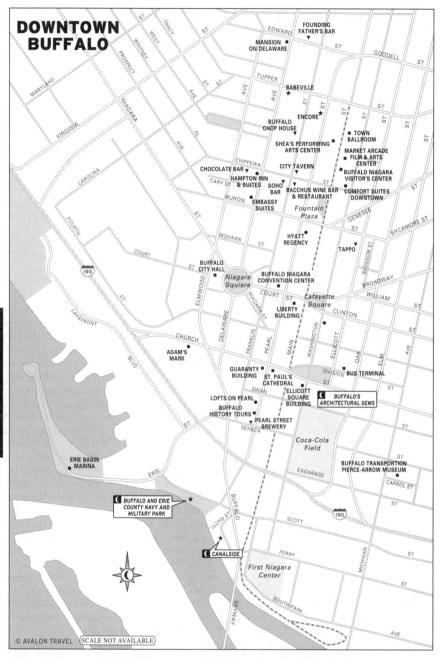

DOWNTOWN BUFFALO

FOUNDING FATHER'S BAR

MANSION ON DELAWARE ●

BABEVILLE ★

ENCORE ★

BUFFALO CHOP HOUSE ●

■ TOWN BALLROOM

SHEA'S PERFORMING ARTS CENTER

■ MARKET ARCADE FILM & ARTS CENTER

CHOCOLATE BAR ▼

CITY TAVERN ▼

■ BUFFALO NIAGARA VISITOR'S CENTER

HAMPTON INN & SUITES ■

SOHO BAR ▼

BACCHUS WINE BAR & RESTAURANT ▼

COMFORT SUITES DOWNTOWN

EMBASSY SUITES ■

Fountain Plaza

HYATT REGENCY ●

TAPPO ▼

BUFFALO CITY HALL ■

Niagara Square

BUFFALO NIAGARA CONVENTION CENTER ■

Lafayette Square

LIBERTY BUILDING ●

ADAM'S MARK ●

GUARANTY BUILDING ■

■ BUS TERMINAL

ST. PAUL'S CATHEDRAL ●

ELLICOTT SQUARE BUILDING ●

LOFTS ON PEARL ■

☾ BUFFALO'S *ARCHITECTURAL GEMS*

BUFFALO HISTORY TOURS ■

PEARL STREET BREWERY ●

Coca-Cola Field

ERIE BASIN MARINA ■

BUFFALO TRANSPORTION PIERCE-ARROW MUSEUM ■

☾ BUFFALO AND ERIE COUNTY NAVY AND MILITARY PARK ★

☾ CANALSIDE ★

First Niagara Center

© AVALON TRAVEL   (SCALE NOT AVAILABLE)

BUFFALO

© ED HEALY

The Guaranty Building is one of many architectural treasures in Buffalo.

which are free. Entertainment includes music acts, historical storytelling, group exercise classes, and street performances.

(Buffalo and Erie County Navy and Military Park

Just north of the Central Wharf is the **Buffalo and Erie County Navy and Military Park** (1 Naval Park Cove, 716/847-1773, www.buffalo-navalpark.org, 10am-5pm daily Apr.-Oct., $10 adults, $6 seniors and children 6-16). This impressive waterfront campus is a living museum to all branches of the U.S. military. Three decommissioned U.S. naval ships dominate the park: a guided missile cruiser, USS *Little Rock;* a destroyer, USS *The Sullivans;* and a submarine, USS *Croaker.* All are open for tours.

Dockside, there is a museum and an outdoor collection of decommissioned tanks, jets, and helicopters that saw action in conflicts from World War II to Vietnam. Some of the displays and educational materials seem dated. Use caution when navigating the bowels of these great ships—stairwells are steep, bulkhead openings are shin-knockers, and there are low clearances.

Plan on at least two hours to tour the ships, museum, and grounds. Chat up some of the volunteer military veteran tour guides stationed throughout the naval park. Their stories bring to life the sacrifices, hardships, and camaraderie of the men and women who joined the armed services.

ERIE BASIN MARINA

The **Erie Basin Marina** (329 Erie St., 716/851-6501, www.eriebasinmarina.org, 24 hours daily May 1-Oct. 15, free) is a wonderful place for a relaxing walk or romantic sunset. Downtown workers often dash out for a quick lunch or snack along the break wall. The marina's beautiful sunsets and cityscapes are best enjoyed by foot or bike. The road to the marina can become congested with vehicles, so park outside the marina; it's free.

Stroll through the gardens, where different flowers and plants are tested each year for their ability to survive Buffalo's climate. Walk to the end of the marina for a bird's-eye view of the waterfront from the lookout tower.

GRAIN ELEVATORS

The mostly abandoned **grain elevators** of Buffalo's waterfront are often referred to as a concrete Atlantis. Plans are under way for one of the grain elevators to be used for rock climbing. Some entrepreneurs are purchasing grain elevators with an eye on creating waterfront entertainment areas with restaurants, bars, and concert spaces.

You can access the area by car via the bridges of Michigan and Ohio Streets. You may walk around some of the elevators that are not fenced off, but it is not advisable to enter any of them. The structures are not open to the public because they are dangerous—some people exploring the silos have been injured or killed. A good driving guide to the grain mills is online (www.buffalohistoryworks.com).

The infrequent, but informative Whole Grain Tour of the grain elevators offered by **Preservation Buffalo Niagara** (617 Main St.,

BUFFALO

LAST STOP ON THE UNDERGROUND RAILROAD

Prior to the Civil War, Buffalo was a hotbed for abolitionist sentiment. Buffalo's proximity to Canada made the city an important and emotional stop on the Underground Railroad. Historians have noted that Buffalo differed from other locales that figured prominently in helping escaped slaves to freedom. Buffalo's tolerance and support of abolition fostered an environment where escaped slaves could move about relatively freely.

There were times when escaped slaves in Buffalo needed shelter. Bounty hunters bent on reclaiming slaves would arrive in Buffalo seeking their quarry. At such times, some slaves were hidden in two secret spaces inside the **Michigan Street Baptist Church** (511 Michigan Ave., 716/837-3226). Call ahead to arrange for an informal tour of the church. Visitors can view a secret spot in the loft of the church, above the choir, as well as a dark recess hidden underneath what appears to be a stairwell. In the basement of the church, there is a modest interpretive center with artifacts and general information on the Underground Railroad. The tour is free, but donations are welcome.

The last stop on U.S. soil for slaves escaping through Buffalo was **Broderick Park** (west end of Ferry St.) along the Niagara River in the shadow of the Peace Bridge. Slaves traveled in secrecy on foot for months to reach this spot—a short boat ride to Canada, then freedom. Proposed improvements to this island park include an amphitheater and improved interpretive signs.

716/852-3300, www.preservationbuffaloniagara.org, $20) occurs about once a month, May-October. The tour takes you inside the massive concrete grain silos that are called Silo City by locals. Those with their own boats, kayaks, and canoes can explore the Buffalo River that winds through the mills.

ALLENTOWN

Head north from downtown Buffalo, and you'll enter the bohemian district known as **Allentown** (www.allentown.org). The epicenter for arts, live music, and gay culture, Allentown is bordered by Plymouth Avenue and North, Edward, and Main Streets.

The heart of Allentown is Allen Street. On weekends, the area is perfect for people-watching as hipsters, live-music lovers, bar hoppers, and college students flow in and out of the numerous bars, restaurants, and cafés. There is just enough grit to keep things interesting, but enough police presence to keep things safe.

Allentown was one of the first and largest communities in the United States to earn recognition as a residential historic district, thanks to well-preserved architectural gems on nearly every street. Within its modest borders are landscapes crafted by Frederick Law Olmsted and Calvert Vaux, a mansion designed by H. H. Richardson, a National Historic Landmark, and a National Historic Site. This small community has more architectural history than many cities.

Historic Architecture

Delaware Avenue is well worth the walk down the street. Of the many notable mansions, highlights include **438 Delaware,** which was designed by H. H. Richardson for William Dorsheimer, a former lieutenant governor of New York.

Although the house where Samuel Clemmons lived at **472 Delaware** is gone, the carriage house remains. **The Midway** is a stretch of stunning row-style houses that comprise 471-499 Delaware Avenue. Among the jewels here is **477 Delaware,** a Georgian revival-style building donated to the Daughters of the American Revolution by wealthy socialite Katherine Pratt Horton.

Just as grand are the structures that line Symphony Circle, Porter and Richmond Avenues, and North and Pennsylvania Streets. This area was originally known as **The Circle.**

At one time Buffalo was the world's busiest port for grain.

Sprawling Victorian houses and impressive mansions ring Symphony Circle, which takes its name from the **Kleinhans Music Hall** (3 Symphony Circle, 716/883-3560, www.kleinhansbuffalo.org). The hall was designed by the father-and-son architectural team of Eliel and Eero Saarinen.

Also here is the **First Presbyterian Church** (1 Symphony Circle, 716/884-7250, www.firstchurchbuffalo.org, 10am-3pm Tues.-Fri.), which houses the city's oldest congregation. The church's Romanesque style and towering 163-foot steeple are reminiscent of the Richardson-Olmsted Complex. Call for times that religious services are offered.

Theodore Roosevelt Inaugural Site

On the southern edge of Allentown is the **Theodore Roosevelt Inaugural Site** (641 Delaware Ave., 716/884-0095, www.trsite.org, 9am-5pm Mon.-Fri., noon-5pm Sat.-Sun., $10 adults, $7 seniors and students,

$5 children 6-18). In this house, the former Wilcox Mansion, Roosevelt took the presidential oath in September 1901, following the assassination of President William McKinley at the Pan-American Exposition in Buffalo. The hasty inaugural event is used as a springboard to explore America at the turn of the 20th century, the optimism of the Pan-American Expo, and the complicated issues facing the first modern-day president.

Guided tours ($10 adults, $7 seniors and students, $5 children 6-18) run about an hour, but budget at least two hours to fully appreciate the site. Check the website for special events such as historical fashion shows, dinners, and Victorian teas during the holidays. The site is fully accessible. The best parking is accessed from behind the building via Franklin Street.

ELMWOOD VILLAGE

The emerging community known as **Elmwood Village** (www.elmwoodvillage.org) overlaps with Allentown and provides visitors with cultural entertainment, shops, and relaxing park spaces. The community is loosely defined as the area bordered by Richmond and Delaware Avenues, North Street, and Delaware Park. Elmwood Village is more bustling than Allentown, but still maintains a unique identity, blending museums, retail shops, parks and a college campus. The village has been named "one of the 10 Great Neighborhoods in America" by the American Planning Association.

The village also boasts green spaces designed by Frederick Olmsted. Olmsted and landscape designer Calvert Vaux designed Bidwell, Chapin, and Lincoln Parkways to connect with Delaware Park.

The Buffalo History Museum

The Buffalo History Museum (1 Museum Ct., 716/873-9644, www.bechs.org, 10am-5pm Tues. and Thurs.-Sat., 10am-8pm Wed., noon-5pm Sun., $7 adults, $5 seniors and students, $2.50 children 7-12) tells the story of western New York via artifacts and displays of historic materials, including the gun used by anarchist Leon Czolgosz to assassinate President McKinley. Frequently changing exhibits keep the narrative relevant and engaging. It is worth a visit just to see the grounds, including the south portico's statue of Abraham Lincoln and the Japanese garden.

TOURS

Preservation Buffalo Niagara (617 Main St., 716/852-3300, www.preservationbuffaloniagara.org, 9am-5pm Mon.-Fri.) offers more than 50 tours of Buffalo throughout the year. Most tours are $10 per person. It provides free tours of Buffalo City Hall at noon Monday-Saturday. **Open Air Autobus** (716/854-3749, www.openairbuffalo.org, $25) gives tours of Buffalo's notable architecture in a school bus that has had its roof removed.

Haunted History Ghost Walks (21 S. Grove St., East Aurora, 716/655-6663, www.hauntedhistoryghostwalks.com, $15) explore the paranormal haunts of Buffalo and surrounding suburbs. Based on more than 10 books on local spirits by Mason Winfield, these walks blend history, folklore, and firsthand ghost stories. Tours are available in summer and autumn.

Buffalo History Tours (92 Pearl St., 716/222-2432, www.buffalohistorytours.com, $5-20) mix history and humor for engaging pub crawls and heritage walking tours of downtown Buffalo. Daily downtown brewery tours are available.

Entertainment and Events

NIGHTLIFE

Buffalo is a city that works hard and plays hard; bars here stay open until 4am. There are four primary districts with clusters of bars and clubs—downtown/Chippewa Street, Allentown, Elmwood Avenue, and Hertel Avenue.

Sportsmens Tavern (326 Amherst St., 716/874-7734, www.sportsmenstavern.com, noon-1am daily, cover $5-40) is not in any of the entertainment districts, but it is the best live music venue in the city. Nestled in the aging working-class neighborhood known as Black Rock (10 minutes north of downtown), Sportsmens is owned and operated by musicians. Owner Dwane Hall has created a space where local musicians can play and also listen to some of the best traveling acts in country, blues, folk, and indie rock. It's easy to believe you are in Austin or Memphis at an authentic honky-tonk. There is no bohemian or dive bar pretention here—just honest music in a perfectly comfortable venue. The kitchen is surprisingly good, serving more than just pub grub. This is truly one of the city's best-kept secrets.

Downtown

For many years, Chippewa Street was *the* entertainment district for Buffalo. Some of its luster has faded, but the Chip Strip still draws the college-age crowd, especially on Friday and Saturday evenings. Business types emerge on Friday after work, but generally clear out by 7pm. Although most venues are open until 4am, this district can get somewhat rowdy and unsafe after 2am.

The City Tavern (51 W. Chippewa St., 716/783-9212, www.buffalocitytavern.com, 9pm-4am Thurs.-Sat.) is everything you want in a downtown bar—good draft beer and attentive bartenders, with a cool sidewalk area. It also has a large open-air patio for enjoying summer evenings. For those who enjoy a smoke while drinking, this could be heaven.

Although the **Chocolate Bar** (114 W. Chippewa St., 716/332-0484, www.originalchocolatebar.com, 11am-midnight Mon.-Thurs., 11am-2am Fri.-Sat., 3pm-midnight Sun.) is both a restaurant and a bar, forget about the entrées. Focus on the desserts and the exotic chocolate drinks. Drinks are expensive, but worth it. The Dirty Girl ($12) is a liquor milkshake that tastes like a Girl Scout

Thin Mint. Martinis start at $10 and include flavors such as Swedish fish, peanut butter cup and banana crème pie.

Close to Chippewa, but a world away, is the **Pearl Street Grill and Brewery** (76 Pearl St., 716/856-2337, www.pearlstreetgrill.com, 11am-1am Mon.-Sat., noon-1am Sun.). The best place to catch a summer sunset is on the New Orleans-style patio here, where you can relax with a pint from the 16 original craft brews on tap. The vibe is casual, and the walls feature enormous murals of life along the Erie Canal in the 1800s. Brewery tasting tours ($10) are offered daily at 11am, 1pm, and 3pm.

The best place for live music near the Chip Strip is the **Tudor Lounge** (335 Franklin St., 716/885-9643, 1pm-2am daily). This unpretentious bar features live acts Thursday-Saturday. The music is eclectic—blues, jam bands, metal—as is the clientele: college students, bikers, hippies, and locals. The selection of beers is sufficient and moderately priced.

On the fringe of the entertainment district, inside an 1863 building, is an Irish tavern, **Eddie Brady's** (97 Genesee St., 716/854-7017, 10:30am-close daily). Stuck in the middle of a sometimes-desolate downtown, it has the ambience of a neighborhood corner bar. Check out the 1950s Iroquois Beer signs, vintage cash register, and picture of owner Eddie's grandfather above the bar. The eclectic jukebox features songs by Tony Bennett, Louis Armstrong, and the Talking Heads. This charming tavern serves a working-class clientele with moderately priced drinks and stick-to-your-ribs food, all cooked on a grill just behind the bar. If your diet permits, try the "Fried Boloney" sandwich ($6).

Almost anything goes at **Club Marcella** (622 Main St., 716/847-6850, www.clubmarcella. com, 10pm-4am Thurs.-Sat.), Buffalo's most exciting LGBT nightclub. The club hosts drag shows and audience-participation beauty pageants (where contestants strip down to their undies). The club attracts both gay and straight patrons for its excellent techno music. If you are looking for a good place to dance, Club

© COLLIGNON JAROSZ AND VISIT BUFFALO NIAGARA

BUFFALO

diners enjoying the outdoor patio at the Pearl Street Grill and Brewery

Marcella is it. Admission varies based on the acts or events each night.

Allentown

The Old Pink (223 Allen St., 716/884-4338, noon-4am daily) is the most venerated dive bar in Buffalo. Unforgettable nights always seem to end at The Pink, affectionately called The Stink. The closer it is to 4am, the more varied the clientele. You'll find college students, urban hipsters, bikers, punks, and cool middle-aged folks gathered over strong, cheap drinks and surprisingly good grilled food. The steak sandwiches ($10) are legendary. They're cooked right before your eyes by the bartender. The Pink is a must for last call.

A stumble away from The Pink, you'll find **Mulligan's Brick Bar** (229 Allen St., 716/881-0545, noon-4am daily). Here you will find inexpensive drinks (but no draft beer). The extroverted barkeeps are entertaining and will even share a shot with you. The front patio is a makeshift porch, usually tightly packed with smokers and those watching the parade of partiers pass by. The atmosphere is playful and skews to the 30-plus crowd, although the clientele is diverse.

Nietzche's (248 Allen St., 716/886-8539, www.nietzsches.com, 5pm-1am Sat.-Wed., 5pm-3am Thurs.-Fri., cover $5 and up) is the place to see live bands in Allentown. Music acts are eclectic (blues, indie, rock, world, funk, jazz, Celtic), as is the crowd. The bohemian ambience and good acoustics are perfect for enjoying the bands. However, the layout is not conducive to dancing, since a bottleneck in the floor design leads to some congestion. But the crowd is cool and, if you are patient, you'll make your way to the cash-only bar. The bathrooms here are grungy. Cover charges vary, based on the musical act.

Elmwood

One of the two anchors for nightlife along the Elmwood Strip is **Mr. Goodbar** (1110 Elmwood Ave., 716/882-4000, www.mrgoodbarbuffalo.com, noon-4am daily). Once a college bar (it's one block from Buffalo State College), it has

kept its comfortable ambience while appealing to a wider age range. You'll find 30 brews on tap at all times, served by bartenders who are happy to chat knowledgeably about the qualities of the beers and ciders they pour. There is live music 10pm-2am on Fridays.

Coles (1104 Elmwood Ave., 716/886-1449, www.colesbuffalo.com, 11am-11pm Mon.-Thurs., 11am-midnight Fri.-Sat., 11am-10pm Sun.) is right next door to Mr. Goodbar. It has embraced the craft beer craze and has 36 beers on tap. You'll pay a bit more here for a pint ($6 and up), but you'll find consistently diverse and interesting selections, including local craft beers. The atmosphere is brighter and cleaner than most bars on the Elmwood Avenue strip. It attracts a healthy mix of adults 25 and older. If you are bar-hopping, Coles is a good place to start, when your wallet is a bit thicker and your taste for alcohol is more discerning.

The Blue Monk (727 Elmwood Ave., 716/882-6665, www.bluemonkbflo.com, 3:30pm-3:30am Mon.-Thurs., 11:30am-3:30am Fri.-Sun.) is designed to feel like a Belgian pub. This bar is deservedly popular, so it gets crowded on weekend evenings. The backyard beer garden is particularly nice, but due to neighborhood noise ordinances, it closes by 9pm.

THE ARTS

The arts scene in Buffalo is thriving, thanks to innovative programming and increased private support after government subsidies shrank over the past few years. The **Albright-Knox Art Gallery** (1285 Elmwood Ave., 716/882-8700, www.albrightknox.org, 10am-5pm Tues.-Sun., $12) is a medium-sized gallery with an impressive collection of contemporary art, including works by Warhol, Pollock, and Gorky. You will also find pieces by Picasso, Gauguin, Van Gogh, and Matisse. Admission is free on the first Friday of some months, but you'll want to call in advance to see when the First Friday program is operating during your visit, as its months of operation vary each year.

Just across the street from Albright-Knox, on the Buffalo State College campus, is the

Burchfield Penny Art Center (Buffalo State College, 1300 Elmwood Ave., 716/878-6011, www.burchfieldpenney.org, 10am-5pm Tues.-Wed., and Fri.-Sat., 10am-9pm Thurs., 11am-5pm Sun., $10 adults, $8 seniors, $5 students). The art center's mission is to showcase works of local artists, the foremost being the watercolors of Charles Burchfield, known for townscapes and nature paintings. The center is an incubator for local artists and displays eclectic artwork, including sculpture, drawings, and photography. Active members of the U.S. military and their families are admitted for free.

Kleinhans Music Hall (3 Symphony Circle, 716/885-5000, www.kleinhansbuffalo.org) is a treat for the eyes and the ears. The rounded building is a beautiful 1940s collaboration of famed Finnish architects Eliel and Eero Saarinen. The acoustics are world-renowned, providing an excellent environment for enjoying the **Buffalo Philharmonic Orchestra** (www.bpo.org) or contemporary music acts. Parking is a challenge, so arrive early to find a spot in the adjacent lot.

Step back into the regal 1920s by catching a show at **Shea's Performing Arts Center** (646 Main St., 716/847-1410, www.sheas.org) in the heart of Buffalo's theater district. A National Historic Site, Shea's hosts Broadway musicals, dramatic productions, ballets, live music performances, and top-notch comedy acts. The theater's design is reminiscent of the grand European opera houses of the 17th century. The interior design by Louis Comfort Tiffany includes massive crystal chandeliers, a huge marble lobby, and beautiful grand staircases.

FESTIVALS AND EVENTS

Cold winters teach Buffalonians to fully appreciate the warmer weather months. In summer, there's a festival going on nearly every weekend in the city. A complete list of festivals is found on the calendar page of Visit Buffalo (www.visitbuffaloniagara.com).

Spring

Everybody is Polish on **Dyngus Day** (www.dyngusdaybuffalo.com), the traditional spring

© JIM BUSH

Shea's Performing Arts Center is located in a stunning restored 1920s building.

BUFFALO

festival held on the Monday following Easter Sunday. Now that the solemnity of Lent is over, it's time to get your polka on, with celebratory events, parades, and parties held throughout the city.

Summer

During the **Allentown Art Festival** (www.allentownartfestival.com), the city shuts down Delaware Avenue for a weekend in June to display the works of more than 400 artists.

Celebrate the culture and contributions of local African Americans at the **Juneteenth Festival** (www.juneteenthofbuffalo.com) in Martin Luther King, Jr. Park. The festival runs on the Saturday and Sunday closest to June 15.

Occurring the second weekend of July, the **Taste of Buffalo** (www.tasteofbuffalo.com) is one of the largest two-day food festivals in the nation. Bring your appetite to Niagara Square to enjoy samples from more than 200 vendors.

Some like it hot, others medium or mild. No matter how you like your wings, the **National Buffalo Wing Festival** (www.buffalowing. com) in August fills Coca-Cola Field (275 Washington St.) in downtown Buffalo with the best wings in the world during the last weekend in August. To sound like a local, be sure to call them chicken wings, not Buffalo wings.

At the **Italian Heritage Festival** (www. buffaloitalianfestival.com) in August, you can *mangi* (eat) to your heart's content along Hertel Avenue in North Buffalo. During the four-day festival, you can try your hand at bocce, grape stomping, and meet the winner of the Miss Italian Festival contest.

Shopping

© KC KRATT

Find unique gifts in the shops along Elmwood Avenue.

The **Buffalo Niagara Shop** (617 Main St., 800/283-3256, www.buffaloniagarashop. com, 10am-4pm Mon.-Sat. Memorial Day-Labor Day, 10am-4pm Mon.-Fri. Labor Day-Memorial Day), on the 1st floor of the historic Market Arcade building, sells authentic, made-in-Buffalo foodstuffs (like chicken wing sauce), poster art, mugs, calendars, stationery, and bumper stickers. The store also provides free information on events in the region. At the shop's Star Theatre, you can sit down and enjoy brief videos about Buffalo and the surrounding region.

Everything Elmwood (740 Elmwood Ave., 716/883-0607, www.everythingelmwood.org, 10am-7pm Mon.-Fri., 10am-6pm Sat., noon-6pm Sun.) is the largest boutique gift store in the Elmwood Avenue shopping district. Because of its size, the store is not as intimate as other boutiques—but it is completely filled (almost cluttered), with gifts from around the world. The large jewelry counter has gifts in the $20-40 range. Whether you're shopping for a baby shower or a 70th birthday, you'll find a unique gift here. The shop offers free gift-wrapping.

Despite its name, **Spoiled Rotten** (831 Elmwood Ave., 716/884-3883, www.spoiledrottenbuffalo.wordpress.com, 10am-8pm Mon.-Sat., 11am-6pm Sun.) has many fresh ideas. The small and quirky shop, with its pink brick exterior, is packed with unique gifts, many with a Buffalo theme. Need a back scratcher, baby outfit, picture frame, or Christmas ornament with a buffalo on it? Spoiled Rotten has you covered. The owner is friendly, as is the resident Boston terrier.

The unique thing about **Thin Ice** (719 Elmwood Ave., 716/881-4321, www.thiniceonline.com, 10:30am-7pm Tues.-Sat., 11am-6pm Sun.-Mon.) is that all the merchandise is locally sourced. You can find jewelry, clothing, pottery, candles, and soap, all created by artists from the region. Gifts range from the creative

and practical (soap made with beer and lime), to the medieval (chain-mail bikini top). The store is open and airy, with three main display areas, hundreds of handcrafted items, and a friendly cat named Atticus.

Walking into **Talking Leaves Books** (3158 Main St., 716/837-8554, www.tleavesbooks. com, 10am-6pm Mon.-Tues. and Fri.-Sat., 10am-8pm Wed.-Thurs.) is like putting on an old, well-worn sweater on a crisp autumn day. The store has a familiar warmth that you won't find at a chain bookstore. You'll likely hear the hushed tones of like-minded readers discussing literature. The eclectic selection of books emphasizes local authors and subject matter. The resident cat is aloof, the floor is worn, and the book displays could have been purchased from various parochial schools or rescued from the curb of a public library.

Sports and Recreation

BOATING

Buffalo is situated where Lake Erie ends and the Niagara River begins, positioning it for great water access. If you are traveling by boat, there are several public and private marinas that rent dock space and provide maintenance and fuel services, including **Erie Basin Marina** (329 Erie St., 716/851-6501, www.eriebasinmarina.org), **NFTA Boat Harbor** (1111 Fuhrman Blvd., 716/828-0027, www.nftaboatharbor.com), and **Rich Marine Sales** (5 Austin St., 716/873-4060, www. richmarinesales.com).

Just outside of the marina, along Erie Street, are two boats offering excursions. **Buffalo Harbor Cruises** (716/856-6696, www.buffaloharborcruises.com, July-Labor Day, $16 adults, $11 children 4-11) provides narrated cruises aboard the venerable *Miss Buffalo II*. If one hull isn't enough for you, try the *moondanceCat* (716/854-7245, www.moondancecat.com, $23 adults, $11.50 children 17 and under), for a ride on a catamaran.

Canalside

Boaters can access the Central Wharf at **Canalside** (www.canalsidebuffalo.com) from the Buffalo River. Docking space is available along the Buffalo River through **First Buffalo Marina** (32 Fuhrman Blvd., 716/867-9271, www.firstbuffalomarina.com). Docking fees are based on vessel size. Spaces are on a first-come, first-served basis and cannot be reserved in advance. Overnight docking is permitted. Daily launch fees are $10.

If you don't own a boat, there are several ways to enjoy the water from Canalside. Housed at the far end of the wharf is **Buffalo Harbor Kayaks** (1 Naval Park Cove, 716/228-9153, www.blfoharborkayak.com, 9am-6pm daily). Stand-up paddleboard (SUP) and kayak (single or tandem) rentals start at $15 an hour, with half-day packages available. One-hour SUP lessons are offered for $30 and there are river tours.

Canalside is the home port for the **Queen City Ferry** (Central Wharf, 716/796-4556,

BUFFALO

The *Spirit of Buffalo* offers cruises of Buffalo's waterfront.

© TERRY CERVI AND VISIT BUFFALO NIAGARA

www.queencityferry.com, noon-8pm daily mid-May-Sept., $8 adults, $6 children). The ferry service connects the inner and outer harbors of Buffalo. This enjoyable, one-hour ride departs from the Commercial Slip on the hour. Service is hop-on/hop-off, making the ferry an excellent way to explore the waterfront at your own pace. The ferry is also the best way to access concerts in the outer harbor area, where pre- and post-concert traffic can be a headache. Queen City also offers daily **historical tours** (10:30am, $14 adults, $10 children), with excellent, passionate narration. It's an educational and entertaining perspective on the era when Buffalo was one of the world's busiest commercial ports. Locals and visitors alike find this boat tour engaging.

The magnificent **Spirit of Buffalo** (Central Wharf, 716/796-7210, www.spiritofbuffalo. com, daily May 15-Oct. 1 $28 adults, $18 children), a 73-foot sailboat, has the best of both worlds: the look and feel of a schooner, but the safety and amenities of a modern boat. These scenic, two-hour cruises are a relaxing way to see the inner and outer harbors of Buffalo. Crew members of this family-operated enterprise share information on landmarks and let passengers help raise the sails. Although the *Spirit of Buffalo* has daily service, you must call for reservations and times. The boat does not sail if there are fewer than 10 reservations for a particular time slot. For families with young children, consider the Saturday morning **pirate cruise** ($23 adults, $19 children under 12) hosted by costumed pirates who will ensure young landlubbers have a good time.

FISHING

If you plan on fishing in the Niagara River, Lake Erie, or Lake Ontario, you'll need a license. One-day licenses for nonresidents are $15 (www.dec.ny.gov). Anglers will find plentiful bass, trout, northern pike, walleyes, and salmon in the local waters. Excellent spots for shore fishing abound, including **Broderick Park** (foot of W. Ferry St.), along the **Riverwalk** (accessed from Niagara St. near Ontario St.), and the **NFTA Boat Harbor** (1111 Fuhrman Blvd.).

PARKS

Frederick Law Olmsted described Buffalo as "the best planned city, as to its streets, public places, and grounds, in the United States, if not in the world." Olmsted and his partner Calvert Vaux planned an ideal cityscape with large parks and beautiful, broad, tree-lined parkways. Most of that envisioned park system remains today.

Delaware Park (199 Lincoln Pkwy., 716/886-0088, www.bfloparks.org, dawn-dusk daily) is the crown jewel of Buffalo's park system. Like New York City's Central Park, it was designed by Frederick Law Olmsted and it serves as a cultural and recreational meeting place. Delaware Park has 350 acres of meadows, woods, and water. It is bordered by the Museum District, Forest Lawn Cemetery, and the Buffalo Zoo. The park includes an 18-hole public golf course, 17 tennis courts, three playgrounds, six soccer fields, and two

FREDRICK LAW OLMSTED'S LEGACY

Regarded as the "Father of American Landscape Design," Frederick Law Olmsted left an indelible mark upon the city of Buffalo and its people. Olmsted is widely remembered for his conservation efforts and his designs of Central Park and Front Park in New York City. Buffalo, some argue, is Olmsted's masterpiece: a system of parks that realized his philosophy about the essential role of recreational space within the fabric of urban communities.

Olmsted believed that parks were needed to temper the alienation, pollution, and pace of emerging American industrial cities. He saw green spaces as having a positive social and political impact on citizens who could use a common area to share their common humanity. Buffalo would be his proving ground.

Olmsted's ambitious plans for Buffalo began in 1868 and were primarily implemented over the next 30 years. The heart of design was three major parks that were connected by broad streets. The parks were dispersed throughout the city so that all citizens could have equal access. The 200-foot-wide parkways that join the parks feature large grassy medians and are lined by trees providing a green oasis for a city heated by coal and shrouded in smog.

The three original parks are now known as Delaware, Front, and Martin Luther King, Jr., Parks. Cazenovia, Riverside, and South Park were added to the design over the years. Olmsted's legacy is a vibrant system of green spaces that play an important role in the lives of everybody in the region. It is in these spaces that we relax, play sports, exercise, congregate, fish, cross-country ski, see Shakespeare productions, and snap wedding photos. In short, Mr. Olmsted has created spaces for us to commune.

Locals and visitors alike can enjoy these interconnected parks for free. The Buffalo Olmsted Parks Conservancy's website (www.bfloparks.org) is the best resource to help you find the parks and learn what is going on at each park. Olmsted's contributions have made Buffalo a much better city in which to live.

lawn-bowling courts. Ring Road encircles the golf course and playing fields, providing an excellent paved route for jogging, biking, and rollerblading. The beautifully restored Marcy Casino building overlooks Hoyt Lake, where people gather to relax and watch kids practice catch-and-release of sunfish. Behind the Marcy Casino is the Rose Garden, a popular place for wedding vows and pictures.

Cazenovia Park (25 Cazenovia St., 716/826-7820, www.bfloparks.org, dawn-dusk daily) is a 186-acre park named after the creek that runs through it. Known as Caz to locals, this pastoral strip of green is the heart of South Buffalo's working-class neighborhood. Originally built in 1893 by Olmsted, the park has been expanded over the years and has some of the most mature stands of trees in the entire city. Cazenovia Creek meanders through the park, eventually joining up with the Buffalo River and Lake Erie. There is also a 9-hole public golf course, swimming pool, playground, jogging trail, three soccer fields, four baseball diamonds, and a public ice-skating rink (Sept. 1-Apr. 7).

Spectator Sports

Buffalo is a sports town, home to the NFL's **Buffalo Bills** (www.buffalobills.com) and the NHL's **Buffalo Sabres** (www.sabres.nhl.com).

The Buffalo Bills play football at **Ralph Wilson Stadium** (1 Bills Dr., Orchard Park, 716/648-1800), about 15 miles south of the city in Orchard Park. No matter what the weather, the tailgating begins as soon as the parking lots open. On game day, it may take an hour to get to the stadium from Buffalo.

The Buffalo Sabres are equally beloved, selling out many of their home ice-hockey games in the **First Niagara Financial Group Arena** (1 Seymour H. Knox III Plaza, 716/855-4444, www.firstniagaracenter.com). Fans jam

BUFFALO

downtown bars and restaurants before games. The arena is also home to the **Buffalo Bandits** (www.bandits.com) of the National Lacrosse League.

The **Buffalo Bisons** (www.milb.com) are a minor league baseball franchise that play at **Coca-Cola Field** (275 Washington St.,

716/846-2000) in the heart of downtown Buffalo. In stark contrast to the excitement and action of Bills and Sabres games, watching the Bisons play is a relaxing experience, best enjoyed with a hotdog and a brew. Friday night games that end with a spectacular fireworks display are popular with families.

Accommodations

The Lofts on Pearl (92 Pearl St., 716/856-0098, www.loftsonpearl.com, $209) give you extra room to relax in a convenient location. Previously loft apartments, these one- and two-bedroom suites (32 in total) feature hardwood floors, fireplaces, full kitchens, and high ceilings. You can't beat the location in the heart of the Brewery District, close to Canalside, First Niagara Arena, and Coca-Cola Field.

Hotel @ The Lafayette (391 Washington St., 716/853-1505, www.thehotellafayette.com, $200) offers style, comfort, and convenience in a renovated 1904 French Renaissance building. Its 57 rooms blend historic and contemporary design, including grand murals of the Buffalo World's Fair in 1901 and modern, European-style bathrooms. Explore the lobby and ballrooms for a sense of life at the turn of the 20th century. Former presidents Woodrow Wilson and Franklin Roosevelt stayed here.

Escape the bustle of downtown at **The Parkside House** (462 Woodward Ave., 716/480-9507, www.theparksidehouse.com, $150) bed-and-breakfast. Snuggled in a residential neighborhood close to Delaware Park, this place has three comfy rooms, excellent food, and many spaces for relaxing or reading a book. The hosts are gracious and knowledgeable about the area; ask them about the nearby Frank Lloyd Wright home on Jewett Avenue, just a few minutes' walk from the hotel.

Buffalo's most lavish boutique hotel is a treat for the weary traveler and a trip back in time. Built in 1867 and completely restored in 2001, the **❰ Mansion on Delaware** (414 Delaware Ave., 716/886-3300, www.mansionondelaware.

com, $300) gives you a taste of how the wealthy lived during the Gilded Age. The 24-hour service by your personal butler includes cocktails in the Fireside Salon, clothes pressing, and shoe shines—all complimentary. Need to head downtown for dinner? A butler will drive you in a Land Rover. The 28 rooms are comfortable yet not too large, with plenty of authentic detail and historic charm. In an area of moderately priced attractions, why not splurge a little?

Hotel @ The Lafayette is located in a grand renovated 1904 building.

© JOEL A. DOMBROWSKI-NIAGARA FALLS WALKING TOURS

Food

FINE DINING

Tasteful elegance is on the menu at 🄲 **Mike A at the Lafayette** (391 Washington St., 716/253-6453, www.mikealafayette.com, 11am-10pm Tues.-Sat., $35). Buffalo's celebrity chef, Mike Andrzejewski, brings cosmopolitan cuisine here, setting the bar for bistros. The 10-course tasting menu takes you around the culinary world with dishes from Asia and Italy, as well as locally sourced food. The bar is perhaps the best in the city for discriminating drinkers. The list of high-end scotch includes both the Balvenie DoubleWood 12-Year and the Laphroaig 10-Year. Cocktails are taken seriously here, with 10 original mixed drinks always on the menu (try Death and Taxes with orange marble rye, $10). The wine list is also substantial, with more than 100 wines from which to choose.

Hutch's Restaurant (1375 Delaware Ave., 716/885-0074, www.hutchsrestaurant.com, 5pm-10pm Mon.-Thurs., 5pm-midnight Fri.-Sat., 4pm-9pm Sun., $32) is a reliable favorite with excellent food and service. Expect American cuisine with an emphasis on seafood. The tables are very close together and the noise level very high, making it good for a family or group gathering, but not for a quiet romantic dinner.

NEW AMERICAN

Enjoy tasty New American cuisine at **The Left Bank** (511 Rhode Island St., 716/882-3509, www.leftbankrestaurant.com, 5pm-11pm Mon.-Thurs., 5pm-midnight Fri.-Sat., 11am-2:30pm and 4pm-10pm Sun., $19). This restaurant finds the perfect balance with an atmosphere that is lively, but the space isn't crowded or loud. Try any of the world-class appetizers and the amazing house ravioli stuffed with pork and zucchini.

ITALIAN

Siena (4516 Main St., 716/839-3108, www.siena-restaurant.com, 11:30am-2pm and 5pm-10pm Mon.-Fri., 5pm-10pm Sat., 4:30pm-9pm Sun., $28) serves contemporary Italian fare in an upscale but casual atmosphere. Among the excellent appetizers, check out the "three ways" fried calamari or the stuffed hot peppers. While the restaurant is famous for its traditional entrées, you won't be disappointed if you try the wood-oven pizzas.

WINGS

In a town famous for chicken wings, **Duff's Famous Wings** (3651 Sheridan Dr., 716/834-6234, www.duffswings.com, 11am-11pm Mon.-Thurs., 11am-midnight Fri.-Sat., noon-10pm Sun., $10) has the best. For the adventurous, "suicidal" and "death" sauces are available; a safe strategy is to order your wings medium or hot, then get a side order of the suicidal or death sauce for dipping.

BARBECUE

Suzy Q's Bar-B-Que Shack (2829 River Rd., 716/873-0757, www.suzy-que.blogspot.com, 11am-8:30pm Tues.-Thurs., 11am-9pm Fri., noon-9pm Sat., $9) does look like a shack, but inside are treats fit for a king. The barbecue served here is authentic, fresh, and inexpensive. If you close your eyes when you're eating the pulled pork, you could easily believe you're in Dixie. Balance your entrée with a side of sweet potato sticks or macaroni and cheese. If you arrive after 7pm, some of the main dishes will be gone, but don't worry: Your second and third choices will still be outstanding.

Duff's Famous Wings

Information and Services

Emergency help is available by calling 911. Non-emergency information requests are fielded by city hall during business hours by calling 311.

The best tourism information and event calendar is found at the **Buffalo Niagara**

Convention & Visitor's Bureau (617 Main St., 800/283-3256, www.visitbuffaloniagara. com, 10am-4pm Mon.-Sat. Memorial Day-Labor Day, 10am-4pm Mon.-Fri. Labor Day-Memorial Day).

Getting There and Around

Being a small city has its advantages. One is the **Buffalo Niagara International Airport** (BUF, 4200 Genesee St., Cheektowaga, 716/630-6000, www.buffaloairport.com), which is easy to navigate because of its small size. Many air travelers from Toronto come here to enjoy significantly reduced fares, easy parking, and faster boarding times. Several air carriers serve the airport, including Southwest,

United, American, Delta, and Jet Blue. From the airport, it's a 15- minute drive to downtown Buffalo and a 25-minute drive to Niagara Falls.

Buffalo's main bus terminal, the **METRO Transportation Station** (181 Ellicott St.) is downtown. All local transit bus routes have stops within a three-block radius of this station. The local transit service, **Niagara Frontier Transit Authority** (716/855-7300, www.nfta.com) operates buses and trains in Erie and Niagara Counties. Bus route 204 ($2.50) connects the METRO Transportation Station with Buffalo Niagara International Airport. Bus route 40 ($2) will take you to Niagara Falls, New York. Check the online schedules, as route coverage changes on weekends and holidays.

Intercity motorcoach service providers that stop at the METRO Transportation Station include **Greyhound** (716/855-7531, www. greyhound.com), **Coach USA** (800/352-0979, www.coachusa.com), **MegaBus** (877/462-6342, www.us.megabus.com), **Neon** (800/231-2222, www.neonbus.com), **New York Trailways** (800/776-7548, www.trailwaysny. com), and **Coach Canada** (800/461-7661, www.coachcanada.com).

Lockport and Niagara Wine Country

To the northeast of Buffalo, fertile land stretches outward, encompassing the historic city of Lockport and eventually reaching Lake Ontario. The Niagara Escarpment cuts through on an east-west axis, creating a perfect microclimate for growing fruit between the ridge and the lake. Wine country spreads northward from the escarpment to Lake Ontario like a green blanket, nurturing nearly 20 wineries. The imposing dolostone of the escarpment yields to Yankee ingenuity and hard labor in Lockport, where the Erie Canal manages to flow uphill.

SIGHTS
Erie Canal Discovery Center
Despite its four-mile-per-hour speed limit, the Erie Canal was the first U.S. superhighway, fundamentally changing both the region and the country as a whole. The **Erie Canal Discovery Center** (24 Church St., Lockport, 716/439-0431, www.niagarahistory.org, 9am-5pm daily May-Oct., 10am-3pm Thurs.-Sat. Nov.-Apr., $6 adults, $4 children 5-13) is the best way to understand the canal, its legacy, and its importance to Lockport. This is no musty museum! This highly educational and entertaining center has contemporary interactive exhibits. Try your hands at piloting a model boat through the locks or take a virtual nighttime ride aboard a packet boat along the canal.

Other displays tell the compelling stories of "canawlers," the men, women, and children whose lives depended upon the Erie Canal. The City of Lockport Visitor's Center is in the

lower level of the complex. The volunteers here can provide excellent information about local attractions and festivals.

◖ Lockport Locks
Diggers of the Erie Canal faced a monumental problem as they excavated the 363-mile waterway in the early 1800s. Engineers needed to find a way to allow boats to climb the 60-foot increase in elevation at Lockport's escarpment. An ingenious series of five twin locks permitted canal boats to safely make the journey up and down the escarpment, the geological ridge over which Niagara Falls originally flowed.

Today, the Erie Canal has transitioned from an essential economic artery for a burgeoning country to a pastoral waterway enjoyed by recreational boaters and curious tourists. Thanks to advances in technology, the original five locks have been replaced by two. The work involved in elevating the boats 60 feet is just as fascinating as it was in 1825 when the Erie Canal opened.

Locks 34 and 35 are the main attractions. They are located in the heart of Lockport, where Pine Street crosses over the canal. You can observe the locks in action from either side of the canal. The west side features a bike path accessible from Canal Street. This path affords a great view of the new locks, as well as old locks that are no longer operational and act as a spillway. Observing from the east side of the canal is the best way to experience the new locks up close as they gently raise and lower the boats. As you walk over the canal on Main

BUFFALO

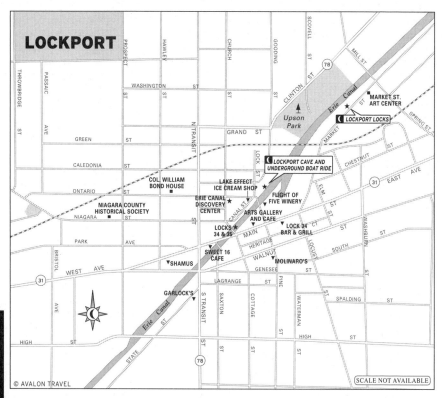

BUFFALO

Street (heading southwest), you will travel over the widest bridge in North America (399 feet wide, but only 129 feet long).

Lockport Locks and Erie Canal Cruises (210 Market St., Lockport, 716/378-0352, www.lockportlocks.com, May-mid-Oct., $17.50 adults, $9 children 4-10) offers a slow-paced, two-hour cruise along the canal and back in time. This ride is an excellent antidote for an otherwise busy vacation, as it forces you to relax and appreciate life at the pace of the canal. The boat's captain provides excellent narration and is eager to answer any questions. If you enjoy America's industrial history, this is a real winner.

Lockport Cave and Underground Boat Ride

Both literally and figuratively, the coolest thing to do in Lockport is to experience the **Lockport Cave and Underground Boat Ride** (5 Gooding St., 716/438-0174, www.lockportcave.com, May-mid-Oct., $12 adults, $7 children 5-12). During the hour-long guided tour, you'll explore a large tunnel blasted out of solid rock in the 1850s. The tunnel provided flowing water to various factories that used it for hydraulic power. Today, the tunnel is an eerie portal to the industrial history of the United States.

The tour also includes what is purported to be "America's longest underground boat ride." While the boat trip is relaxing, be prepared to do some uphill walking and stair climbing—the attraction is not wheelchair-accessible. Your tour guide will talk about the locks and the history of Lockport as you walk along the canal and before you enter the cave.

Take a trip back in time by cruising on the Erie Canal.

© NIAGARA TOURISM AND CONVENTION CORPORATION

WINERIES

New York State is second only to California in American grape production. For many years, the farmers of this area were able to grow peaches, apples, and table grapes. It wasn't until the 1990s that winegrowers began to seriously cultivate grapes for wine. The **Niagara Wine Trail** (www.niagarawinetrail.org) has blossomed into a region supporting nearly 20 wineries. After the Wisconsin glaciation ended, some 11,000 years ago, it left behind soil perfect for growing temperamental wine grapes.

The wineries are as diverse as the vintages they create, with some focusing on handcrafted traditional wines, while others experiment with wines made from apples, apricots, and cherries. **The Winery at Marjim Manor** (7171 E. Lake Rd., Appleton, 716/778-7001, www.marjim-manor.com, 10am-6pm Mon.-Sat., noon-6pm Sun., $3 tasting fee) serves fruit-based wines with a side helping of ghost stories. Owners Margo and Jim Bittner began farming in the early 2000s. Today, they make wines using

apples, plums, pears, apricots, blueberries, and many other fresh fruits, along with locally grown grapes. There are tastings at Marjim Manor, a beautiful, historic building from the 1850s that boasts a spooky history. Although there are no on-site wine-making facilities, it is nonetheless one of the best stops on the Niagara Wine Trail.

A Gust of Sun Winery (4515 Baer Rd., Ransomville, 716/731-4878, www.agustof-sun.com, by appointment only Mon.-Thurs., noon-6pm Fri. and Sun., 10am-6pm Sat. Jan.-Apr., noon-6pm Sun.-Fri., 10am-6pm Sat. May-Dec., $5 tasting fee) is a true family-owned and -operated enterprise. Erik and Shane Gustafson moved here to try their hand at wine making shortly after they were married. The couple planted vines and renovated an old Amish barn into a tasting room and lounge in the loft. Their hard work has paid off with their sweet and dry white wines winning medals at competitions regionally and in the Midwest. A partnership with a local chocolate maker has led to a novel tasting where five wine samples are paired with five chocolates custom made to complement the Gustafson's wine.

Vizcarra Vineyards at Becker Farms (3724 Quaker Rd., Gasport, 716/772-2211, www.beckerfarms.com, 11am-6pm daily May-Nov., noon-5pm Wed.-Mon. Dec.-Apr., $3 tasting fee) believes in growing the best fruit on its 340-acre farm, then making it into wine for people to enjoy. In addition to traditional grape wines, Vizcarra offers apple, plum, strawberry-rhubarb, cherry, and raspberry wines. The most recent addition is the "sinful series"—heavily fortified, port-style wines fermented to 17 percent alcohol by volume. Vizcarra is part of the Becker Farms estate, which includes a microbrewery, farmers market selling fresh fruits and vegetables, and a small bakery and snack shop.

For the founders of **Freedom Run Winery** (5138 Lower Mountain Rd., Lockport, 716/433-4136, www.freedomrunwinery.com, noon-6pm Sun.-Wed., 10am-6pm Thurs.-Sat., tasting fees vary), wine is art. The sweeping elegance of their winery was designed to enhance the wines. The contemporary and

© NIAGARA TOURISM AND CONVENTION CORPORATION

This cave once supplied hydraulic power to Lockport's industries.

airy tasting rooms are alive with works from local artisans, with an emphasis on stunning handcrafted glass. The wines crafted here are works of art as well—they've won several medals from regional tasting competitions. Among Freedom Run's successful vintages are pinot noirs that thrive in the heavy clay soils of their vineyards.

It's a story of "gravel to grapes" at the **Spring Lake Winery** (7373 Rochester Rd., Lockport, 716/439-5253, www.springlakewinery.com, noon-5pm daily, $3 tasting fee). Before it was a winery, Spring Lake was a gravel pit. The Varallo family saw the potential of the pit and purchased 78 acres of land surrounding the excavation. The pit filled with natural spring water and is now a small lake with a beautiful vista for wine tasting, picnics, and weddings. The land's unique sandy soil is best suited to growing riesling grapes. Spring Lake's Rieslings have won medals at tasting competitions nationally and internationally. Visitors can walk among the vines, see the processing machinery, and explore the pastoral area around the lake.

The lakeside gazebo is a picturesque place to sip wine or to host a wedding. When enough staff is available, informal tours of the grounds are offered.

ENTERTAINMENT AND EVENTS
The Arts

The **Market Street Art Center** (247 Market St., Lockport, 716/478-0239, www.market-streetstudios.com, 10am-5pm Tues.-Sat., 11am-4pm Sun., free) features the multimedia works of local artists and offers art classes, too. The building that houses the artists is an old factory built in the 1880s, which provides the perfect industrial backdrop for the labors of local artists. The art center has large interior spaces with brick walls, I-beams, and large steel pipes. Artists who rent the spaces are involved with creating watercolor paintings, photography, pottery, jewelry, chainsaw sculptures, embroidery, quilting, leatherwork, and finely crafted furniture.

Fine art pieces by local artists are found at

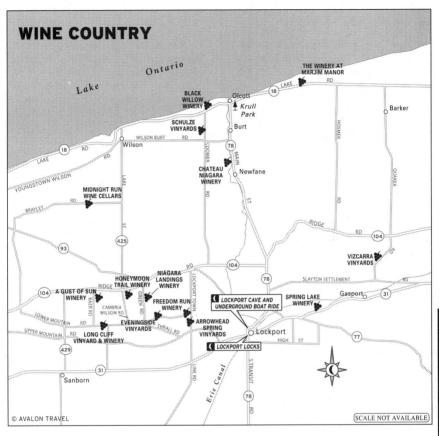

WINE COUNTRY

Lake Ontario

THE WINERY AT
MARJIM MANOR
RD

BLACK
WILLOW
WINERY

Olcott

Krull
Park

Barker

SCHULZE
VINYARDS

Burt

WILSON BURT   RD

Wilson

18   RD   RD

COOMER

78

MAIN

CHATEAU
NIAGARA
WINERY

Newfane

ST

YOUNGSTOWN WILSON

LAKE

RD

BRAYLEY   RD

MIDNIGHT RUN
WINE CELLARS

RIDGE   RD

104

ST

425

93

104

VIZCARRA
VINYARDS

HONEYMOON
TRAIL WINERY

NIAGARA
LANDINGS
WINERY

SLAYTON SETTLEMENT   RD

78

104   A GUST OF SUN
WINERY

RIDGE RD

FREEDOM RUN
WINERY

LOCKPORT CAVE AND
UNDERGROUND BOAT RIDE

SPRING LAKE
WINERY

Gasport   31

BAKER RD

GREEN RD

CAMBRIA
WILSON RD

LOWER MOUNTAIN   RD

EVENINGSIDE
VINYARDS

THRALL RD

ARROWHEAD
SPRING
VINYARDS

Lockport

UPPER MOUNTAIN   RD

LONG CLIFF
VINYARD & WINERY

LOCKPORT LOCKS

HIGH   ST

77

429

31

78

Sanborn

LINE RD

Erie Canal

S TRANSIT

RD

HOSMER

QUAKER

LAKE   18

BUFFALO

© AVALON TRAVEL

SCALE NOT AVAILABLE

the **Kenan Center House Gallery** (433 Locust St., Lockport, 716/433-2617, www.kenan-center.org, noon-5pm Mon.-Fri., 2pm-5pm Sun., June-Labor Day, noon-5pm Mon.-Fri., 2pm-5pm Sat.-Sun., Labor Day-May, free) in Lockport. The gallery hosts an eclectic array of works, including paintings, sculptures, graphic designs, metal work, pottery, and prints. The Kenan Center is a 25-acre campus that includes the gallery, a sports arena, theater, and educational building. The gallery dates back to 1858 and was the home of businessman William Rand Kenan. A portion of this sprawling Victorian-style building houses the gallery, while the rest is used for administrative offices.

Festivals and Events

Niagara's longest running juried art show, the **100 American Craftsmen Art Show** (www.kenancraftshow.com, $6) displays the works of local artists. It is hosted at the beautiful **Kenan Center Arena** (195 Beattie Ave., Lockport) for three days in late May each year.

In August, **Canal Fest** (www.canalfest.org) is a fun community celebration where Tonawanda and Ellicott Creeks meet in downtown Tonawanda. It runs for one week in mid-July and has a parade, fireworks, live music, and numerous food vendors. Highlights include an arts-and-crafts show, a classic car night, and a charity toy duck race in the creek.

Olcott's **Niagara Celtic Heritage Festival**

Vizcarra Vineyards offers tastings of wine and craft beers.

and Highland Games (www.niagaraceltic.com) in Krull Park (6108 Lake Rd., Olcott) celebrates all things Celtic for a weekend in mid-September. The festival provides seminars on Celtic customs and genealogy, with costumed re-enactors. Traditional Scottish Highland games are played, such as the caber toss, in which men wearing kilts throw 19-foot wooden poles in an attempt to land them upright. During the festival, you can enjoy contemporary Celtic music, falconry, and a demonstration of kilt folding. If you enjoy the music, foods, and traditions of Ireland, Scotland, and Wales, you'll enjoy this festival.

SPORTS AND RECREATION
Parks
In Wilson, **Wilson Tuscarora State Park** (3371 Lake Rd., Wilson, 716/751-6361, www.nysparks.com, dawn-dusk daily, free) has more than 450 acres of woods and meadows to explore, along with a four-mile nature path, picnic facilities, and a boat launch ($7). Located on Lake Ontario, the park allows for swimming, fishing, and hiking.

Krull Park (6108 Lake Rd., Olcott, 716/778-7711, www.niagaracounty.com/parks, dawn-dusk daily Memorial Day-Labor Day) is a 325-acre community park on the shore of Lake Ontario, with a splash pool, beach, playground, and picnic shelters.

Fishing
The Lower Niagara River and Lake Ontario afford numerous opportunities for fishing from shore or a chartered vessel. Careful stewardship of area waterways has allowed for sustainable populations of bass, trout, pike, catfish, sunfish, salmon, and many other freshwater species. Adult anglers need to obtain a fishing license from the state (www.dec.ny.gov).

Wilson Tuscarora State Park (3371 Lake Rd., Wilson, 716/751-6361, www.nysparks.com) and **Golden Hill State Park** (9691 Lower Lake Rd., Barker, 716/795-3885, www.nysparks.com) provide boat launches ($7) and good spots for shore fishing. A good resource listing all public places to fish, as well as guidelines and regulations, is found at the website for the Department of Conservation (www.dec.ny.gov).

ACCOMMODATIONS
Brookins Inn & Suites (2697 Maple Ave., Newfane, 716/870-6244, www.brookinsinn.com, $130) has three suites and two guestrooms, all with private baths. It's a convenient location for people on the Niagara Wine Trail. Home-baked chocolate chip cookies are a nice plus.

Lockport Inn & Suites (315 South Transit Rd., Lockport, 716/434-5595, www.lockportinnandsuites.com, $150) is a good value, especially the suites, which have fireplaces and whirlpool tubs. The rooms to the rear (farther from the road) are newer and quieter.

FOOD
Lockport's **Shamus Restaurant** (98 West Ave., Lockport, 716/433-9809, www.theshamus.com, 11am-9pm Mon.-Thurs., 11am-10pm

Wilson Tuscarora State Park

Fri.-Sat., $12-34) is where the locals enjoy good food at reasonable prices. A few steps away from the canal locks, Shamus serves generous portions, as well as craft beer.

You can usually find a reliable Greek food joint wherever you go. In Lockport, **Kalamata Family Restaurant** (5690 S. Transit Rd., 716/433-2626, www.kalamatafamilyrestaurant.com, 7am-9pm Sun.-Wed., 7am-10pm Thurs.-Sat., $9-13) is it. The wide selection of food comes in huge portions. They are everything you'd expect from a great Greek restaurant.

GETTING THERE AND AROUND

Lockport is approximately 20 miles north of Buffalo (40 min.) and 19 miles northeast of Niagara Falls (35 min.). Driving from Buffalo, use Route 78 (Transit Rd.) to reach Lockport; Route 31 joins Lockport with Niagara Falls.

Public transit is provided by **Niagara Frontier Transit Authority** (716/855-7300, www.nfta.com). Bus route 44 ($2 one way) joins Buffalo and Lockport. The trip takes about 90 minutes. The main bus stop in Lockport is located at Locust and Main Streets.

NIAGARA-ON-THE-LAKE AND WINE COUNTRY

When war-weary Winston Churchill came to Niagara Falls, Ontario, in August 1943, he found relaxation and beauty during the 13-mile drive from the falls to Niagara-on-the-Lake. The prime minister remarked that the trip is "the prettiest Sunday afternoon drive in the world." Those words ring true as you wind your way along the Niagara River Gorge, stopping to visit any of the dozens of wineries in the area.

The Canadian vineyards literally have their roots in Europe. Local vintners imported European grape vines to this region for grafting experiments. Grafting allowed wine-quality grapes to be grown in this climate, yielding sophisticated vintages. Ice wine festivals in February feature outdoor tasting bars carved from ice. People gather around fires toasting marshmallows made from wine sugar.

During the War of 1812, American soldiers burned the village of Niagara-on-the-Lake. The entire village was rebuilt and stands today preserved in Victorian time, with most homes and buildings dating from 1814. This is the most romantic place to window-shop and enjoy a perfectly paired wine with dinner.

Lake freighters circumvent the Niagara River via the Welland Canal. This 26-mile waterway joins Lake Erie with Lake Ontario, allowing enormous ships safe passage. The canal is used in equal measure for commerce and leisure, coming alive in the summer with numerous festivals in the major towns dotting its edges. The region hosts a tall-ship regatta, Canada's largest single-day music festival (S.C.E.N.E.), Shakespeare in the Vineyard, and many other events year-round.

HIGHLIGHTS

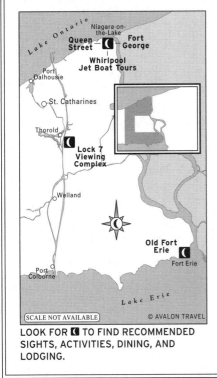

◖ Fort George: Experience the dangerous and difficult life of soldiers and civilians who called Fort George home during the War of 1812 (page 108).

◖ Queen Street: Explore the heart of the "Prettiest Town in Canada." Stroll, shop, and sip along this street that appears frozen in Victorian times (page 109).

◖ Whirlpool Jet Boat Tours: Challenge the rapids of the Niagara River in an open-air jet boat (page 109).

◖ Lock 7 Viewing Complex: Enjoy the spectacle of massive freighters gently gliding by as they navigate the locks of the Welland Canal (page 121).

◖ Old Fort Erie: Guarding the mouth of the Niagara River, Fort Erie's buildings and grounds survived Canada's bloodiest battle. Historical reenactments bring the drama to life (page 123).

LOOK FOR ◖ TO FIND RECOMMENDED SIGHTS, ACTIVITIES, DINING, AND LODGING.

HISTORY

The two indigenous groups that dominated Ontario prior to European exploration were the Algonquins and Iroquois. At times, these groups struggled against each other, and they eventually sided with each of the two main European powers that explored the region.

By 1615, both the French and the English were exploring Ontario with an eye on trade and colonization. The Algonquins primarily allied themselves with the French, while the Iroquois sided with the English. Following much bloodshed, the English defeated the French during the Seven Years' War, also known as the French and Indian War. By

1780, more than 9,000 English loyalists settled in Ontario, along with many Iroquois who fled New York State following the American Revolution.

Ontario was in the breach during the War of 1812, witnessing the bloodiest engagements of that conflict. In the end, no land was lost or gained, but the region began moving toward a unified country of Canada. By 1867, Ontario was declared a province and Canada was an autonomous dominion, eventually becoming an independent nation with historic and symbolic ties to England.

Southern Ontario is culturally diverse. Immigrants from Europe and elsewhere settled here to seek opportunities in agriculture

NIAGARA-ON-THE-LAKE

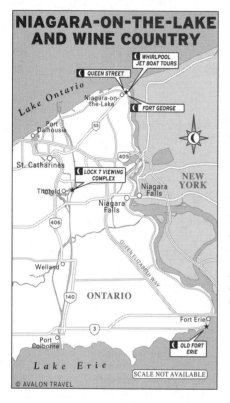

NIAGARA-ON-THE-LAKE AND WINE COUNTRY

and industry. The region has successfully balanced the challenges and benefits of its three major industries—tourism, farming, and light manufacturing. Transportation is another important economic driver, due to the region's international border and proximity to Toronto, the fourth-largest city in North America.

PLANNING YOUR TIME

This region forms a crescent that surrounds Niagara Falls. It is largely rural, with excellent roadways for easy driving and cycling. Though the regional highlights can be seen during a long (and hectic) day trip, it's better to take two days at a relaxed pace. Some travelers use Niagara Falls as their base, but you may prefer staying overnight in Niagara-on-the-Lake at an inn or bed-and-breakfast.

Visit the towns along the Welland Canal on a single day's adventure. Niagara-on-the-Lake and the wine country are a perfect escape for a separate one-day jaunt.

Niagara-on-the-Lake

Niagara-on-the-Lake (NOTL), a small town of 15,000 residents, has emerged as the center of a region unrivaled in beauty, charm, and historic significance. Located on the shore of Lake Ontario, it is surrounded by thousands of acres of vineyards. In the 1970s, NOTL was at the vanguard of the movement to bring wine-quality grapes from Europe to Canada. Over the years, this area has attracted internationally acclaimed winemakers and chefs. High-end wineries and restaurants thrive because of NOTL's unique proximity to Toronto and Niagara Falls.

SIGHTS
Queenston Heights Park

Queenston Heights Park (14184 Niagara Pkwy., 877/642-7275, www.niagaraparks.com, 24 hours daily, free) is a memorial park with a magnificent view of the Niagara River and lands stretching from the escarpment ridge to Lake Ontario. The strategic value of this perch along the Niagara Gorge was not lost on the combatants in the War of 1812. The British occupied it, and the Americans needed to take it. Thus came the Battle of Queenston Heights, fought on October 13, 1812. The park serves as a memorial of that battle.

This park is all about the view. The Niagara

NIAGARA-ON-THE-LAKE

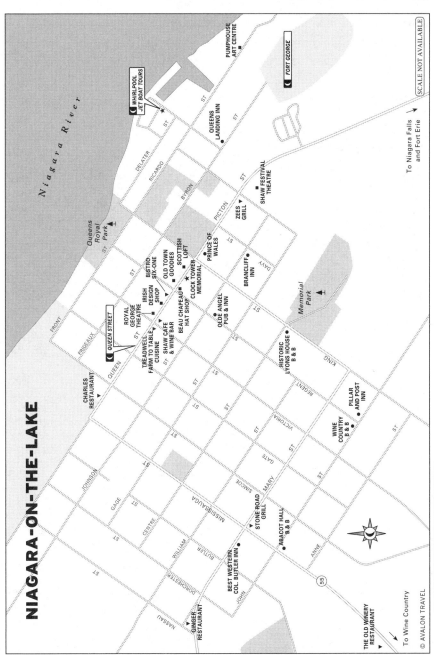

Niagara River

Queens Royal Park

WHIRLPOOL JET BOAT TOURS

FORT GEORGE

PUMPHOUSE ART CENTRE

QUEENS LANDING INN

SHAW FESTIVAL THEATRE

ZEES GRILL

PRINCE OF WALES

SCOTTISH LOFT

BISTRO SIX-ONE

OLD TOWN GOODIES

BRANCLIFF INN

IRISH DESIGN SHOP

CLOCK TOWER MEMORIAL

BEAU CHAPEAU HAT SHOP

QUEEN STREET

ROYAL GEORGE THEATRE

OLDE ANGEL PUB & INN

TREADWELL FARM TO TABLE CUISINE

SHAW CAFE & WINE BAR

HISTORIC LYONS HOUSE B & B

CHARLES RESTAURANT

PILLAR AND POST INN

WINE COUNTRY B & B

STONE ROAD GRILL

ABACOT HALL B & B

BEST WESTERN COL. BUTLER INN

GINGER RESTAURANT

THE OLD WINERY RESTAURANT

Memorial Park

To Niagara Falls and Fort Erie

To Wine Country

FRONT ST
PRIDEAUX ST
QUEEN ST
JOHNSON ST
GAGE ST
CENTRE ST
WILLIAM ST
BUTLER ST
DORCHESTER ST
NASSAU ST
JOHN
MISSISSAUGA
SIMCOE
GATE
MARY
VICTORIA ST
REGENT ST
KING
ANNIE
DELATER ST
RICARDO ST
BYRON ST
PICTON ST
DAVY
ST

DELATER ST

(55)

© AVALON TRAVEL

SCALE NOT AVAILABLE

NIAGARA-ON-THE-LAKE

© JOEL A. DOMBROWSKI·NIAGARA FALLS WALKING TOURS

Queenston Heights provides a commanding view of the fertile plain that stretches to Lake Ontario.

NIAGARA-ON-THE-LAKE

Parkway runs through Queenston Heights. Along it, there's a small paved parking lot (just after a hairpin turn) with a panorama of the green glacial plain that stretches from the escarpment (where you're standing) to Lake Ontario seven miles away. From here, you can see white dots in the water that are not rapids, but sailboats. The river slows and widens, cutting an irregular line that separates Canada from the United States. In summer, the vista is verdant; in fall, it is a festive palette of orange, red, and brown.

Within the park, at the top of **Brock's Monument** (Queenston Heights Park, 905/468-6621, www.friendsoffortgeorge.ca, 10am-5pm daily May-Aug., 11am-4pm Wed.-Sun. Sept.-Oct. 13, $4.50 adults, $3.50 children 6-16) is another magnificent vista. Reaching the top of the 185-foot monument involves climbing a seemingly endless circular staircase, which requires some maneuvering to accommodate visitors who are descending (there is no elevator). The journey is worth it, but be advised that it is equal to climbing 18 stories' worth of stairs.

Brock's Monument is dedicated to the audacious general, Isaac Brock, who died while rallying his troops to repel the invading American forces during the Battle of Queenston Heights. Brock turned the tide of the battle in favor of the British; he is regarded as "the hero of Upper Canada." Just outside the monument, there are interpretive plaques that tell the story of the Battle of Queenston Heights, as well as a memorial to Laura Secord, another hero of the War of 1812.

The grounds at Queenston Heights are everything you'd expect from Niagara Parks, including meticulously groomed greenery, acres of open space, well-maintained picnic facilities, clean restrooms, and plenty of parking. It is the best location in the region for family picnics.

The entrance to the park is at the traffic circle on Niagara Parkway. Bear right to park near Brock's Monument; turn left to park next to the picnic areas.

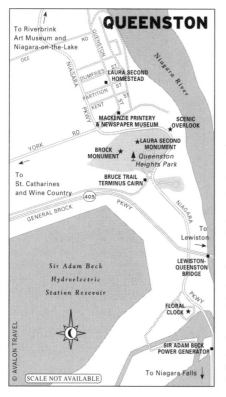

favored British-born subjects at the expense of those who had emigrated from the United States. Mackenzie was elected to office, led an ill-fated and ineffective revolt, spent time in jail, and helped create reform in Canada's government. Docents bring to life Mackenzie's firebrand advocacy and his principled resistance to government cronyism.

Docents also discuss printing press history over 500 years. The museum's collection of eight working presses includes the Louis Roy Press, which dating back to 1770 and the oldest printing press in Canada. Docents supervise as visitors create documents using vintage linotype technology and a hand-operated wooden heritage press. The printery is a hidden gem, and will take about an hour to explore.

Laura Secord Homestead

The **Laura Secord Homestead** (29 Queenston St., 905/262-4851, www.niagaraparksheritage. com, 10am-5pm daily May-Aug., 10am-4pm Wed.-Fri., 10am-5pm Sat.-Sun. Sept.-mid-Oct. $9.50 adults, $6.25 children 6-12). is the home of Canada's most famous heroine. Restored to its original condition, the homestead affords a glimpse into the life of settlers who lived in this area in the early 1800s.

Laura Secord is remembered for her heroism during the War of 1812. Upon overhearing a remark from American soldiers about an impending attack against British troops, she set out on a 20-mile trip to relay the information to the British Military Command. Visitors are led through the homestead by a costumed guide who relates the compelling story of settlers who came to southern Ontario. The homestead itself becomes a character in the narrative, as your guide uses furniture, kitchenware, and other artifacts to explain the experience of 19th-century settlers.

History fans will like this attraction; fans of Canadian history will love it. Plan on spending 30-60 minutes here.

McFarland House

Drink in the history and some wonderful tea at the **McFarland House** (15927 Niagara Pkwy.,

Mackenzie Printery and Newspaper Museum

The power of the press in determining Ontario's fate is on display at the **Mackenzie Printery and Newspaper Museum** (1 Queenston St., 905/262-5676, www.niagaraparksheritage. com, 10am-5pm daily May-Aug., 10am-5pm Sat.-Sun. Sept.-Oct., $5 adults, $3.75 children 6-16). The printery is a restoration of the home of William Lyon Mackenzie, a 19th-century publisher and advocate for government reform. The museum is a stately limestone, Federal-style home built using the original plans of Mackenzie's 1850s home. The museum is small, but allows for hands-on learning on a historical printing press.

Mackenzie was a businessman who wanted to change the existing political framework that

Operate vintage printing presses at the Mackenzie Printery.

© THE NIAGARA PARKS COMMISSION

905/468-3322, www.niagaraparksheritage. com, noon-5pm daily mid-May-Aug., noon-5pm Sat.-Sun. Sept.-Oct., $5 adults, $3.75 children 6-12). This restored home welcomes visitors into the well-mannered world of the early 1800s.

Built and occupied by ship builder John McFarland, this structure is unique because it survived the burning of Niagara-on-the-Lake in 1813, likely because it was used as a hospital during the war for wounded U.S. and British soldiers. The McFarland House is also the oldest structure owned and maintained by the Niagara Parks Commission; it was built in 1800. The house is surrounded by parkland with ample parking, picnic shelters, and a baseball diamond.

Guides dressed in period costumes provide tours of the home and share stories about 19th-century life in southern Ontario. They inform you of the civility and customs of the Georgian era against an authentic backdrop. Look for the antique rope bed that demonstrates the origin of the term "sleep tight."

For a relaxing break, try the afternoon tea, with freshly baked scones and light sandwiches (if you order scones, ask for the ice wine jelly). Choose among many teas, including the vividly named Delirium Blossom Flowering Tea. Grab a table at the conservatory, overlooking the river.

Allot 30 minutes to visit this house, and 45 minutes more if you stay for tea or a meal.

◖ Fort George

The fortifications, buildings, and grounds of **Fort George** (51 Queen's Parade, 905/468-6621, www.friendsoffortgeorge.ca, noon-4pm Sat.-Sun. Dec.-Mar., 10am-5pm Sat.-Sun. Apr. and Nov., 10am-5pm daily May-Oct., $11.70 adults, $5.80 children 6-16) are wonderful, but the employees here make it a must-see.

Costumed docents really get into character here, where they depict life during the War of 1812. From your first interaction with the guardhouse sentry (who may play a tune on his penny whistle for you) to the cannon-firing demonstration, there is an emphasis on authenticity. These lively docents know their history; they can easily answer questions and entertain with improvised interactions.

The fort is not just for history buffs. Children can try on uniforms and participate in some demonstrations. The Fife and Drum Corps fills the air with music while marching across the parade grounds with pageantry. Take a walk to the southern portion of the fort to find the Powder Magazine, the only original structure remaining from when the fort was first constructed in 1796. The thick stone walls of this single-story rectangular building are designed to withstand cannon fire. Inside the magazine are dozens of barrels representing the black powder that was stored here during the War of 1812, as well as interpretive signs describing the safety measures taken by soldiers who worked here. Do not miss the barracks, officers' quarters, and blacksmith—each reveals an engaging story about the simple, but hard and dangerous life in the fort.

The fort hosts many special events throughout the year, such as battle reenactments and holiday festivals. Check the website's events calendar for more information. Budget at least 2-4 hours to fully appreciate Fort George.

◖ Queen Street

Queen Street is the main thoroughfare of Niagara-on-the-Lake, and the heart of the charming village, which appears to have been frozen in Victorian times. The village was destroyed in 1813 by American soldiers fleeing across the river, and then rebuilt, so many of the structures date back to the early 1800s.

Queen Street is quaint, picturesque, and romantic. The street is lined with shops, restaurants, hotels, and theaters. Flowers are everywhere, bursting with color from planters and hanging baskets. Most visitors spend their time leisurely strolling the street, checking out the wares in one-of-a-kind shops like the Scottish Loft, Irish Design, and Beau Chapeau Hat Shop. NOTL draws visitors from culturally diverse Toronto, so you're likely to overhear conversations in four or five different languages.

The village's identity is intertwined with the world famous Shaw Festival, which features new productions of George Bernard Shaw's plays each year. Two of the four theaters participating in the festival are located on Queen Street.

A list of Queen Street shops and restaurants is found on the official NOTL website (www.niagaraonthelake.com).

◖ Whirlpool Jet Boat Tours

The number one white-knuckle, death-defying attraction in the entire Niagara region is the **Whirlpool Jet Boat Tours** (61 Melville St., 888/438-4444, www.whirlpooljet.com, $61 adults, $51 children). Jet boats are uniquely designed vessels capable of surviving the severe white-water conditions of the Lower Niagara River.

Tours are in covered boats (Jet Domes) and open-air boats (Wet Jets). If your courage permits, choose the Wet Jet. The experience is exhilarating, frightening, and saturating. Each tour begins with a safety discussion and an explanation of what gear you need to wear. If you choose the Wet Jet, you and all your personal effects will be drenched. Do not take cameras or other electronic devices aboard, unless specifically designed for underwater use.

The ride begins quietly as the boat glides through the relatively smooth waters of the river near the entrance to Lake Ontario. Heading south on the river, the boat can increase speed and perform a few stunts like 360-degree spins. A crew member narrates the trip, discussing the nature of the river's white water.

The jet boats take you through stretches of torturous Class V rapids in the narrow parts of the Lower Niagara. (Class VI waves are considered the most dangerous.) Here the boat manages to navigate standing waves 15-20 feet high. At times, there will be a foot or more of water inside the boat—but don't worry, the boat's design allows it to safely conquer white water. Certain maneuvers result in a wall of water slamming over the boat and, though you are warned in advance, nothing can quite prepare you for this experience.

The exhilarating ride is scary, but safe. It takes 90 minutes to complete the tour. There are two other locations to board the boats, at the Aero Car attraction on the Canadian side of the river and in Lewiston on the U.S. side.

ENTERTAINMENT AND EVENTS

The Arts

NIAGARA PUMPHOUSE VISUAL ART CENTRE

The **Niagara Pumphouse Visual Art Centre** (247 Ricardo St., 905/468-5455, www.niagarapumphouse.ca, noon-4pm Mon.-Fri., 1pm-4pm Sat.-Sun. May-Nov., free) reminds us not to judge a book by its cover. The outside of this brick building is Victorian and blocky, but the interior explodes with creativity. This building once housed the pumps that brought water to the village of Niagara-on-the-Lake. Today, it is home to the work of local artists and provides a space for new artists to learn their craft. Exhibitions change frequently, so check the website for updated information.

RIVERBRINK ART MUSEUM

The benefactor of the **Riverbrink Art Museum** (116 Queenston St., 905/262-4510, www.riverbrink.org, 10am-5pm daily late May-Oct., 10am-5pm Wed.-Sat. Nov.-late May, $5 adults, $4 seniors and students, children 12 and under free), Samuel Weir, liked the facility so much that he is buried in the yard. Weir, an eccentric art collector and successful lawyer, found beauty in many things, especially art. His passion for collecting works is manifest in this museum, which was his home and is now his permanent resting place.

The museum focuses on the works of Canadian fine artists, as well as other works of historical events. Many pieces depict life in southern Ontario, including a collection of paintings from the War of 1812 era. The museum is also well known for its Inuit sculpture. There are more than 1,000 pieces in its collection, plus a robust exhibition schedule.

Festivals and Events

Start the new year properly by attending the **Niagara Icewine Festival** (www.niagarawinefestival.com), hosted by wineries throughout the Niagara region in the latter three weeks of January. Imagine drinking wine from a glass made of freshly carved ice or roasting ice wine marshmallows over a fire accompanied by a perfectly paired vintage. This festival marries two things for which southern Ontario is famous: good wine and freezing cold weather! It's a great reason to be outside. Tasting fees vary by winery. Events are open to people of all ages; sparkling grape juice is substituted for wine for underage participants, or those who avoid alcohol.

April-September, the stage is set in Niagara-on-the-Lake for the **Shaw Festival** (www.shawfest.com, $24-117). The Shaw Festival started in 1962 and has grown to become a major Canadian festival, drawing 250,000 people to performances each year. Each year, at least 10 new productions are brought to the stages of four theaters in NOTL. The festival is known for encouraging ingenious twists on

© JOEL A. DOMBROWSKI-NIAGARA FALLS WALKING TOURS

All of Niagara-on-the-Lake is a stage during the Shaw Festival.

existing plays. One such production, of *Joan,* the story of Joan of Arc, portrayed the story as occurring during the Balkan conflicts of the 1990s. The Shaw Festival has attracted dignitaries like Queen Elizabeth II, Indira Gandhi, and Canadian prime minister Pierre Trudeau.

SHOPPING

Queen Street has an eclectic group of shops where you can buy wine, clothing, and Canadian-themed gifts. Shops here tend to skew to the high end, but given the unique nature of many of the shops, including ones that specialize in authentic Irish and Scottish wares, it's worth the splurge. A listing of Queen Street shops is found on the official NOTL website (www.niagaraonthelake.com).

The **Beau Chapeau Hat Shop** (42 Queen St., 905/468-8011, www.beauchapeau.com, 9:30am-6pm Mon.-Thurs., 9:30am-8pm Fri. and Sun., 9am-8pm Sat.) is a gorgeous, 1920s-themed store. It has more than 6,000 hats and accessories for men and women.

The 560-mile Bruce Trail follows the Niagara Escarpment.

© JOEL A. DOMBROWSKI-NIAGARA FALLS WALKING TOURS

Irish Design (75 Queen St., 905/468-7233, www.irishdesign.com, 9:30am-5:30pm Mon.-Fri., 9:30am-6pm Sat., 10am-6pm Sun.) is as quaint as Ireland is green. The selection of women's and men's sweaters, jackets, and coats is truly grand. In addition to clothing, you'll find accessories and official Guinness merchandise. Relax in the shop's Irish Tea Room and try a slice of Bushmills whiskey cake.

For the wee bit of Scot in all of us, try the **Wee Scottish Loft** (13 Queen St., 905/468-0965, www.scottishloft.com, 10am-5pm daily). This small shop caters to those interested in gifts, foods, and media from England, Wales, and Scotland. If you're in the market for a kilt, a Union Jack pillow, authentic sticky toffee sponge pudding, or Benny Hill DVDs, you've found your place!

Find thousands of reasons to ignore your diet at the **Rocky Mountain Chocolate Factory** (70 Queen St., 905/468-0800, www.rockychoc.com, 10am-7pm daily May-Oct., 10am-5pm daily Nov.-Apr.). Many of the confections are handmade on-site, including caramels, candy apples, nut clusters, and toffees. For calorie-counters, there are sugar-free sweets and frozen yogurt. The shop also sells pet treats that are cocoa bean free, and safe for your pooch to eat.

RECREATION
Hiking

The granddaddy of Ontario hiking trails is the **Bruce Trail** (http://brucetrail.org), which stretches 550 miles north of Queenston to Tobermory along Georgian Bay. The Bruce Trail generally follows the Niagara Escarpment and is Canada's oldest and longest footpath. It's also a UNESCO World Biosphere Reserve that traverses public and private lands.

The Niagara section of the Bruce Trail covers an 11.5-mile route from Queenston to St. Catharines through forested, rural, and urban areas. Hiking this portion of the trail will take you past the Niagara River, along vineyards, and through mature forests as you ascend 40 feet in elevation. The Bruce is an out-and-back trail, so consider turning around where the Bruce Trail intersects the Upper Canada Heritage Trail (at 2.6 miles on the Bruce Trail).

The Queenston to St. Catharines section of the Bruce Trail is well maintained and accessible for hikers of all levels. The southern terminus for the Bruce Trail is in Queenston Heights Park (14184 Niagara Pkwy.). Look for a cairn in the main parking lot of Queenston Heights, near the entrance roundabout, and follow the white blaze markers.

Cycling

The **Vineyards & Blossoms Trail** is a 25-mile bike route that gives an excellent overview of NOTL. The route begins in the heart of NOTL, looping along the Niagara River Recreational Trail, the Lake Ontario Waterfront Trail, and through miles of vineyards. Should you desire a rest stop, there are eight wineries for you to investigate on this trail.

Looking to rent a bike? **Zoom Leisure Bikes** (431 Mississauga St., 905/468-2366, www.zoomleisure.com, 9am-5pm daily June-Aug., full-day rental $30) will rent you everything you need. Reservations are required September-May.

ACCOMMODATIONS

One of the finest hotels in Niagara-on-the-Lake is the 🄲 **Queen's Landing** (155 Byron St., 888/669-5566, www.vintage-hotels.com, $300). Styled as a Georgian mansion, the hotel is close to all the main attractions in NOTL and just a few steps from the waterfront. Standard rooms are not overly large, but have nice amenities, including a Keurig coffeemaker and turndown service with a rose left on the pillow. Queen's Landing is one of three luxury properties operated by Vintage Hotels in NOTL. The other two, **Prince of Wales** (6 Picton St., 905/468-3246, www.vintage-hotels. com, $320) and **Pillar and Post** (48 John St. W., 905/468-2123, www.vintage-hotels.com, $300) offer similar excellent accommodations.

Niagara-on-the-Lake is home to more than 150 bed-and-breakfasts. The **BranCliff Inn** (40 Platoff St., 905/468-8800, http://bran> cliffinn. com, $210) is among the top choices. Located just one block away from Queen Street and the Shaw Festival Theatre, BranCliff exudes charm and comfort. All six rooms have bathrooms en suite, and five have gas fireplaces. The inn dates back to 1859 and has been tastefully renovated to maintain the historic sense of the structure, while providing modern comforts such as Wi-Fi and refrigerators stocked with complimentary drinks.

Enjoy English elegance at the **Historic Lyons House B&B** (8 Centre St., 905/468-2297, www.lyonshouse.ca, $195). Inside this 1835 home are three spacious guestrooms with a Georgian period theme and paintings by local Canadian artist Linda Hankin. Outside, enjoy the half-acre traditional English garden with its lush green lawn, fountain, shade trees, and friendly cat.

Abacot Hall B&B (508 Mississagua St., 905/468-8383, www.abacothall.com, May-Dec., $155) is a short walk away from NOTL's shopping, dining, and theater district. The B&B's three suites are decorated in a Victorian theme and include en suite bathrooms. Free Wi-Fi, a full breakfast, and the use of bicycles are also provided, compliments of the owners, Irene and Ed.

A three-course breakfast served on a spacious veranda is among the treats awaiting you at the **Wine Country B&B** (75 John St. W., 905/468-8701, www.winecountrybb.com, $155). All three guestrooms have en suite baths, comfortable queen-size beds, and warm color schemes. The largest of the three rooms, the Queenston Suite, has rich redwood furniture and a private balcony. Your hosts, Jeff and John, will make recommendations for visiting wineries and attractions. The front veranda is excellent for enjoying a glass of wine while you watch the sunset and recover from a long day of touring.

FOOD

Pub fare, history, and a ghost are on the menu at the 🄲 **Olde Angel Inn** (224 Regent St., 905/468-3411, www.angel-inn.com, 11am-1am daily, $17). This authentic British pub serves pub grub, such as ploughman's lunch (traditional English midday meal of bread, cheese,

Old Town Goodies lives up to its name.

eggs, and beer) and shepherd's pie. The food is reasonably priced and served promptly. The hand-hewn wood beams of the short ceiling and wood-burning fireplace feel as if you're stepping into a pub in the misty English countryside. Olde Angel is reportedly haunted by the ghost of Colonel Colin Swayze, a British officer who was killed by American soldiers while visiting his beloved, a woman who worked at the former pub here. Legend has it that an apparition appears in the mirror of the ladies' restroom and that the taps of American draft beers mysteriously open, causing the American beer to flow into the drain.

If you're on Queen Street and you need good food fast, head to **Old Town Goodies** (29 Queen St., 289/868-9603, 10am-9pm daily, $7.50). The shop is set up for takeout orders only. The food is fresh and prepared quickly while you wait. The menu is a good selection of paninis and salads, with no item over $8. The Red Coat Reuben ($7) and the Butler's BBQ Steak ($8) are both wonderfully satisfying and a bit messy to eat, so take plenty of napkins with you. Old

Town Goodies is also great for a quick espresso or an ice-cream cone. In a town of high-end eateries, this ma-and-pa joint (operated by generations of the Pullman family) is short on pretense and big on value.

The **Charles Restaurant** (209 Queen St., 905/468-4588, www.niagarasfinest.com, 5pm-8pm Mon.-Fri., 11am-3pm and 5pm-8pm Sat.-Sun., $35) offers fine dining in a distinguished atmosphere. Meals are served in the exquisite dining room of the 1832 mansion in the northern end of NOTL. Entrées are uniformly good, but don't skimp on the appetizers. The spiced sweet potato velouté and the roasted pear salad are pricey, but worth it.

For great Asian food at reasonable prices, go to the **Ginger Restaurant** (390 Mary St., 905/468-3871, www.gingerrestaurant.ca, 5pm-9pm Wed.-Sun., $22). The dining room is small, with a capacity of only 40 people, but it's warm and inviting. Ginger's menu is a fusion of Japanese, Chinese, and Thai cuisine served American style. Reservations are recommended, especially if you are planning to eat before or after a performance at one of the Shaw Festival theaters, all within walking distance.

Bistro Six-One (61 Queen St., 905/468-2532, www.bistrosixone.com, 11am-9pm Sun.-Thurs., 11am-10pm Fri.-Sat., $18) offers an alternative to high-priced restaurants along Queen Street. The feel is casual and the menu is contemporary Canadian, as evidenced by the wonderful maple salmon dish. Another highlight is the pizza cooked in wood-burning brick ovens—try the potato bacon pizza for a warm and filling meal. The bistro provides tastings of local wines at the bar.

Find contemporary Mediterranean food at the **Old Winery Restaurant** (2228 Niagara Stone Rd., 905/468-8900, www.theoldwineryrestaurant.com, 11:30am-9pm Sun.-Wed., 11:30am-10pm Thurs., 11:30am-midnight Fri.-Sat., $18). As the name suggests, the building is a renovated winery that is now a casual restaurant and wine bar. As soon as you walk in the door, you can see and smell the brick pizza oven. If you enjoy dining to live music, take a table in the Wine Lounge where they have music acts each Friday and Saturday evening.

You'll never be late for a show at the Shaw Festival if you dine at **⟨** **Zees Grill** (92 Picton St., 905/468-5715, www.zees.ca, 8am-10am, 11:30am-2:30pm, and 5pm-9pm daily May-Nov., $25). Zees is right across the street from the Shaw Festival Theatre. Weather permitting, reserve a table on the front patio and experience one of the most beautiful dining venues in NOTL. Chef Jason Dobbie takes pride in adding creative twists to traditional dishes at this casual fine dining joint, such as his wonderful Nova Scotia lobster poutine. Several popular dishes also have vegan versions and there is a wide variety of local wines. Appetizers are a bit pricey ($14 average); desserts are wonderful, especially the local honey and ginger crème brûlée.

Chef Stephen Treadwell has a simple food philosophy. Prepare dishes with as few ingredients as possible, and be sure they're locally sourced. This has been a recipe for success at **Treadwell Farm-to-Table Cuisine** (114 Queen St., 905/934-9797, www.treadwellcuisine.com, 11:30am-3pm and 5pm-10pm Wed.-Mon.,

$30). Treadwell's restaurant has the feel of a modern bistro with small tables tightly packed and a serving counter where patrons can watch food being prepared as they eat.

The **Stone Road Grill** (238 Mary St., 905/468-3474, www.stoneroadgrille.com, 11:30am-2pm and 5pm-10pm Tues.-Sun., $27) is a truly hidden gem. Tucked inside a bland strip mall, the restaurant has no sign. Despite this, the Stone Road Grill is widely known by locals as the best place to eat in NOTL. Inside, the restaurant is dark, eclectic, and perfect for casual fine dining. As the menu changes to accommodate seasonally available ingredients, it is difficult to single out any specific dish for recommendation—they are all excellent. Attached to the restaurant is a separate takeout counter that operates the same hours as the restaurant. The grill's exterior signs read "REST," the remnants of the previous owner's restaurant sign. The new owners embraced the mistake and have not changed it since they first opened in 2003.

GETTING THERE AND AROUND

Most motorists driving to Niagara-on-the-Lake from Niagara Falls take the Niagara Parkway, which takes you directly to NOTL. There are other, more complicated routes that involve highways and back roads, but they won't get you there any faster. Resign yourself to driving 35 miles per hour and enjoy the scenic 25-minute ride.

Street parking in the main tourist area is metered, as are the five nearby public parking lots. Rates are reasonable and range $1-1.50 per hour. Machines accept credit cards or Canadian coins, but not U.S. currency. A complete map of street parking and public parking lots is online (www.niagaraonthelake.com).

This area is easily navigated on foot. The main drag is Queen Street, where you'll find many restaurants, shops, and theaters. The area of interest to visitors is roughly a seven-by seven-block area bisected by Queen Street. There is a small public transit system in NOTL, but it is geared toward transporting residents into central NOTL for work. There is one portion of the NOTL Transit System (www.notl.org) that may be of use for travelers. From May-October, daily **shuttle buses** connecting the Old Court House and Fort George run every 10 minutes. One-way fare is CAN$3; you'll need exact change in Canadian currency.

Hours of operation vary by day and month, so check the website for the most accurate information. The Old Court House faces Queen Street, but the bus stop is located behind the building on a service road connecting two public parking lots.

Wine Country

You may think Canada is all cold weather and maple syrup. Think again! The Niagara-on-the-Lake region contains more than 30 wineries and is the center for the crafting of world-class wines in Canada. Whether you tour by car, bus, or bike, you can taste the spirit of Niagara in every wine you sample in this region.

"Wine country" refers to the approximately 42 square miles of fertile plain bounded by Route 405 to the south, the Niagara River to the east, Lake Ontario to the north, and the Welland Canal to the west.

Most people exploring wine country find accommodations in Niagara-on-the-Lake. A majority of people use their cars to explore while others hop on a tour bus. It is impractical to walk to wineries because of the distances involved, but cycling through wine country is gaining in popularity.

WINERIES
Inniskillin Winery

All contemporary Canadian wineries have roots that reach back to the **Inniskillin Winery** (1499 Line 3 Rd., NOTL, 888/466-4754, www.inniskillin.com, 10am-6pm daily May-Oct., 10am-5pm daily Nov.-Apr., tasting fee $1 per sample). In the early 1970s, the founders of Inniskillin decided to create world-class wines and were granted the first winery license in Ontario since the Prohibition era.

Their work of cultivating wine grapes adapted to Ontario's unique climate launched an entire industry. Driving into the winery, you'll notice architecture with hints of Frank Lloyd Wright. The estate originally belonged to

Darwin Martin, who employed Wright to build several structures in the Buffalo area.

Although many of the vintages have received medals at tasting competitions, Inniskillin is particularly known for its ice wines. Tours ($5) are available and the Market Grill (open daily during summer) offers food pairings to complement their wines.

Château de Charmes

Another pioneer in Ontario winemaking is the Bosc family, owners of the **Château de Charmes Winery** (1025 York Rd., St. Davids, 905/262-4219, www.fromtheboscfamily.com, 10am-6pm daily, tasting fee $10). The Bosc family championed the exclusive cultivation of *vitis vinifera,* the European grape varieties known to yield the finest wines. They were on the vanguard of agritourism and built the sprawling Château des Charmes Winery and Visitors Centre. Tours are held daily ($10) in English, French, and Japanese.

Peller Estates

On the outskirts of Niagara-on-the-Lake, just before you drive into the village, there's a stunning estate surrounded by vineyards. **Peller Estates** (290 John St. E., NOTL, 905/468-4678, www.peller.com, 10am-9pm Fri.-Sat., 10am-7pm Sun.-Thurs., tasting fee $7) is a gorgeous winery with a first-class restaurant that should not be missed.

Upon entering the winery, a fireplace with comfortable couches greets you. The structure is spacious, yet warm and inviting. To the left is the wine boutique, where tastings are available. To the right is the winery's restaurant, which

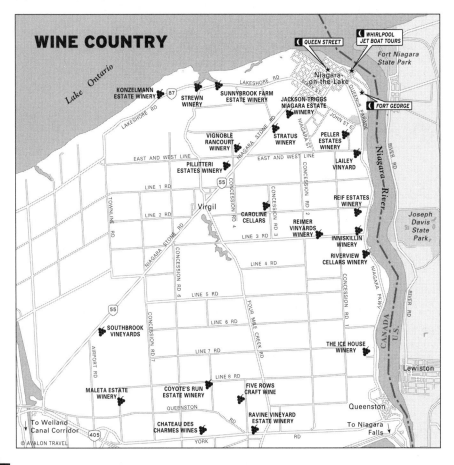

WINE COUNTRY

Lake Ontario

To Welland Canal Corridor

To Niagara Falls

© AVALON TRAVEL

has received Zagat's highest culinary rating (Extraordinary). Tours are offered daily ($10); the cost is deducted from any purchases made.

Stratus Vineyards

Stratus Vineyards (2059 Niagara Stone Rd., NOTL, 905/468-1806, www.stratuswines. com, 11am-5pm daily May-Dec., noon-5pm Wed.-Sun. Jan.-Apr., tour and tasting fee $20) is a modern winery dedicated to making top-quality wine while reducing the impact of that process on the environment. This is the only LEED (Leadership in Energy & Environmental Design) certified winery in Canada. The wines

here are limited production, which means that many vintages are only available on-site and not sold in stores. Stratus is renowned for its premium single-varietal reds and whites.

Jackson-Triggs Niagara Estate Winery

The architecture is as stunning as the wines at **Jackson-Triggs Niagara Estate Winery** (2145 Niagara Stone Rd., NOTL, 905/468-4637, www.jacksontriggswinery.com, 10am-6:30pm daily June-mid-Sept., 10am-5:30pm daily mid-Sept.-May, tasting fee $1-3). A magnificent, modern glass-and-metal barn greets you at the entrance. Its two huge sliding doors open in the summer, allowing visitors to pass through the building directly to the vineyards. The atmosphere is open, airy, and inviting. Tours (10:30am-5:30pm daily, $5) are offered every half-hour.

Jackson-Triggs offers a full spectrum of wines. The Entourage Grand Reserve Sparkling Brut 2009 is among its best. The winery also has a summer season of live concerts at its 500-seat outdoor amphitheater.

Reif Estate Winery

While many NOTL winery operations have an Italian or French heritage, **Reif Estate Winery** (15608 Niagara Pkwy., NOTL, 905/468-9463, www.reifwinery.com, 10am-6pm daily Apr.-Oct., 10am-5pm daily Nov.-Mar., tour and tasting fee $5) has its roots in the Rhine River Valley of Germany. The winery produces a complete range of good varietals; try Reif's Vidal Icewine ($47), which is an international medal winner.

Caroline Cellars

Caroline Cellars (1028 Line 2 Rd., Virgil, 905/468-8814, www.carolinecellars.com, 10am-5pm daily Jan.-Mar., 10am-6pm daily Apr.-Dec., free tastings) is a family-owned and -operated winery that distinguishes itself by producing fruit wines in addition to traditional reds and whites. Both the Plum Wine ($11.50) and the Cranberry Winter Harvest Wine ($22.50) were medal winners in 2013.

Coyote's Run Estate Winery

Coyote's Run Estate Winery (485 Concession 5 Rd., St. Davids, 905/682-8310, www.coyotesrunwinery.com, 10am-6pm daily June-Oct., 10am-5pm daily Nov.-May, $10 tasting fee) has two different types of soil within its vineyards, and you can taste the difference in the wines. This attention to detail has helped Coyote's Run earn a ranking as one of Canada's top 20 wineries. The winery features small-batch, nuanced wines, with a reputation for excellent pinot noirs (2011 Black Paw Vineyard Pinot Noir $29.95).

Trius Winery at Hillebrand

Trius Winery at Hillebrand (1249 Niagara Stone Rd., NOTL, 905/468-7123, www.triuswines.com, 10am-9pm daily Apr.-June, 10am-7pm Sun.-Thurs., 10am-9pm Fri.-Sat., Sept.-May, $10 tasting fee) was the first winery in NOTL to have a restaurant on-site. Today, this spirit of innovation continues. Hillebrand focuses on the wine-tasting experience, with an emphasis on the splendor of pairing wine with the proper food. Throughout the year, more than a dozen different tours and tastings are offered, each a unique experience. If you like red wine, try the Trius Red ($23). It is a blend of cabernet franc, cabernet sauvignon, and merlot grapes and was designated as the world's best red wine at the prestigious International Wine and Spirits Competition in London.

Between the Lines Winery

You'll taste local pride in every bottle of wine at the **Between the Lines Winery** (991 Four Mile Creek Rd., NOTL, 905/262-0289, www.betweenthelineswinery.com, 10am-6pm daily Apr.-Oct., 11am-5pm Tues.-Sun. Nov.-Mar., tasting fee $1 per sample). This small family winery is operated by the Wertsch brothers who believe that vintners should trust the local grape varieties, rather than imitate those grown elsewhere. Their philosophy has resulted in wines that lack pretense, with the true taste of Niagara.

At this proud boutique winery, wines are small-batch and only sold on-site in the big red barn. For a unique wine, try the Lemberger Red. Between the Lines is the only local winery to use Lemberger grapes. Finding the winery is easy. It's on Four Mile Creek Road, between Line Five and Line Six Roads.

FOOD

Not content with simply baking their own bread, staff members at **☾ Ravine Winery Restaurant** (1366 York Rd., St. Davids, 905/262-8463, www.ravinevineyard.com, 11am-9pm Wed.-Sun., $25) locally source all their ingredients. That means growing their own grapes and herbs and raising their own livestock. This über-organic philosophy results in well-paired food and wine, along with interesting conversations with employees who enjoy describing your dish's origin. The restaurant's exterior is that of a simple prairie home, while the interior has a simple, but warm ambience with plenty of wood and rustic earth tones. For every entrée on the menu, there is a suggested wine pairing. The braised lamb shank and 2010 Estate Merlot perfectly complement each other.

Most restaurants could learn a thing or two from **Benchmark** (135 Taylor Rd., NOTL, 905/641-2252, www.niagaracollege.ca, 11:30am-2pm Tues., 11:30am-2pm and 5pm-9pm Wed.-Sat., $25), a teaching restaurant on the campus of Niagara College, where students cook under the supervision of teachers and professional chefs. The emphasis here is on locally sourced ingredients. The grain-fed Ontario chicken has a wonderful ice wine stuffing ($25) and the slow braised lamb shank has a side of feta cheese made from Ontario goat milk. The restaurant is modern, mixing wood and metal in its design, with glass windows overlooking the local vineyards and farms.

You can savor the art of wine and food pairing at the **Trius Winery Restaurant** (1249 Niagara Stone Rd., NOTL, 905/468-7123, www.triuswines.com, 10am-9pm daily Apr.-June, 10am-7pm Sun.-Thurs., 10am-9pm Fri.-Sat. Sept.-May, $50-120), located on the grounds of the Trius Winery. The menu optimizes the wine-food relationship. Dinner pairings at Trius start at $50 per person; a special five-course pairing dinner is $120 per person. The restaurant is a stunning stone building with high ceilings, hardwood floors, and a contemporary feel. Large floor-to-ceiling windows add to the bright and natural ambience of the dining area. When the weather is nice, head to the outdoor patio. It has a beautiful view of the vineyards gently rolling out before the distant escarpment, and the sound of the large fountain drowns out background noise.

The **❲** **Peller Estates Winery Restaurant** (290 John St. E., NOTL, 888/673-5537, www.peller.com, noon-2:30pm and 5:30pm-8:30pm Sun.-Fri. noon-2:30pm and 5pm-8:30pm Sat.,

$41) sets the standard for winery dining in NOTL. The winery is a massive French château surrounded by picturesque lawns and vineyards. At the entrance, you are greeted by a large, warm fireplace and stairs that wrap around to the restaurant. The vaulted ceiling of the indoor dining area creates a spacious yet intimate setting. The outdoor patio is wonderful, affording great views of the vineyards while you eat. The menu philosophy here is different from other restaurants, with dishes served à la carte. However, many diners come here for Chef Jason Parsons' signature menu, which features five-course ($129) and seven-course ($154) dinners with wine pairings. Although pricey, the seven-course dinner is a real treat. If you choose this option, make reservations by a window or out on the patio for 6:30pm and enjoy the beautiful sunset.

As you walk into the **Pie Plate Bakery and Cafe** (1516 Niagara Stone Rd., Virgil, 905/468-9743, www.thepieplate.com, 10am-6pm Tues.-Sun., $11), your nose immediately will confirm that all the food here is homemade. This delightful restaurant is small, comfortable, and warm, with a French country ambience. The Pie Plate shines if you're looking for a light lunch served quickly at a reasonable price. Try the pear-and-brie sandwich on a baguette ($9). The thin-crust pizzas are superb, especially the Chicken Run ($14) with roasted chicken, marinated artichoke hearts, and asiago cheese. As you might imagine, the baked goods are wonderful, too. Pies, tortes, and other flaky confections are made with local fruit and are perfect for dessert or a midday snack with coffee. You may dine here or take out.

GETTING THERE AND AROUND

The most popular ways to tour wineries are by car, bus, or bike. If you're making a day of it and want to include lunch or dinner, planning ahead is essential. You can make your own map or use an online map generator (www.winecountryontario.ca).

Bus tours are popular in NOTL because they

are safe, fun, and convenient. Many tour operators will pick you up and drop you off at your hotel. **Grape and Wine Tours** (855/682-4920, www.grapeandwinetours.com) provides pick-up service from Niagara Falls or NOTL. Its four-hour, three-winery tour is $65. **Grape Escape Wine Tours** (866/935-4445, www.tourniagarawineries.com) offer pick-ups in NOTL (Niagara Falls pick-up is extra) for its four-hour, four-winery tour ($59). **Niagara Wine Tours International** (800/680-7006, www.niagaraworldwinetours.com) makes pick-ups in NOTL, Niagara Falls, or St. Catharines. The four-hour, four-winery tour is $65.

A fun and healthy way to tour wine country is by bike. Several reputable companies provide bike rentals and escorted bike winery tours. **Grape Escape Wine Tours** (215 King St., NOTL, 866/935-4445, www.tourniagarawineries.com) has a six-hour tour that includes bike rental, lunch, and several winery visits ($69). Free pick-up and drop-off shuttle service is provided. **Zoom Leisure Bikes** (431 Mississauga St., NOTL, 905/468-2366, www.zoomleisure.com, June-Aug.) offers a three-hour tour to three wineries ($69). There's also a five-hour picnic lunch winery tour ($90). Both tours include bike rental.

Niagara Getaway (92 Picton St., NOTL, 905/468-1300, www.niagaragetaways.com, $65-139) is located directly across from the Shaw Festival Theatre in NOTL. This company has the greatest variety of guided and self-guided bicycle winery tours available in the area. **Niagara Wine Tours International** (32 Queen St., NOTL, 905/468-7367, www.niagaraworldwinetours.com, $69-89) is conveniently located on Queen Street in NOTL, where bike tours originate from. Tours are self-guided and include lunch.

Welland Canal Corridor

A 25-mile line cuts through Ontario's Niagara peninsula joining Lake Ontario and Lake Erie: the Welland Canal. The canal has shaped the economic fortunes of this region, drawing people to small towns along it since the early 1800s. Towns such as St. Catharines, Welland, Thorold, and Port Colborne were founded and then thrived because of this waterway.

Today, the towns along the canal look to the Welland Canal for transportation, as well as recreation, tourism, and community identity. Together, they make up a vibrant corridor that redefines the role of the Welland Canal and embraces its industrial heritage. Tourists who view the magnificent lake freighters on the canal are discovering reasons to stay longer: engaging museums, heritage sites, and entertaining festivals.

Adjacent to the southern portion of the canal is Fort Erie. This fort is steeped in the history of the War of 1812, when it guarded the mouth of the Niagara River and witnessed Canada's bloodiest battle. Today, the fort's guns are quiet; the former fortress is now a symbol of 200 years of peace between Canada and the United States.

ST. CATHARINES

Known as the garden city because it contains more than 1,000 acres of parkland and trails, St. Catharines is the Niagara region's largest municipality. This region is where the Welland Canal was developed by its tireless champion William Hamilton Merritt. Merritt had served for the crown during the War of 1812 when he devised the idea to create a canal to bypass Niagara Falls. St. Catharines grew in population, political importance, and wealth as the Welland Canal prospered.

During the mid-1800s, the city earned a reputation for supporting the abolitionist movement. Former and escaped slaves found a welcoming community in St. Catharines; by 1850, 800 of the town's 6,000 residents were black.

The city's population soared from 40,000 in

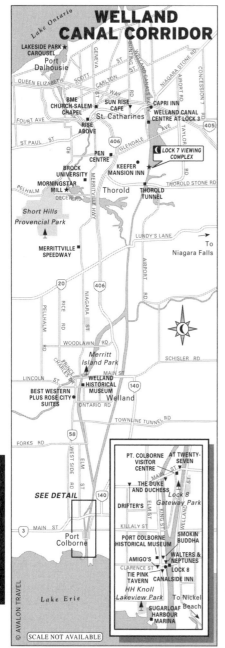

1950 to 130,000 by the 1980s due to the availability of manufacturing jobs at plants like GM of Canada. Since the turn of the century, St. Catharines has seen manufacturing jobs being replaced by jobs in the service industry, especially for call centers.

St. Catharines Museum and Welland Canals Centre

To get any closer to a lake freighter, you'd have to be a sailor! The **St. Catharines Museum and Welland Canals Centre** (1932 Welland Canals Pkwy., 905/984-8880, www.stcatharines.ca, 9am-5pm daily, $4 suggested donation) gives you a front-row seat as huge ships ascend and descend 45 feet in this lock. You'll be amazed at how these behemoth vessels ease through the lock with just a few feet to spare on either side. Wave to the sailors and try to guess what the ship is carrying (40 million metric tons of goods traverse the canal each year).

The museum is small, but packed with information on the Welland Canal and local history. The staff is quite friendly and knowledgeable. Ships ply the Welland Canal April-December. Call on the morning of your visit to find out when ships are passing through Lock 3. The Lock 3 viewing platform is free and open to the public. Visitors usually spend about an hour here, watching the lock in action and investigating the museum.

The Salem Chapel, British Methodist Episcopal Church

When slavery was legal in the United States, many escaped slaves found freedom and refuge in Canada. **The Salem Chapel, British Methodist Episcopal Church** (92 Geneva St., 905/682-0993, www.salemchapelbmechurch.ca, tours by appointment, $3) is among the most important stops on the Underground Railroad.

Originally built in the 1820s, the church was expanded in 1851 to meet the needs of the growing congregation. Abolitionist Harriet Tubman lived in St. Catharines in 1851-1858 and was among the church's members. The church functioned as Tubman's home base as she rescued slaves from plantations in the southern United States. The building today is a simple chapel, having retained some of its original 1851 architecture, including benches hewn from walnut logs. The predominantly black congregation is believed to be the oldest of its kind in Ontario. This church is one of many Underground Railroad heritage sites in southern Ontario.

Port Dalhousie and Lakeside Park Carousel

At one time, **Port Dalhousie** (www.port-dalhousielife.com) was the terminus for the Welland Canal. Modern improvements have changed that, but Port Dalhousie still maintains its waterfront charm. This community of St. Catharines has waterfront access, beaches, historic lighthouses, and the original pier of the second Welland Canal. While most of St. Catharines is urban, Port Dalhousie is more like a beachside resort. On weekends, locals and visitors alike take the 15-minute drive from the city center to enjoy Port Dalhousie's lake views, beaches, and sunsets.

One of the major attractions in Port Dalhousie is the **Lakeside Park Carousel** (1 Lakeport Rd., 905/934-1221, www.stcatharines.ca, 10am-9pm daily June-Aug.) This stunning antique carousel was donated to the local government with one string attached—the fare for riding the carousel could never be more than a nickel. That promise has been kept and, for just five cents, you can hop aboard and ride upon any of 68 different animals.

The ride was originally built between 1898 and 1905 in Brooklyn. It has been lovingly restored and maintained. Depending on the weather, visitors can spend an hour or more exploring the lighthouses, shops, and sights in Port Dalhousie.

Morningstar Mill

Step back in time with a visit to the **Morningstar Mill** (2714 Decew Rd., 905/688-6050, www.morningstarmill.ca, 9am-1pm Tues. and Thurs., 10am-3pm Sat.-Sun. mid-May-Oct., free). After emigrating from Bavaria,

Wilson Morningstar settled in the American colonies. Being a loyalist, he left the states and moved to Canada during the American Revolution. Eventually, he purchased this tract of land near the Decew Falls and harvested the moving water to power a grist mill.

Today, the original Morningstar house and mill remain. Other structures here are faithful reproductions of 19th-century agricultural buildings. You can tour the buildings as volunteer docents recount the story of the Morningstar family and life during the early 1800s. The grounds are quite picturesque. Plan on spending an hour here. Call ahead to check if the mill is open for tours, since it is staffed by volunteers and hours of operation can vary day to day.

THOROLD

Just five minutes south of St. Catharines is the historic canal city of Thorold (www.thoroldtourism.ca). It is here that the Welland Canal climbs up the Niagara Escarpment.

◖ Lock 7 Viewing Complex

The **Lock 7 Viewing Complex** (50 Chapel St. S., 905/680-9477, www.thoroldtourism.ca, 9am-7:30pm daily July-Aug., 9am-4pm daily June and Sept., free) is perched atop the Niagara Escarpment, which allows you to view Locks 4-7. From this vantage point, you also can see Niagara Falls in the distance as freighters pass through the locks and climb the escarpment. It is truly amazing to see ships 740 feet by 77 feet glide through the locks with just a few feet to spare on either side. When a vessel completes its journey through the Welland Canal, it has been raised or lowered more than 30 stories.

When the indoor viewing area is open, enjoy a complimentary maple syrup cookie and a copy of *Tommy Trent of the Welland Canal*, an informative guide to the basics of the Welland Canal. The staff at the complex can answer questions about the canal and the region's attractions. They may tell you about the legend of the Kissing Rock, which is along the canal near the viewing complex. Lore has it that a

The Welland Canals Centre has viewing platforms so you can watch boats traverse the canal.

handsome sailor known as Charles Snelgrove would bring his lady friends to the rock for one last kiss before setting sail. Other mariners heard of this ritual and soon began bringing their partners to the rock for a proper send-off. Sailors are a superstitious lot so the Kissing Rock became a tradition, and is said to bring good luck to those who use it wisely.

Plan on spending an hour at the viewing complex, depending on how many boats are in the locks and how long you'd like to embrace at the Kissing Rock.

PORT COLBORNE

Port Colborne (www.portcolborne.ca) is the southernmost lock on the Welland Canal. It has the ambience of a small canal town. Emigration here started in 1790, with the population surging after completion of the first Welland Canal in 1833. As a gateway to Lake Erie, Port Colborne serves as a hub for many seasonal cottage residents who flock to the quaint canal area for its shops and restaurants.

The **Port Colborne Historical and Marine Museum** (280 King St., 905/834-7604, www.portcolborne.ca, noon-5pm daily May-Dec., free) is a treasure for history lovers. The museum consists of a small campus of buildings restored to their 19th-century charm. The museum's main site is the 1869 Georgian revival-style home and carriage house of Arabella Williams. The campus also includes a log cabin schoolhouse, a marine blacksmith shop, and a reproduction of the parapet of Port Colborne's lighthouse. The museum has marine artifacts such as the wheelhouse from a tugboat and a lifeboat from the S.S. *Hochelaga*. Top off your visit to the museum with a light afternoon tea at Arabella's Tea Room, a fully restored 1915 Edwardian cottage that is small, but elegant.

Port Colborne is a great spot for watching massive boats navigate through the locks. Port Colborne's Lock 8 is among the longest in the world, at 1,380 feet. Most visitors will only need to spend two hours in Port Colborne.

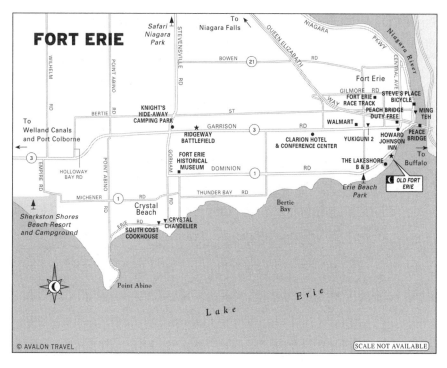

FORT ERIE

Fort Erie (www.forteriecanada.com) is a vibrant border town, just across the Niagara River from Buffalo, and 18 miles south of Niagara Falls. In the heart of vacation country, Fort Erie's population swells from 30,000 to 40,000 each summer as cottage dwellers flock to the area's beautiful beaches.

(Old Fort Erie

The site of Canada's bloodiest battlefield, **Old Fort Erie** (350 Lakeshore Rd., 905/871-0540, www.niagaraparksheritage.com, 10am-5pm daily mid-May-Aug., 10am-4pm Mon.-Fri., 10am-5pm Sat.-Sun. Sept.-Oct., $12.25 adults, $8 children 6-16) dates back to the late 1700s. In 1764, after Britain won the French and Indian War, redcoats built a modest fort near the water's edge along the Lake Erie shoreline. After the American Revolutionary War, Britain built a much larger fort a little farther inland,

which still guarded Lake Erie and the entrance to the Niagara River.

This national historic site comes alive each July when reenactors dramatize the 1814 siege of Fort Erie, which was Canada's most deadly battlefield. More than 1,000 British troops lost their lives, were injured or captured. The reenactment is a dramatic retelling of the violent clash that occurred when British troops attempted to capture the fort held by American forces. During the two-day reenactment, visitors can take guided tours of the fort as well as British and American troop encampments. The evening tour by lantern light is fun. Visitors will also witness various reenactments of skirmishes and assaults from the siege battle.

The fort offers visitors an authentic glimpse into the lives of the soldiers and families who occupied the fort in the 1800s. Restored buildings include the Guard Room, Soldiers' Barracks, and the Powder Magazine. The

Old Fort Erie stands guard over the eastern end of Lake Erie, where the Niagara River begins.

© THE NIAGARA PARKS COMMISSION

Officer's Quarters have real artifacts from an officer who lived here, such as the "traveling bed" of Capt. Kingsley of the 8th Regiment of Foot. The canopy bed and other portable furniture were constructed so officers could easily transport them.

Fort Erie is great fun for families; a visit will take about two hours.

FESTIVALS AND EVENTS

For 16 days from mid-May through early June, St. Catharines hosts the **Niagara Folk Art Festival** (St. Catharines, www.folk-arts.ca). Canada's longest running heritage festival celebrates diversity by highlighting the numerous cultures that call Ontario home. You'll experience music, dancing, food, and arts from a spectrum of cultures, including artists from Africa, Europe, and Asia. Events are hosted throughout St. Catharines, including the opening ceremonies on the front steps of St. Catharines City Hall.

St. Catharines also hosts Canada's largest single-day music festival. Known as **S.C.E.N.E.**

(St. Catharines, www.scenemusicfestival.com), it draws more than 140 bands and other musical acts to the city on the second Saturday in June. The Market Square (91 King St.) is the hub, with all music stages and venues within walking distance of each other. Music ranges from alternative to rock to folk, and the acts are mostly independent bands from Canada, although the festival now attracts international artists.

Have a blooming good time throughout June at the **Welland Rose Festival** (Welland, 905/732-7673, www.wellandrosefestival.on.ca). At several venues throughout the city, various events highlight Welland's traditions and talented citizens. Festivities include a baby contest, grand parade, juried art show, and coronation ball. The **Friendship Festival** (Fort Erie, 905/871-6454, www.friendshipfestival.com) celebrates the 200 years of peace shared by Canada and the United States, and is celebrated in both Fort Erie and Buffalo. Festivities are based at the Mather Arch (11 Niagara Pkwy.) in Fort Erie and include a midway with amusement rides, a kids/family fun zone, an art show, live music, and fireworks. The festival runs June 28-July 4.

In the first week of August, Port Colborne comes alive during its **Canal Days Festival** (Port Colborne, 888/767-8386, www.port-colborne.ca). For four days, tall sailing vessels arrive at Port Colborne and become the highlight of the festival. Visitors can board the ships, learn about maritime history, and go for a sail on Lake Erie. Each year, more than 300,000 visitors travel to Port Colborne to see the ships and other attractions, including a classic car show, a craft show, and nightly music entertainment.

SHOPPING
The Pen Centre

With more than 180 stores, **The Pen Centre** (221 Glendale Ave., St. Catharines, 905/687-6622, www.thepencentre.com, 10am-9pm Mon.-Fri., 9am-6pm Sat., 11am-6pm Sun.) is this area's largest mall. Among the most popular stores are Aeropostale, American Eagle, Sears, and The Bay. The Pen also features four restaurants and a 10-screen multiplex.

SPORTS AND RECREATION
Cycling

Cycling is growing in popularity in this region, and many adventurous cyclists are discovering the **Greater Niagara Circle Route** (www.regional.niagara.on.ca), an 86-mile loop of paved paths that join Lakes Erie and Ontario. The path is an amalgam of five trails along the Niagara River to the shore of Lake Ontario. The route follows the Welland Canal and then connects Port Colborne with Fort Erie.

There are 12 smaller bike loop routes within the region as well. Maps and descriptions are online at the **Cycle Niagara** website (www.cycleniagara.com), which has excellent information on accommodations and bike repair shops near the loop routes.

The wineries of Niagara-on-the-Lake are increasingly becoming a top destination for novice and veteran cyclists. Several retail tour operators offer escorted group tours through

wine country. For those who want to go at their own pace and customize a route, there's a map and an app online (www.niagararegion.ca).

For bike rentals in Fort Erie, contact **Steve's Place Bicycle and Repair** (181 Niagara Blvd., Fort Erie, 905/871-7517, www.cycleman.com, noon-6pm Tues.-Fri., 10am-3pm Sat., $25/day).

For bike rentals in Thorold, contact **Canal City Cycle** (23 Front St. S., Thorold, 905/964-8056, www.canalcitycycle.com, 8am-8pm daily, $30/day).

Horseback Riding

HorsePlay Niagara (11061 Ellsworth Rd. N., Port Colborne, 905/834-2380, www.horseplayniagara.com, daily by reservation only, $45/hr.) puts you in the saddle for leisurely rides along nature trails near Port Colborne. More experienced riders can gallop on the sands of a Lake Erie beach with their instructor ($60-$75).

Motorsports

Got the need for speed? **Merrittville Speedway** (2371 Merrittville Hwy., Thorold, 905/892-8266, Apr.-Sept., $12 adults, $5 children 8-12) has fast-paced action. Saturday evening stock-car races are the most popular events at the one-third mile banked clay speedway.

ACCOMMODATIONS

Thorold's Keefer Mansion Inn (14 St. Davids St. W., Thorold, 905/680-9581, www.keefermansion.com, $170) is the epitome of Victorian ambience. Once the 9,000-square-foot mansion of the prominent Keefer family, it now accommodates six B&B suites, each named after a Keefer family member. Rooms all have bathrooms en suite, queen-size beds, and antique touches right out of a Dickens novel. Rooms with east-facing windows allow a great view of ships passing through the Welland Canal's locks.

Cyclists will feel right at home at the **Talwood Manor** (303 Fielden Ave., Port Colborne, 905/348-5411, www.talwoodmanorbb.com, $120). The manor is a B&B with four rooms and all the comforts of home. Cyclists will like the manor's proximity to trails and indoor overnight bike storage. The B&B's hostess makes you feel right at home by providing wine before dinner, tea, cookies, and genuinely caring service.

Affordable, clean, and conveniently located, the **Capri Inn** (391 Ontario St., St. Catharines, 905/684-8515, www.capriinn.com, $105) in St. Catharines has everything a value-conscious traveler needs. The guestrooms and front desk at this two-story motel have benefitted from a 2010 renovation. There is no elevator, so choose a room on the first floor to avoid carrying gear up the stairs. Try to reserve a room on the back side of the property for good views of the canal and less traffic noise.

The **Lakeshore Bed and Breakfast** (667 Lakeshore Rd., Fort Erie, 289/320-9907, www.lakeshorebedandbreakfast.ca, $140) opened in 2012 and is right on the waterfront. It offers the amenities and services of top boutique hotels, whichthe owners experienced during their own world travels. Each of the three rooms has warm robes, super-comfy beds, and an in-room coffeemaker. The location is wonderful, right on the shore of Lake Erie and a few minutes away from historic Old Fort Erie.

FOOD

Every region has its legendary breakfast joint, and in St. Catharines it's the **Sun Rise Cafe** (136 Bunting Rd., St. Catharines, 905/685-1100, 6am-2pm Mon.-Wed., 6am-3pm Thurs.-Sun., $10). The restaurant is clean and simple, with everything you'd want in a great breakfast place. The reasonable prices are why it gets crowded here. Service is fast and the wait times are minimal. Try the banana-split breakfast parfait.

The best vegan restaurant in southern Ontario is found in St. Catharines. **Rise Above** (120 St. Paul St., St. Catharines, 289/362-2636, www.riseaboverestaurant.com, 11am-10pm Tues.-Sat., 11am-3pm Sun., $11) has an ambitious but tasty menu. The mac-and-cheese is so good that you won't believe it doesn't contain cheese. The most expensive entrée is $13.

This place is also a vegan bakery. The desserts rock and you can always order goodies to go.

Enjoy fine breakfasts and lunches at the **Bleu Turtle** (215 St. Paul St. W., St. Catharines, 905/688-0330, www.bleuturtle.com, 8am-2pm Wed.-Sun., $14), a trendy bistro with a hip vibe. Prices are a bit high compared to other breakfast places, but commensurate with the quality of the food. The pork-belly eggs Benedict ($14) is a tremendous way to start the day. All ingredients are locally sourced. The basic breakfast ($9) is a good option for traditional breakfast favorites.

Of the many good Asian restaurants in southern Ontario, **Ming Teh** (126 Niagara Blvd., Fort Erie, 905/871-7971, 5pm-10pm Mon., 11am-10pm Tues.-Sun., $12) is among the best. For years, Americans have crossed over the Peace Bridge to dine at this wonderful restaurant. Portions are large. The food is always made to order and fresh. Ask to be seated along the rear of the restaurant to view the swift waters of the Niagara River on its 18-mile journey toward the falls.

The best Japanese restaurant in Fort Erie is **Yukiguni 2** (660 Garrison Rd., Fort Erie, 905/994-8506, noon-9pm daily, $14). The exterior is a little drab, but the inside is warm and inviting, and the staff is very personable. Consistently fresh seafood is the key to this restaurant's success. The dinner menu is varied and the Yukiguni Box (separate portions of chicken teriyaki, shrimp tempura, *gyoza,* and California rolls in a compartmentalized dish, $16) is a local favorite. Try the two-appetizers-for-$10 deal; the portion sizes are enough to qualify as an entrée at most sushi places.

Just down the shore from Fort Erie is Crystal Beach and cottage country, lovingly referred to by locals as Canada's South Coast. The **South Coast Cookhouse** (423 Derby Rd., Crystal Beach, 905/894-7037, 11:30am-11pm Sun.-Thurs., 11:30am-midnight Fri.-Sat., $16) is a casual, family-friendly restaurant close to the beach, with a kitchen open longer than most other eateries in the area. The Cookhouse has a lot of typical pub fare, but it's known for its large chicken wings. Unless you are a veteran wing consumer, stay away from the suicide-style wings (very, very hot), and instead try the chipotle mango-sauce wings. On summer weekends, there is live music, a wonderful accompaniment to watching the sun set and enjoying a choice of 20-plus beers.

The small community of Crystal Beach doesn't have any fine dining establishments, but it does have **The Crystal Chandelier** (3878 Erie Rd., Crystal Beach, 905/894-9996, www.thecrystalchandelier.com, 4pm-9pm Wed.-Thurs., 4pm-11:30pm Fri., 11:30am-11:30pm Sat.-Sun., $22), with a romantic ambience and good food. The menu is contemporary, with a few surprises such as the meatloaf Calabrese—a nice Italian twist on an old favorite. The patio is a wonderful place to dine during the summer as the beachgoers pass by and the sun sets over the water. On summer evenings, the Chandelier hosts live music. If you want a quiet meal, make reservations by 6pm. The music, featuring local acts, is lively and begins at 9pm on Saturdays and Sundays.

The **Bridgewater Cafe** (91 E. Main St., Welland, 905/788-9339, www.bridgewatercafe.ca, 11am-3pm Wed.-Fri., 8am-2pm Sat.-Sun., $7) offers a unique menu for down-home fine dining. Chef Randy Dupuis has 20-plus years of experience at some of the best restaurants in Niagara, and he has applied it to traditional breakfast and lunch dishes. They're all served in a relaxed, contemporary atmosphere. Try the Cuban grilled cheese (pulled pork, smoked ham, and Havarti cheese, $9) for a fine spin on a traditional lunch-time favorite.

If you're looking for pub grub served in an English pub atmosphere, then pop into **Ye Olde Squire Restaurant** (800 Niagara St., Welland, 905/714-7821, www.yeoldesquire.com, 10am-11pm Mon.-Thurs., 10am-midnight Fri., 10am-11pm Sat., 10am-10pm Sun., $13). If you love a lighthearted atmosphere and prompt service (especially at lunch), then you'll like the Squire. The head chef has an "aversion to anything frozen," so all meals are prepared fresh. The diverse menu includes typical pub favorites such as fish and chips ($11), steak and Guinness

mushroom pie ($13), and Memphis-style ribs ($17). Reservations are a good idea on Friday and Saturday evenings when the restaurant becomes crowded after 6pm.

GETTING THERE AND AROUND

Most visitors drive as they explore this region. Fort Erie is 18 miles away from Niagara Falls. Take the Niagara Parkway along the Niagara River for a scenic route. St. Catharines is about 12 miles away from the falls, a 15-minute drive on the QEW (Queen Elizabeth Way).

Driving south from St. Catharines to Port Colborne (22 miles) should take less than 30 minutes. The major roads are Routes 406 and 140. You'll pass through Thorold and Welland on the way.

The QEW connects Fort Erie to St. Catharines. Route 406 joins the QEW in St. Catharines and then goes south, generally parallel to the QEW, and passes through Thorold, then Welland, and terminates in Port Colborne. Highway 3 connects Port Colborne to Fort Erie.

Niagara Regional Transit (www.niagararegion.ca) connects St. Catharines, Welland, Port Colborne, Thorold, Fort Erie, and Niagara Falls with buses that run Monday-Saturday. One-way fares ($6) cover transfers to each town's municipal transit service.

For-profit bus operators offer fewer options—**MegaBus** (www.ca.megabus.com) provides daily motorcoach service between Fort Erie (Vince's Robo Mart, 21 Princess St.) and St. Catharines, at the St. Catharines bus terminal (70 Carlisle St.), but there are no other stops in the region. The journey from Fort Erie to St. Catharines costs less than $10.

Rail service is minimal in this area as well; trains stop at St. Catharines (5 Great Western St.), but no other communities in the area. **VIA Rail** (www.viarail.ca) has daily service between Niagara Falls, Ontario, and St. Catharines with a 21-minute trip ($23). **GO Transit** (www.gotransit.com) offers service connecting Niagara Falls and St. Catharines, but only on summer weekends.

NIAGARA-ON-THE-LAKE

BACKGROUND AND ESSENTIALS

The Land

Geography both divides and unites this region. The U.S. and Canadian sides of Niagara Falls are physically separated by the Niagara River, but they share these same geographical features that give the region its identity.

About 12,000 years ago, the entire area was covered by a glacier that was more than a mile thick. As the earth's climate warmed, the glacier retreated. The glacier's movement created the basins of the Great Lakes, and the melting glacier filled the lakes with freshwater. Today, the Great Lakes contain 20 percent of all the liquid freshwater in the world.

The Great Lakes flow from Lakes Superior to Michigan to Huron to Erie, and then to Lake Ontario. Lake Erie is more than 320 feet higher in elevation than Lake Ontario, which means the water flows downhill (via the Niagara River) between the two bodies of water. The river flows over an escarpment during its journey downstream, resulting in Niagara Falls. Just 12,000 years ago, Niagara Falls was seven miles downstream. The erosive power of the water cut a gorge from its original location, causing the waterfall to recede to where it is today.

The region's soil is fertile and allows for cultivation of diverse crops, including corn,

tomatoes, strawberries, potatoes, beans, grapes, gourds, and lettuce. The region is known for production of tree fruits, including apples, cherries, peaches, and pears. It also has abundant forests, woodlands, meadows, and small rolling hills. Gorges such as Niagara's can be formed because much of the area's rock is sedimentary and relatively soft, making it that much easier for erosion and changes in the landscape to occur. Fossils abound here, evidence from a warm and shallow sea, teeming with life, that existed many millions of years ago. Most of these fossils were formed 240-425 million years ago. The most often spotted fossils are Trilobita (sea floor crustaceans), Crinoidea (sea lilies), and Gastropoda (snail shells).

CLIMATE

Summer and autumn are the best times to visit the Niagara region. Winters are cold, snowy, and windy. Spring is unpredictable and can have snow, rain, and sunshine all in the same day.

The average July temperature is 81°F; the average January temperature is 32°F. Summers are moderate and comfortable, with temperatures rarely reaching 90°F. In the fall, highs average 60°F.

The annual precipitation is 35 inches (New York City averages about 50 inches). In winter, Niagara Falls can expect a total of 76 inches of snow. Portions of Buffalo receive 100 inches of snow.

FLORA AND FAUNA

Niagara has a healthy mix of urban, suburban, and rural spaces, from cities to sprawling farmlands and forests.

Animals

The largest animals here are whitetail deer, bobcats, coyotes, turkeys, and foxes. In the parks surrounding the falls, you'll see squirrels (black and grey), but may also encounter chipmunks, rabbits, groundhogs, woodchucks, skunks, turtles, snakes, and raccoons in nearby hiking areas.

Bird-watchers trek to the Niagara area because it's along a major migratory path that annually attracts birds from as far north as Greenland and as far south as Florida. The Niagara River corridor has gained international recognition by conservation groups as a "Globally Significant Important Bird Area"— the first such designation in all of North America. The National Audubon Society designated the entire river as "Globally Significant" in 1996 to raise awareness of the river as a major food source for migrating birds.

Because Niagara's waters are generally free of ice, migrating birds can find fish, whereas many other sources of food on their path are frozen over. In November, the river is visited by more than 100,000 gulls of 19 different species, some of which have traveled from Siberia. Most of these birds are traveling south from arctic Canada and Greenland. Numerous species of swans, ducks, and geese live here year-round or migrate through the area. Many waterfowl gather near the base of Niagara Falls, where there is a large supply of dead or stunned fish.

Other birds typically found in this area include robins, hummingbirds, blackbirds, cardinals, chickadees, cormorants, doves, finches, jays, and crows. Larger birds such as herons, cranes, owls, and hawks are seen regularly, with rare appearances by falcons and eagles.

THE MEANING OF "NIAGARA"

The origins of the name "Niagara" are shrouded in mystery because the native people who lived here did not have a written language. Some scholars believe the word comes from a group of local people named the Niagagarega. Others say Niagara is derived from "Onguiaahra," an Indian word for "the strait." Local guides may tell you that the term means "neck" or "thunder water."

Plants and Trees

Although nearly all the old-growth forest is gone, there is a remarkable diversity of trees in the woodlands of the Niagara region. Maple, elm, birch, beech, ash, dogwood, sycamore, oak, cherry, chestnut, and willow trees thrive. By 1833, nearly all the white oak trees on Grand Island were harvested and milled, eventually shaped into barrels for rum in the West Indies and planks for Yankee boats in Boston.

Some of the more common plants of the region include goldenrod, irises, geraniums, roses, milkweed, and various grasses. Poison ivy, poison sumac, and stinging nettles may be found near woodland paths in the area.

ENVIRONMENTAL ISSUES

Niagara Falls, New York, is still recovering from the legacy of generations of high-polluting industries that once operated here. In the early 1900s, manufacturers were drawn to Niagara Falls because of the inexpensive and reliable electric power. Many of the major names in industry, including Alcoa, Union Carbide, Olin, Dupont, Hooker, Carborundum, and Occidental, generated jobs, economic growth, and chemical by-products. The boom lasted through World War II and into the 1970s.

Although many of the industrial plants have closed, a toxic legacy remains. The first U.S. Federal Superfund clean-up site was Love Canal, a school and community about seven miles from the falls (and within city limits) built on a chemical landfill. In the late 1970s, the federal government purchased the homes of 950 families near the dump site, paid to relocate them, and then began remediating the area. According to government officials, there are pollution concerns for dozens of similar sites in the region.

Thanks to aggressive clean-up efforts, tougher environmental regulations, and a decline in heavy manufacturing, the region is much cleaner and safer. A more symbiotic relationship between industry and regulators has emerged as the community balances the need for both manufacturing jobs and a livable environment. Wise conservation measures have led to an abundance of fish and game for sportsmen. Several species have enjoyed resurgence in the region, including wild turkeys, red-tailed hawks, eagles, and foxes.

History

EARLY PEOPLES

Long before Europeans visited the Niagara region, native peoples inhabited the land. Some groups were attracted to the area because outcroppings of flint yielded important tools, such as arrowheads and hide scrapers. Others came here for the abundance of nature—forests filled with wild game and waters packed with fish. Many who stayed cultivated the soil and harvested corn, squash, pumpkins, and beans.

Prior to the 1500s, the various tribes within the area fought against each other. Around 1570, the Cayuga, Onondaga, Mohawk, Seneca, and Oneida tribes banded together to form the Iroquois League, an advanced confederacy with social laws and government institutions designed to promote peace among its members. In 1722, a sixth nation, the Tuscarora, joined the Iroquois League.

The Iroquois Confederation dominated the region and greatly influenced the fate of all natives in this area. The Iroquois went to war with two local tribes, the Eries and the Neutrals, resulting in the destruction of those tribes. The remaining Eries and Neutrals fled, were killed, or were assimilated into other tribes.

EUROPEAN SETTLEMENT

Europeans began exploring this region in the 1600s. The French and the British traded with the native peoples, swapping iron tools, firearms, blankets, and other wares for beaver pelts. During the French and Indian War, the alliance of the Iroquois with the British was instrumental in allowing England to gain control of the region in 1759.

For a few years, there was peace in the area. The region's sparse population began to grow as the American Revolutionary War started. Many American colonists who were loyal to Great Britain sought refuge across the border in Ontario. For the six tribes of the Iroquois Confederacy, the American Revolutionary War was the source of massive in-fighting. The Tuscarora and Oneida leaders sided with the Americans, while the Cayuga, Mohawk, Seneca, and Onondaga leaders allied with England. When England lost, American troops pushed the English-allied tribes from central and western New York in a sustained military campaign in 1779. Some of these Iroquois crossed the border and settled in Canadian territory.

WAR OF 1812

By the turn of the 19th century, the region saw modest population growth as yeoman farmers began clearing fields and planting crops. The War of 1812 erupted as the United States declared war on Great Britain over trade policies and English impressment of U.S. sailors, a practice where English soldiers boarded U.S. vessels and seized any American sailors who deserted from the British Navy. Many contemporary historians believe that the conflict was, in reality, a thinly veiled attempt by the United States to annex Canadian territory.

The bloodiest fighting of that war occurred in the Niagara theater. In October 1812, U.S. forces crossed the Niagara River and briefly took control of the cannon that was strategically placed atop Queenston Heights. The U.S. invaders were eventually repelled, but Canada lost its most able young general, Isaac Brock. In another dark chapter of the war, retreating U.S. forces burned down the village now known as Niagara-on-the-Lake. In retaliation, British forces crossed the border and burned Lewiston, Niagara Falls, and Buffalo. At the end of the conflict, neither side gained or lost territory. Eventually, peace negotiations yielded an agreed-upon, fixed boundary between Canada and the United States.

EVOLUTION OF CANADIAN GOVERNANCE

Following the war, Ontario struggled to define itself politically. Some residents favored an aristocratic form of government with access to positions of power limited to an elite group, many of whom were British-born transplants. This type of governance was opposed by others loyal to the Crown, but resistant to the creation of a powerful class of unelected "nobles."

Building resentment led to unrest and a brief and unsuccessful armed rebellion in 1837 by William Lyon MacKenzie. The seeds of reform were sown, and Great Britain recognized that its colony in Canada was capable of limited autonomy. A governor would preside over a territory or colony, but that governor would implement the will of a democratically elected legislature. The first steps were taken toward Canada's complete autonomy and the creation of Ontario as a province.

ECONOMIC DEVELOPMENT

The opening of the Erie Canal in 1825 fundamentally changed the region's economic destiny. The canal placed Buffalo at the terminus of the world's first superhighway, making it the crossroads for raw materials traveling east and immigrants heading west. Buffalo became the 6th busiest port in the world and, by 1900, it had more millionaires per capita than any other American city.

The Canadian side of the border prospered as well, although the growth was more measured. The Welland Canal was built as a competitor to the Erie Canal, and was improved over the years. In Niagara Falls, Canadians considered tourism to be the main industry. Americans embraced Niagara for tourism, but also fostered heavy industrialization of the area. Both regions experienced population and economic growth through the 1950s.

THE SCHOELLKOPF POWER PLANT DISASTER

When humans try to harness the power of nature, sometimes nature strikes back. A good example is the Schoellkopf Power Plant disaster. As you look along the U.S. side of the gorge just north of the Rainbow Bridge, you'll see that the wall of the gorge is interrupted by an artificial facade. It is here that the Schoellkopf Power Plant harnessed flowing water for electricity, starting in the late 1800s. In June 1956, the water turned the tables and caused catastrophic damage to the plant, killing one worker.

On the day of the power plant collapse, employees noticed water leaking into the plant along the wall adjacent to the gorge. Soon the trickle turned into a torrent and within a few hours, a large portion of the plant was pushed from the gorge and slid to the water below. The explosive force of the event propelled debris across the river and onto the Canadian shore. Forty workers escaped the collapsing building, but 39-year-old Richard Draper, a maintenance foreman, was not as fortunate and was killed in the mishap. The exact cause of the disaster is still debated, although most believe groundwater pressure or a small earthquake caused the collapse.

THE GRIP OF THE RUST BELT

The United States was rocked by two events that paralyzed the economic fortunes of Buffalo-Niagara. In 1959, the St. Lawrence Seaway opened, allowing large oceangoing ships to bypass the port of Buffalo. Buffalo's waterfront slowly atrophied, changing from a robust, vibrant center of trade and transport to a graveyard for massive grain silos that were no longer needed. The knockout punch came in the form of the general decline of manufacturing in the United States, which was particularly acute in the Northeast during the 1970s and 1980s. Buffalo and Niagara Falls joined cities such as Pittsburgh, Cleveland, Milwaukee, and Detroit in what became known as the Rust Belt.

The Rust Belt cities witnessed the closure of many manufacturing plants, loss of jobs, and inner city decay. Both Niagara Falls, New York, and Buffalo saw their populations decrease by 50 percent, which led to a shrinking tax base and concentrations of poverty. Attempts to bring jobs back to the region were hampered by high tax rates, labor unions, and a bureaucracy that was unfriendly to business. The Canadian region near Niagara Falls suffered a similar fate, although not as severe as Buffalo.

BRIGHTER FUTURE

By the late 1980s, Canada recognized that Niagara Falls needed more attractions to become a multiday vacation destination. Federal, provincial, and local leaders collaborated on a plan to build up their side of the border with a casino, high-rise hotels, golf courses, and infrastructure that significantly enhanced the visitor experience. Public and private spending helped create a heritage-and-tourism corridor that now stretches from Fort Erie to Niagara-on-the-Lake. This effort is evident today, as you stand at the falls and see that the Canadian side is much more commercially developed than the American side.

On the U.S. side, Buffalo and Niagara Falls are experiencing positive change. In 2012, New York State committed $25 million to upgrade facilities within Niagara Falls State Park. A movement to increase access to the gorge by changing roadways is gaining speed. Tourism agencies are trying new ideas that give tourists a reason to stay here longer than one day. One such initiative is bringing more live entertainment, food vendors, and free family-oriented activities to Old Falls Street in downtown Niagara Falls.

Buffalo's once-slumbering waterfront and downtown area are enjoying a true renaissance, with private developers transforming historic buildings into loft apartments, boutique hotels, and entertainment venues. Grain silos on the inner harbor are being used for tours, rock climbing, and music festivals. Former high-polluting factories are now facilities for high-tech light manufacturing, requiring a skilled labor force. A city that was once known for its low self-esteem and lack of desirability has found growth and confidence by embracing its industrial, political, and economic heritage.

Government

New York's government is led by a governor who holds power over hundreds of appointments, and a legislature consisting of a 61-member Senate and 150-member Assembly. Members of both houses are elected for two-year terms, and each house has standing committees concerned with public policy issues. The governor also appoints non-legislative commissions to investigate such problems as education aid and welfare administration. The state's finances are overseen by an independently elected state comptroller.

New York is divided into 62 counties that are subdivided into towns. The towns contain cities and villages, most governed by an executive, usually a mayor. Despite its decreasing population, Buffalo is still the second largest city in New York State. Niagara Falls' population of 50,000 ranks it as the 13th largest city in the state. Both Buffalo and Niagara Falls are governed by mayors who work with elected councils. Buffalo is located in Erie County; Niagara Falls is in Niagara County. The combined population of the two counties is 1.1 million.

Canada is a democratic constitutional monarchy in which a sovereign acts as head of state, but the national Parliament makes decisions and holds power. The monarch of England functions as a symbolic and ceremonial representative.

Canadians elect a prime minster who heads the parliamentary government, which is comprised of two chambers, the Senate and the House of Commons. Members of the House of Commons are elected by citizens, while Senate members are appointed by the governor-general with the prime minister's recommendation. Government responsibilities are shared between federal, provincial, and territorial governments.

Ontario is 1 of 10 provinces, analogous to state in the United States. Citizens in the Province of Ontario elect representatives to a legislature known as the Assembly of Ontario. The party with the most elected members in the Assembly forms the government and chooses a premier for the province who acts as an executive.

Ontario is divided into 444 municipalities. These can be as large as Toronto, or as tiny as a village of 100 people. There are several types of municipalities, and each has different governing responsibilities, such as raising taxes, maintaining highways, or administering emergency services. It is typical for a mayor and several councillors to make decisions at the municipal level.

Niagara Falls, with its population of 80,000, is the 23rd largest city in Ontario. The City of Niagara Falls, Ontario, has a mayor and eight councilors who are elected to four-year terms.

Getting There and Around

GETTING THERE
By Air
The largest airport in the region is Toronto's **Pearson International Airport** (YYZ, 6301 Silver Dart Dr., Mississauga, 416/247-7678, www.torontopearson.com). Pearson handles flights from 64 different airlines and is Canada's busiest airport. Pearson is large, time-consuming to navigate, and expensive. Many Canadian travelers use the Buffalo airport because flights are less costly and the airport is small and easy to use. The **Buffalo Niagara International Airport** (BUF, 4200 Genesee St., Buffalo, 716/630-6000, www.buffaloairport.com) is a 25-minute drive from Niagara Falls. The **Niagara Falls International Airport** (IAG, 2035 Niagara Falls Blvd., Niagara Falls, 716/297-4494, www.niagarafallsairport.com) is conveniently located close to the falls, but is only serviced by two regional air carriers, **Allegiant Air** (www.allegiantair.com) and **Spirit Airlines** (www.spirit.com), so flight options are limited.

By Train
Amtrak (800/872-7245, www.amtrak.com) offers service between Buffalo and Niagara Falls with stops on both sides of the border. Amtrak's **Empire Route** joins New York City and Niagara Falls with three daily runs. The **Maple Leaf Route** runs once daily, connecting New York City with Toronto via the falls.

By Bus
Intercity motorcoach service providers with routes that link downtown Buffalo, Niagara Falls, and Toronto include **Greyhound** (800/661-8747, www.greyhound.com) and **MegaBus** (877/462-6342, www.megabus.com).

By Organized Tour
There are several tour companies that provide transportation and guide service for those seeking to join a group tour of Niagara Falls. All tour companies listed here will provide customer pick-ups at the address you specify. Among the reputable providers are **Niagara Airbus** (800/268-8111, www.niagaraairbus.com), **Bedore Tours** (800/538-8433, www.bedoretours.com), and **Gray Line** (877/285-2113, http://graylineniagarafalls.com). Customized private tours that include transportation are available through **Niagara Falls Walking Tours** (716/997-2245, www.niagarafallswalkingtours.com), **See Sight Tours** (888/961-6584, www.seesight-tours.com), and **Buffalo Limousine Tours** (800/599-2088, www.buffalolimousine.com).

For heritage tours of Buffalo, try **Buffalo History Tours** (716/222-2432, www.buffalohistorytours.com) or the **Preservation Society** (716/852-3300, www.preservationbuffaloniagara.org).

GETTING AROUND
The vast majority of visitors to Niagara arrive by car. Outside of Niagara Falls, Ontario, public transportation is not robust and is designed to serve locals, not visitors.

In New York, I-90 is the main highway running east-west, from Albany to Buffalo. In Buffalo, big-city traffic is virtually nonexistent, although congestion can occur during weekday commute times. The statewide speed limit for open highway driving is 65 miles per hour. Speed limits for cities, towns, villages, and smaller roads are considerably slower and are posted. If visiting in the winter months, snow may make for less-than-ideal driving conditions. Local radio stations and highway signs provide warnings and weather information.

The main thoroughfare on the Canadian side of the border is Queen Elizabeth Way (QEW), which joins the Niagara region to Toronto. The QEW's top posted speed limit is 100 kilometers per hour (60 mph), although traffic moves faster the closer you get to Toronto. Except for construction areas, there is not much traffic in the Niagara region. Most of the traffic laws are the same for Canada as New York, except that radar detectors are not legal.

Major car-rental companies operating out of the Buffalo airport include **Alamo** (800/327-9633), **Avis** (800/831-2847), **Budget** (800/283-4387), **Enterprise** (800/736-8222), **Hertz** (800/654-3131), and **National** (800/227-7368).

Tips for Travelers

CROSSING THE BORDER

U.S. citizens crossing the border into Canada must have a passport, passport card, Nexus card, or Enhanced Drivers License (issued by a select number of U.S. border states). Technically, U.S. citizens do not need a passport to enter Canada; however, U.S. regulations require that you have the proper documentation to re-enter the United States. The typical border inspection lasts less than three minutes, especially if you are prepared.

Have your documentation ready to present to the inspector. Remove your sunglasses, mute your radio, and pay attention (ask everyone in the car to put away electronic devices). Inspectors are concerned if there is inconsistent information among people within the vehicle. Make certain that everybody knows where you're going and how long you are staying. You may not bring mace, pepper spray, or stun guns across the border. If one parent is traveling with a child, it is recommended that the absent parent create and sign an informal letter of permission.

Travelers with criminal records are likely to receive extra scrutiny when crossing into Canada. Infractions including DUI may prevent your entry into Canada. Border agents have much discretion in these matters, so it pays to be respectful, sincere, and honest. If someone in your vehicle has a criminal conviction, the entire group may be asked to remain in the car while that person is questioned further inside the immigration offices.

If you are not a U.S. citizen and you're entering Canada, find out if you need a visa or other documentation by using an interactive form on Canada's Immigration and Citizenship website (www.cic.gc.ca).

For the current wait times at border crossings, call (800/715-6722) or go online (www.niagarafallsbridges.com) for updates on which border crossing to use based on traffic volume.

MONEY

Banks on both sides of the border are usually open 9am-3pm Monday-Friday, with some branches open 9am-1pm Saturday. Many banks offer 24-hour ATMs. Check with your bank to see if your debit card will work at Canadian ATMs. Most larger banks participate in international networks that permit cash withdrawals in other countries. There may be fees associated with these transactions.

U.S. and Canadian currency fluctuate in relative value, which means that sometimes the U.S. and Canadian dollar are at par and sometimes not. Businesses set their own exchange rates and policies on accepting foreign currency. There are two ways to make certain that you know the exchange rate you're receiving. The first is to use your own credit card for all transactions; the other is to purchase Canadian currency at your local bank before you leave the United States.

CELL PHONES

It is important to know your cell phone carrier's policy on roaming charges if you intend on using your phone in Canada. Roaming charges, especially for data, can quickly add up. If your carrier charges roaming fees for service in Ontario, you may consider turning off phone functions that require data roaming and data sync. Switching your phone to airplane mode insures that your phone will not roam, but you cannot make or receive calls in this mode.

WHICH IS THE BEST SIDE?

During the 1800s and for much of the 1900s, Niagara Falls, New York, was considered *the* destination when visiting Niagara. Since the 1960s, that situation has changed, and Niagara Falls, Ontario, dominates in tourism (number of visitors, hotel rooms, etc.). A friendly rivalry exists across the border as each destination claims to be number one. But which side is better?

The answer is they *both* are.

Each side has its own distinct advantages and challenges. The Canadian side of the border boasts the better view. Without a doubt, this is true—you can see all three of the waterfalls that make up Niagara Falls from the Canadian side. The vista here is clearly superior. However, the Ontario side is also more crowded and is ringed with high-rise hotels that some feel detract from the natural beauty of the falls.

The New York State Park at Niagara Falls has many more opportunities to experience the water up close. The park facilitates a relationship with nature that is much more visceral. By state law, the park is prohibited from becoming over-commercialized and over-developed. Fewer tourists make for shorter lines at attractions. But the U.S. side faces its own challenges—outside of the park, the downtown area is not nearly as vibrant as its Canadian counterpart. Top-quality hotels and restaurants are few in comparison to Niagara Falls, Ontario.

The best advice is to experience both sides of Niagara Falls. Think of Niagara as a region, not just a single attraction. If your situation permits, explore both sides of the border and you'll discover that each has its unique charm and character.

You can, however, use Wi-Fi in airplane mode. Another option is to contact your carrier and see if they have a service package for Canada, which would allow you full use of your phone's functions, while avoiding roaming fees.

RECREATION
Parks

The Niagara region abounds in lovely green spaces most of the year. New York has an excellent park system that includes Niagara Falls State Park and Fort Niagara State Park in Youngstown. Admission is free, although there may be a charge for parking. If you visit multiple parks during the same day, you only need to pay for parking one time—just show your receipt from the first park as you enter subsequent ones. Of the state's 178 parks, 17 are in the Niagara region. For the best information on park amenities and activities, call 518/474-0456 or go to the state's website (www.nysparks.com).

Also on the U.S. side of the border, **Erie County** (www2.erie.gov) and **Niagara County** (www.niagaracounty.com) operate regional parks. Look online (www.bfloparks.org) for information on Buffalo's historic Olmsted system of parks.

Not to be outdone, **Niagara Parks** (www.niagaraparks.com) provides many outdoor attractions, such as Queen Victoria Park, Fort Erie, Queenston Heights, Niagara Glen, and the Botanical Gardens. Niagara Parks is governed by the Niagara Parks Commission, a special administrative body created by the province. Niagara Parks is financed by park revenue.

Camping

Camping is very popular in the Niagara region, with dozens of campgrounds with tent and RV spaces as well as cabins. Camping spots in New York State's campgrounds start at $15 a night; there are four in the region and it is wise to reserve spaces online (www.newyorkstateparks.reserveamerica.com) well in advance of your trip. Across the border, Ontario Parks offers camp spots starting at $33 a night. For more information and reservations, call 888/668-7275 or visit the website (www.ontarioparks.com).

HEALTH AND SAFETY
Outdoor Safety

Before heading onto the hiking trails of Niagara, be sure you know where you're going and what you're doing. Check with park officials about trail conditions and weather. Be sure your equipment is functioning properly, and don't head out alone.

Lyme Disease

Anyone who spends much time outdoors in this region should be aware of the symptoms of Lyme disease. The bacterium that causes the disease is carried by the deer tick, which lives in brush, meadows, forests, and even lawns. In early stages, the disease is easily treatable with antibiotics, but if left unattended, it can lead to serious neurological, heart, and joint problems.

Many—*but not all*—of those infected develop a red circular rash around the bite location within three days to one month. The rash usually begins with a small red dot that expands to a diameter of one to five inches. The expanded rash may feature a bright red border and a hard, pale center, often resembling a bullseye on a target.

The rash is usually accompanied by flu-like symptoms. These may include fatigue, nausea, vomiting, diarrhea, pain in the muscles and joints, stiff neck, swollen lymph glands, headaches, fevers, chills, sore throat, dry cough, dizziness, sensitivity to the sun, and chest, ear, and/or back pain.

Wear light-colored clothing to make it easier to spot ticks, and long pants and long-sleeved shirts to discourage them from coming in contact with your skin. Tuck pants cuffs into socks, and use an insect repellent with a 25-30 percent DEET content around clothing openings and on exposed skin.

Use gloves and tweezers to remove ticks; grasp the tick's head parts as close to your skin as possible and apply slow, steady traction. Wash both your hands and the bitten area afterward. Do not attempt to remove ticks by burning them or coating them with anything like nail polish remover or petroleum jelly. If you remove a tick before it has been attached for 24 hours, you greatly reduce the risk of infection.

Crime

In Niagara Falls, New York, the state park has its own police force that caters to the needs of visitors. The Parks Police Headquarters is located on Goat Island, which keeps response times short and provides maximum visibility for visitors. The tourist area adjacent to the park is patrolled by the Niagara Falls city police. Some neighborhoods beyond this zone are depressed and have higher crime rates. Because of the importance of tourism to the local economy, police frequently patrol the tourist areas downtown.

In Niagara Falls, Ontario, Niagara Parks also has their own police force, with headquarters in Queen Victoria Park. Officers here are highly visible and patrol in cars, on bikes, and on foot.

No matter where you visit, always put valuables such as cameras and GPS units inside your car's trunk and lock your car doors. Using common sense and staying alert are the best ways to avoid crime while on vacation in Niagara.

ACCESS FOR TRAVELERS WITH DISABILITIES

Travelers with disabilities will find many accessible attractions in the region. Nearly all the attractions on the U.S. side are ADA-compliant. Niagara Falls State Park features curb cuts and paved paths for wheelchairs. All buildings in the park are accessible, including restrooms, visitor centers, restaurants, theaters, the Observation Tower, and the Maid of the Mist.

Ontario does not mandate sweeping accessibility regulations, although many businesses and government agencies are striving to increase access. Major attractions such as Table Rock Welcome Centre, the Skylon Tower, WEGO buses, Niagara Hornblower Cruises, and the Butterfly Conservatory are all accessible.

Help for travelers with disabilities is available through the **Society for Accessible Travel and Hospitality** (212/447-7284, www.sath.org), a nationwide, nonprofit membership organization that collects data on travel facilities around the country.

New York State residents with disabilities should apply for the **Access Pass,** which provides free entry to most state parks and recreation areas. For an application, contact **New York State Parks** (Empire State Plaza, Albany, NY 12238, 518/474-2324, www.nysparks.com).

SENIOR TRAVELERS

The **Golden Age Program** provides New York State residents age 62 or older with free entry to state parks and recreation areas any weekday, excluding holidays. Simply present your current driver's license or non- driver photo ID card at the entrance gate.

WORK STUDY

The **Council on International Educational Exchange** (CIEE, 7 Custom House St., 3rd floor, Portland, ME 04101, 207/553-7600 or 800/407-8839, www.ciee.org) provides information on low-cost travel and work-study programs in the United States, including New York State. The CIEE also sells the International Student Identity Card, good for travel and entertainment discounts.

RESOURCES

Suggested Reading

HISTORY

Aherns, Edward W. *The Devil's Hole Massacre*. Sanborn, NY: Rissa Productions, 2004. Well-researched tale of a dark chapter in Native American and settler relations.

Berton, Pierre. *Niagara: A History of the Falls*. Albany, NY: State University Press, 1992. An accessible and thoughtful history of the falls from a prolific Canadian author.

Gromosiak, Paul. *Water Over the Falls: 101 Most Memorable Events at Niagara Falls*. Buffalo, NY: Western New York Wares Inc., 1996. Humorous vignettes of interesting people and events in Niagara.

Jackson, John N., John Burtniak, and Gregory P. Stein. *The Mighty Niagara: One River—Two Frontiers*. Amherst, NY: Prometheus Books, 2003. The most comprehensive study of the border that separates and unites the United States and Canada.

Kriner, T.W. *In the Mad Water: Two Centuries of Adventure and Lunacy at Niagara Falls*. Buffalo, NY: J and J Publishing, 1999. Captures the dark side of those who've made their final journey at Niagara.

Malcomson, Robert. *A Very Brilliant Affair: The Battle of Queenston Heights, 1812*. Toronto: Robin Brass Studio, 2003. Well written and balanced account of the Battle at Queenston Heights in the War of 1812.

NATURE AND RECREATION

Duling, Gretchen, Dennis Duling, Karen Noonan, Toby Jewett, and Linda Fritz. *From the Mouth of the Lower Niagara River: Stories of Four Historic Communities*. Buffalo, NY: Western New York Wares Inc., 2012. Fascinating study by local authors of communities along the Niagara River.

Freeman, Rich and Sue. *Bruce Trail: An Adventure Along the Niagara Escarpment*. Fishers, NY: Footprint Press, 1998. An excellent hiking guide to the Bruce Trail.

Gromosiak, Paul. *Goat Island: Niagara's Secret Retreat*. Buffalo, NY: Western New York Wares Inc., 2003. A quick read on the beautiful details of Goat Island.

Schuman, Michael and Deborah Williams. *Natural Wonders of New York: Exploring Wild and Scenic Places*. Toledo, OH: Country Roads Press, 1999. Describes many of the state and local parks in Western New York.

TRAVEL

Kowsky, Frank. *Buffalo Architecture: A Guide*. Cambridge, MA: MIT Press, 1981. Complete and scholarly guide to Buffalo's architecture.

Sheridan, Jan. *Buffalo Treasures: A Downtown Walking Guide and Driving Tour of Frank Lloyd Wright Homes*. Buffalo, NY: Western New York Wares Inc., 2006. Quick guide on the architecture of Buffalo.

Wooster, Margaret. *Somewhere to Go on Sunday: A Guide to Natural Treasures in Western New York & Southern Ontario.* Buffalo, NY: Prometheus Books, 1991. Practical guide to many natural areas that are off the beaten path.

Internet Resources

EVENTS

Gusto
www.buffalonews.com/gusto
Gusto is the entertainment guide for Buffalo's only daily newspaper, *The Buffalo News.*

Niagara This Week
www.niagarathisweek.com
Use this site to find out what's going on in southern Ontario during your stay.

Old Falls Street
www.fallsstreet.com
Old Falls Street is a vibrant area immediately adjacent to Niagara Falls State Park. Check their schedule for daily activities in the summer.

Winter Festival of Lights
www.wfol.com
Best site for information on the Festival of Lights in Niagara Falls, Ontario.

HISTORY

The Erie Canal
www.eriecanal.org
Discover how this humble waterway shaped a nation and why it is still important today.

Niagara Falls Public Library
www.nflibrary.ca
The Niagara Falls Public Library has many images and books available online. The historical images section is well worth a look.

Niagara Falls Thunder Alley
www.niagarafrontier.com
Grassroots website detailing the history of the falls, as well as information on current attractions; emphasizes the natural beauty of the region.

RECREATION

Cycling the Erie Canal
www.ptny.org/canaltour
This site offers ways to enjoy the Erie Canal on a bike.

Hiking Trails in Western New York
www.wnyhikes.com
Informative site listing the best hiking trails in Erie and Niagara Counties.

New York State Office of Parks, Recreation & Historic Preservation
www.nysparks.com
New York State's listing of all state-operated parks, with excellent information on amenities and fees.

Ontario Trails Council
www.ontariotrails.on.ca
Non-profit organization promoting hiking in Ontario.

TOURIST INFORMATION

Clifton Hill
www.cliftonhill.com
Guide to the über-touristy area of Niagara Falls, Ontario, that's known as Clifton Hill.

Niagara Parks
www.niagaraparks.com
Official site of Ontario's Niagara Parks. Very reputable and informative.

Niagara Falls State Park
www.niagarafallsstatepark.com
The official site of Niagara Falls State Park.

Niagara Falls Tourism
www.niagarafallstourism.com
Commercial site featuring attractions, restaurants, and accommodations on the Canadian side of the falls.

Niagara USA
www.niagara-usa.com
Comprehensive website listing attractions and events in Niagara Falls, NY, and Niagara County.

Tourism Niagara
www.tourismniagara.com
Promotes attractions in southern Ontario.

Look here for convenient packaged regional itineraries.

Visit Buffalo Niagara
www.visitbuffaloniagara.com
Check here for information on Erie-Niagara County attractions, plus excellent suggestions for adventures.

Visit Niagara Canada
www.visitniagaracanada.com
Easy-to-navigate site with information on Canadian attractions. The itinerary listings are particularly interesting.

Index

List of Maps

Acknowledgments

Thanks to my family, especially my wife Jennifer, the kids, and Biff—your love and support allowed me to take this amazing journey. I could not have completed this task without the assistance of Visit Buffalo, the Niagara Tourism and Convention Corporation, Ontario Tourism, Niagara Parks, Empire State Development and New York State Parks. Among the tourism professionals who helped me on this quest are Angela, Arlene, Stephanie, Matt, Joey, Darren, Holly, Ed, Karen, Joel N., and the Keklak family.

The people from Avalon Travel including Larissa, Grace, Darren, and Mike are the best friends an author could have. A special thank you goes to Leah Gordon, editor extraordinaire, whose patience, insights, and talents have made this book much more useful, readable, and interesting. She is more than an editor, she is a partner.

Finally, thank you to my grandfather who planted the seeds of curiosity, kindness, and humor in me. Everything that is good in our family is rooted in you and Grandma. Your love is as powerful as the Falls and as gentle as the mist. It continues to run through us, never stopping, never ending, just like Niagara.

MOON NIAGARA FALLS

Avalon Travel
a member of the Perseus Books Group
1700 Fourth Street
Berkeley, CA 94710, USA
www.moon.com

Editor: Leah Gordon
Series Manager: Kathryn Ettinger
Copy Editor: Shelley Bance
Graphics and Production Coordinator: Darren Alessi
Cover Design: Faceout Studios, Charles Brock
Moon Logo: Tim McGrath
Map Editor: Mike Morgenfeld
Cartographer: Brian Shotwell
Indexer: Rachel Kuhn

ISBN-13: 978-1-61238-777-2
ISSN: 2334-0681

Printing History
1st Edition — June 2014
5 4 3 2 1

Front cover photo: © Rolf Hicker / All Canada Photos
/ SuperStock
Back cover photo: © ishtygashev / 123rf.com
Title page photo: © Niagara Tourism and Convention
Corporation
Interior color photos: page 4 © Niagara Tourism and
Convention Corporation; page 5 © The Niagara Parks
Commission; page 6 (top left) © The Niagara Parks
Commission, (top right) © Ontario Tourism Marketing
Partnership Corporation 2014, (bottom) © The
Niagara Parks Commission; page 7 (top) © Angel Art
Limited, (bottom left) © Ontario Tourism Marketing
Partnership Corporation 2014, (bottom right) ©
Angel Art Limited; page 10 © Joel A. Dombrowski;
page 11 © The Niagara Parks Commission; page 12 ©
Niagara Tourism and Convention Corporation; page
13 © The Niagara Parks Commission; page 15 © The
Niagara Parks Commission

Printed in Canada by Friesens

KEEPING CURRENT

If you have a favorite gem you'd like to see included in the next edition, or see anything
that needs updating, clarification, or correction, please drop us a line. Send your com-
ments via email to feedback@moon.com, or use the address above.